The Golden Hands
Book of Knitting Patterns

Marshall Cavendish Publications, Ltd,
58 Old Compton Street, London W1V 5PA.

Credits
Golden Hands Book of Knitting Patterns

Photographs by Camera Press   Femina Design, 29, 35, 36, 39. GMN, 18, 38, 45, 46, 57, 58, 59. Kamerabild, 27, 28, 32. Jan Ralf, 48. Lars Larsson, 50. Bo Appeltofft, 68. Svante Stostedt, 25. Stephen Hiett, 30, 31, 41. Sandra Lousada, 49. Jim Williams, 1. Simis Press, 14, 15, 16, 17, 19, 21, 23, 24, 26, 33, 37, 40, 44, 47, 52, 61, 66. Chris Lewis, 64, 65, 67, 70, 71, 72, 73. Peter Pugh Cook, 55. Mahoney, 20. Pingouin, 62, 63, 74, 75.

Accessories
31. Coat at Peter Robinson. Brooches and bangles by Adrien Mann. 32. blue shirt at Peter Robinson. Jewellery by Adrien Mann. 41. Suede culottes by Morel at Peter Robinson, Oxford Street, London, W.1. Silk shirt at Annacat, 270, Brompton Road, London, S.W.3. Bangle by Adrien Mann at Dickins & Jones, Regent Street, London, W.1. 49.Jewellery by Adrien Mann at Marshall & Snelgrove, Oxford Street, London, W.1. 61. Linen and blankets from Heals, 196, Tottenham Court Road, London, W.1. 69-70. Tea and coffee pot from John Lewis, Oxford Street, London, W.1. 62. Blanket and book from Heals, 196, Tottenham Court Road, London, W.1.

Diagrams by: Barbara Firth
                    Paul Williams
                    Trevor Lawrence

Published by Marshall Cavendish Publications Ltd.
58 Old Compton Street
London, W1V 5PA

© Marshall Cavendish Ltd. 1972
58 Old Compton Street
London, W1V 5PA

This material first published by Marshall Cavendish Ltd.
1971–1972, in:
Golden Hands New Guide
Golden Hands Monthly
All You Can Knit and Crochet for Babies
All You Can Knit and Crochet for Children
All You Can Knit and Crochet for Women
All You Can Knit and Crochet for the Home
All You Can Knit and Crochet for Men

This volume first printed 1972.
Second Impression 1972.

Printed by Proost, Turnhout, Belgium.

This volume is not to be sold in the U.S.A.,
Australia, New Zealand and South East Asia.

About this book . . .

Here is a special collection of garments
for every member of your family and a
variety of colourful and original items
to enhance your home.

There are layettes and play suits for
babies, fashionable sweaters and dresses
for mums and teenage daughters, smart
cardigans and ties for dads, and cheerful
tablecloths, curtains and bedcovers for
the house.

The collection is technically definitive,
too. It should encourage the beginner
and challenge the expert.

If you are a newcomer to the art of
knitting, then turn to our Crash Course
on page 121 which will lead you to that
stage of confidence and skill in which
you can tackle everything in the book.
We suggest that you start with one of
the simple items and then move on to
the more complicated designs.

Knitting can be a totally absorbing and
worthwhile hobby — even more so when it
involves those nearest to you. Knitting
can save you money, delight those who
receive the finished articles and
provide a satisfying creative outlet for
your leisure time.

Other books in this series are The Golden Hands
Book of Crochet Patterns and The Golden Hands
Book of Embroidery Designs.

CONTENTS

YARNS AND TENSIONS

Yarns and qualities vary from year to year and country to country. The secret of using this book at any time, in any country, is to use a yarn which knits up to the right tension. To check, knit a tension sample before embarking on a garment. The needle size is only a guide —the point is to have the right number of stitches and rows to the inch. To do this you may need to use needles a size larger or smaller than suggested because some people knit more loosely or tightly than others. You will notice that we give the basic yarn tensions in the chart on pages 6, 7 and 8—while in the book there are specific tensions for each pattern. To find what yarns should knit up to the same tension as any yarn given in a pattern, find the basic tension of that yarn in the chart and use any other yarn in that group.

Because it is difficult to judge how to count, say, $3\frac{1}{2}$ or $4\frac{1}{2}$ stitches to the inch, it is worth counting stitches over four inches and then dividing by four.

If the tension reference includes a $\frac{1}{3}$ measure over three inches to get a whole number of stitches, then divide by three. Even a $\frac{1}{4}$ of a stitch in an inch should be considered—if a 36in sweater in double knitting yarn has a $\frac{1}{4}$ stitch to the inch too few, the finished garment will be almost two inches too tight.

Some yarns made overseas carry the same name as a similar British yarn but are made up to a different specification. Always double check with a tension square. In some cases, yarns knit up to the same number of stitches to the inch but give a slightly different number of rows to the inch. An experienced knitter should be able to adjust garment lengths to her own requirements. When you use a yarn different from the one originally quoted, you may need a different number of balls or ounces, so keep a spare ball band showing the dye lot number.

Yarns and Metrication

When purchasing yarns it is also advisable to check with your stockist as to the weight of the balls, since they now vary due to the introduction of the metric system. Metrication has been adopted by some manufacturers, while others are still in the process of changeover. Also large stocks of balls in standard ounces will take time to run out, so this confused situation will be with us for some time. Most spinners opt for the safety of not mentioning weight at all so we suggest that, if you are at all worried, it is always better to overbuy, than to run short.

KNITTING NEEDLE SIZES		
British	**French**	**American**
14	2	0
13	—	—
12	2.50	1
11	3.00	2
10	3.25	3
—	3.50	4
9	4.00	5
8	4.50	6
7	4.75	7
6	5.00	8
5	5.50	9
4	6.00	10
3	7.00	$10\frac{1}{2}$
2	8.00	11
1	9.25	13

Spinners' Addresses

Lister yarns—Lister & Co (Knitting Wools) Ltd, PO Box 37, Providence Mills, Wakefield, Yorks.
Mahoney yarns—Martin Mahoney (Great Britain) Ltd, The Coal Road, Seacroft, Leeds, Yorks, LS14 2AQ.
Pingouin yarns—French Wools Ltd, Lexington Street, London, W1R 4BJ.
Hayfield yarns—John G. Horsfall & Sons Ltd, Hayfield Mills, Glusburn, Nr Keighley, Yorks, BD20 8QP.
Mail order stockist—Messrs Abbey Dale, 8 Ilkley Road, Addingham, Uttley, Yorks.
Sirdar yarns—Sirdar Ltd, PO Box 31, Bective Mills, Alversthorpe, Wakefield, Yorks.
Sirdar Wools (Australia) PTY Ltd, PO Box 472, Goulbourn, New South Wales 2580.
Sirdar Wools (New Zealand) Ltd, PO Box 4199, Auckland, New Zealand.
Sirdar Wools (PTY) Ltd, PO Box 49072, Rosettenville, Johannesburg, South Africa.
Emu yarns—Emu Wools Ltd, Low Street, Keighley, Yorks.
Robin yarns—Robert Glew & Co Ltd, Robin Mills, Idle, Bradford.
Patons yarns—Patons & Baldwins (Sales) Ltd, PO Box 22, Darlington, Co Durham.
Coats Patons (Australia) Ltd, PO Box 110, Mount Waverley, Melbourne, Australia.
Coats Patons (New Zealand) Ltd, PO Box 6149, Auckland, New Zealand.
Patons & Baldwins South Africa (PTY) Ltd, PO Box 33, Desert Street, Randfontein, Transvaal, South Africa.
Lee Target yarns—George Lee & Sons, PO Box 37, Wakefield, Yorks.
Templeton yarns—James Templeton & Sons, Ayr, Scotland.
Jaegar yarns—Jaegar Hand Knitting, PO Box 5, Suttington Road, Shepshed, Loughborough, Leics, LE12 5BR.

Basic Yarn Tension	UK	Canada	Australia	South Africa	New Zealand
8½ sts and 11 rows on No. 11 needles	**Wendy** Peter Pan 3-ply yarns	**Wendy** Peter Pan 3-ply		**Wendy** Peter Pan 3-ply	
7½ sts and 9½ rows on No. 10 needles	**Emu** All 4-ply yarns (inc. Super Crepe) **Sirdar** All 4-ply yarns (inc. Talisman Baby Nylon) **Ladyship** Countryman	**Emu** All 4-ply yarns including Super Crepe and Diadem **Robin** Baby Nylon 3-ply **Ladyship** Siesta	**Sirdar** Fontein Crepe 4-ply Baby Nylon 4-ply Baby Courtelle **Villawool** Superknit 4-ply **Patons** Easy-care Bri-nylon Baby Silversheen 4-ply	**Emu** All 4-ply yarns including Super Crepe and Diadem **Sirdar** Fontein Crepe 4-ply Baby Nylon 4-ply	**Sirdar** Fontein Crepe 4-ply **Mosgiel Woollens** Aotea Super Botany Baby (9 rows)
7½ sts and 10 rows on No. 10 needles	**Twilleys** Goldfingering Lysbet Lyscordet **Lee Target** All 3-ply yarns including Cherub **Wendy** Invitation Cotton	**Patons** Beehive 4-ply Scotch Fingering Canadiana Carefree 4-ply Fingering **Twilleys** Goldfingering Lysbet Lyscordet Baby Bri-Nylon Super Crimp **Wendy** Invitation Cotton	**Twilleys** Goldfingering Lyscordet **Lincoln** 4-ply Bri-Nylon Cleckheaton 4-ply wool	**Twilleys** Goldfingering Lyscordet **Wendy** Invitation Cotton	**Twilleys** Goldfingering Lyscordet
7 sts and 9 rows on No. 10 needles	**Pingouin** Age d'or Coton **Lister** All 4-ply yarns **Robin** All 4-ply yarns **Hayfield** All 4-ply yarns **Patons** 101 Courtelle Crepe All 4-ply yarns 101 Courtelle Soft Quickerknit Beehive Baby Wool 4-ply **Wendy** All 4-ply yarns **Twilley** Crysette Stalite **Templeton** Antler 4-ply	**Lister** Lavenda Crisp Crepe 4-ply Bel Air Courtelle 4-ply Crepe Bel Air Courtelle Starspun **Pingouin** Age d'or **Patons** Beehive Astra 4-ply Patwin Knitting Wool with Nylon **Robin** Casino Crepe 4-ply **Wendy** Peter Pan Courtelle 4-ply Peter Pan Bri-nylon 4-ply **Twilley** Crysette Stalite **Hayfield** All 4-ply yarns **Templetons** Antler 4-ply	**Jaeger** Doppelwul **Twilleys** Crysette Stalite **Villawool** Pinto **Lee Target** Cherub 4-ply	**Lister** Lavenda Crisp Crepe 4-ply Lavenda 4-ply Nursery Time Baby 4-ply Bri-nylon Bel Air 4-& 7-ply Crepe Bel Air Courtelle Starspun **Pingouin** Golden Age **Patons** Beehive Baby Wool 4-ply 101 Courtelle Soft Quickerknit Quickerknit Baby Wool Purple Heather 4-ply **Robin** Super Crimp Bri-nylon 4-ply **Wendy** All 4-ply yarns **Twilleys** Crysette Stalite **Hayfield** 4-ply yarns	**Lister** Lavenda Crisp Crepe 4-ply **Mosgiel Woollens** Aotea 4-ply Worsted Fingering Aotea 4-ply Worsted Crepe Aotea 4-ply Super Spiral Spun Exlan Aotea Super Botany 4-ply Baby yarn
7 sts and 10 rows on No. 10 needles	**Pingouin** Coton Cordonnet Coton Perle 4-ply Twille...	**Pingouin** Coton Cordonnet Twilleys...	**Villawool** Pinto	**Pingouin** Golden Age	**Twilleys** Crysette

6¼ sts and 8½ rows on No. 9 needles	6¼ sts and 8 rows on No. 9 needles	6 sts and 8 rows on No. 9 needles	5½ sts and 7½ rows on No. 9 needles	5 sts and 7 rows on No. 9 needles	6 sts and 8 rows on No. 8 needles	5¾ sts and 7½ rows on No. 8 needles	5½ sts and 8 rows on No. 8 needles
		Mosgiel Woollens Aotea Super Botany Bambino Baby yarn; **Lister** 2-spun Double Crepe; **Sirdar** Courtelle Crepe Double Knitting	**Twilley** Knitcot	**Sirdar** Double Knitting / Double Crepe / Arctic Moss			
		Lister Lavenda Double Crepe; **Jaeger** Celtic Spun; **Lee Target** Leemont Double Crepe; **Sirdar** Courtelle Double Crepe / Double Bouclé; **Mahoney** Killowen; **Templetons** Wool Double Crepe	**Twilley** Knitcot	**Jaeger** Sunlin	**Pingouin** Gemini Double Crepe / Taurus Double Crepe; **Robin** Bri-nylon Double Knitting; **Wendy** Double Knitting Nylonised / Ciro Double Knitting Crepe; **Sirdar** Double Crepe / Arctic Moss; **Patons** Promise	**Patons** Fiona	**Emu** All double knitting yarns
	Patons Lambswool / L'Amour	**Jaeger** Celtic Spun; **Lee Target** Duo Double Crepe; **Sirdar** Courtelle Crepe Double Knitting / Double Bouclé 6-ply Goldseal Courtelle	**Sirdar** 8-ply Gold Seal Courtelle	**Jaeger** Sunlin	**Sirdar** Double Crepe Random Courtelle; **Lincoln** Cleckheaton 8-ply; **Villawool** Bouclé; **Patons** Katie	**Patons** Double Knit (7¾ rows); **Villawool** Super Knit DC 8	**Patons** Mohair (7 rows)
Templetons H & O Shetland Fleece		**Lister** Double knitting yarns; **Jaeger** Celtic Spun; **Lee Target** Leemont Double Crepe; **Mahoney** Killowen; **Templetons** Wool Double Crepe / Antler Double Crepe / H & O Shetland Charm	**Patons** Excelsior Scotch Fingering 4-ply	**Jaeger** Sunlin	**Pingouin** Madame Pingouin; **Patons** Beehive Astra; **Robin** Double Knitting Crepe; **Wendy** Carolette / Peter Pan Baby Nylon; **Ladyship** Allure / Safari		**Emu** All double knitting yarns
Templetons H & O Shetland Fleece	**Patons** Ninepin Midi Knitting	**Lister** Lavenda Double Knitting; **Jaeger** Donegal / Celtic Spun; **Lee Target** Motoravia D.K. and all double knitting yarns.; **Sirdar** Courtelle Double Crepe; **Templetons** Wool Double Crepe / Antler Double Crepe / H & O Shetland Charm; **Mahoney** Killowen Extra Double Knitting	**Twilley** Knitcot / Health Vest Cotton No. 1.; **Pingouin** Classique Crylor / Multipingouin	**Jaeger** Sunlin	**Pingouin** Double Double Knitting / Double Knitting\Jaspee\Super; **Robin** All double knit yarns; **Sirdar** All double knits yarns; **Ladyship** County Double Knitting; **Wendy** Double Knitting Nylonised / New Tricel Nylon Double Knitting; **Twilleys** Afghan	**Patons** Fiona	**Emu** All double knitting yarns (inc. Carella)

Tension					
5½ sts and 7½ rows on No. 8 needles	**Jaeger** Spiral-spun **Patons** Limelight Courtelle Double Crepe Four Seasons Courtelle	**Jaeger** Spiral-spun **Patons** Beehive Superior Double Knitting Beehive Double Knitting	**Patons** Bonny Courtelle (5¼ sts) **Sirdar** Octo	**Jaeger** Spiral-spun **Patons** 101 Courtelle Double Crepe Four Seasons courtelle	**Mosgiel Woollens** Aotea Romney Double Knitting Lyric Super Double Crepe
5½ sts and 7 rows on No. 8 needles	**Lister** All double knitting yarns **Hayfield** All double knitting yarns **Wendy** Peter Pan Courtelle Baby Quick	**Lister** All double knitting **Lee Target** Motoravia D.K. **Wendy** Peter Pan Courtelle Baby Quick **Hayfield** All double knitting yarns	**Patons** Caressa	**Lister** All double knitting yarns **Lee Target** Motoravia D.K. **Wendy** Peter Pan Courtelle Baby Quick **Hayfield** All double knitting yarns	
5 sts and 7½ rows on No. 8 needles	**Jaeger** Spiral-spun	**Jaeger** Spiral-spun	**Patons** Bonny Courtelle (5¼ sts)	**Jaeger** Spiral-spun	**Mosgiel Woollens** Aotea Romney Double Knitting
5 sts and 6½ rows on No. 8 needles	**Wendy** Kinvara **Sirdar** Candytwist Sportswool	**Patons** Carefree Aran Fisherman's Knit	**Sirdar** Candytwist	**Wendy** Kinvara **Sirdar** Candytwist Sportswool	**Sirdar** Candytwist Sportswool
4¾ sts and 7½ rows on No. 8 needles	**Patons** Camelot				
5½ sts and 7½ rows on No. 7 needles	**Pingouin** Classique Crylor Multipingouin **Patons** Double Wool **Wendy** Peter Pan Courtelle Quickerknit **Jaeger** Spiral-spun	**Pingouin** Classique Crylor Multipingouin **Jaeger** Spiral-spun **Patons** Beehive Double Knitting	**Patons** Double Knitting Snow White Sports Sea Urchin Totem (Patonised) Bonny Courtelle **Sirdar** Octo	**Pingouin** Classique Crylor **Wendy** Peter Pan Courtelle Quickerknit **Patons** Double Knitting **Jaeger** Spiral-spun Camelhair and Wool	**Mosgiel Woollens** Aotea Royal Worsted Fingering Lyric Super Double Crepe Caress Supersoft Worsted Fingering Aran Worsted Showerproof Fingering Crofter Woollen Spun Fingering
4½ sts and 6½ rows on No. 7 needles	**Mahoney** Blarney Bainin. **Wendy** Pompadour	**Mahoney** Blarney Bainin	**Mahoney** Blarney Bainin	**Mahoney** Blarney Bainin **Wendy** Pompadour	
5 sts and 4½ rows on No. 6 needles	**Templetons** 3 Glens Crepe Double Knitting	**Templetons** 3 Glens Crepe Double Knitting		**Templetons** 3 Glens Crepe Double Knitting	
4½ sts and 5½ rows on No. 6 needles	**Lister** Lavenda Double Six Triple Knitting	**Lee Target** Motoravia Triple Special Quality for Aran Knitting	**Villawool** Concorde	**Lister** Lavenda Double Six Triple Knitting	**Mosgiel Woollens** Aotea Sable Soft Triple Knitting
4¼ sts and 5¼ rows on No. 5 needles	**Patons** Doublet	**Patons** Carefree Double Double Knitting	**Patons** Skol (5¾ rows)	**Wendy** Diabolo Double Double Knitting	
4 sts and 5¼ rows on No. 5 needles	**Jaeger** Mohair Spun	**Jaeger** Mohair Spun	**Jaeger** Mohair Spun	**Jaeger** Mohair Spun	**Jaeger** Mohair Spun
3½ sts and 5 rows on No. 3 needles	**Lister** Prema Bulky Knitting		**Sirdar** Pullman **Lee Target** Super Flecknit	**Sirdar** Pullman **Lister** Prema Bulky Knitting	**Sirdar** Pullman

75 designs for the family

1

Here are the most original and appealing baby togs to appear for years—'patchwork' bell bottoms teamed with a jersey sporting epaulettes and arm-bands. The mock patchwork is most effective and yet quite simple to work.

*Knit
Sizes: to fit 18 [20:22] inch chest.*

2, 3

Matinée coat in triple spot pattern edged with garter stitch (above).

Knit
Size: to fit 18 [19] inch chest.

Arrowhead eyelet pattern gives a lively texture to this matinée coat (below).

Knit
Size: to fit 18 [19] inch chest.

4

Double moss stitch gives the pixie hood and matinée coat of this pram set a crisp texture. Leggings and mittens are in plain stocking stitch.

Knit
Sizes: to fit 18 [20 : 22] inch chest.

5

Long sleeve rompers with ridge stitch bodice—pants button at crutch. Matching cardigan.

Knit
Sizes: to fit 18 [20:22:24] inch chest.

6,7

Back buttoning cardigan (left) with lace trimmed neck.

Knit
Sizes: to fit 20 [22] inch chest.

Garter stitch jersey (right) with lace edged yoke.

Knit
Sizes: to fit 17 [20:23] inch chest.

8

Snug long sleeve zip fronted jumpsuit and matching hat.

Knit
Sizes: to fit 18 [20: 22:24] inch chest.

9

A honey of a dress, with a beautiful lacy stitch used for the short sleeves and the skirt. It buttons up at the back.

Knit
Sizes : to fit 16/18 [20:22] inch chest.

10

Tinker-ball—a large knitted ball with a bell inside. Each of the six sections can be worked in 2 colours which makes 12 colours in all.

Knit
Diameter : 18 inches.

11

The brightest dressing gown in town for little boys and girls—made in a marvellous Fair Isle pattern with soft, machine-washable pure new wool which comes in pretty baby colours too. (If you adjust the length it also makes a dishy cardigan).

Knit
Sizes: to fit 20 [22:24] inch chest.

12

Yoked matinée coat worked in eyelet ridge stitch, with matching bonnet and mittens, all trimmed with bows.

Knit
Sizes: to fit 18 [19] inch chest.

13

This layette in bramble stitch includes dress, matinée coat, bonnet, bootees and shawl.

Knit
Size: to fit 18 [20] inch chest.
Shawl: 36 inches square.

*Perfect for holidays this
all-in-one shorts suit
zips up the front, and
is edged with double
crochet and a single row
of contrast colour.*

Knit
Sizes: to fit 22 [24:26]
inch chest.

15

Practical and striking jersey and trousers with dungaree top and big striped pockets. The jersey is worked in wide rib and the dungarees in stocking stitch.

Knit
Sizes: to fit 22 [24:26] inch chest.

16

Fringed and braided bolero—warm and gay. Knitted in stocking stitch and trimmed with a crochet fringe and picot edge.

Knit
Sizes: to fit 24 [26:28] inch chest.

17

Crisp cotton knitted dress with narrow bands of contrasting colour. The demure collar is trimmed with a bow.

Knit
Sizes: to fit 22 [24:26] inch chest.

18

Simple and delightful playsuit. The short sleeves are worked in wide two-colour stripes and the two pockets have matching stripes.

Knit
Sizes: to fit 22 [24] inch chest.

19

Classic jersey in simple three-colour Jacquard design.

Knit
Sizes : to fit 26 [28:30:32] inch chest.

20

Tough and warm Aran jerseys with V or crew neck and raglan sleeves. Work in cables and lattice stitches.

Knit
Sizes : to fit 20 [22:24] inch chest.

21

A warm and husky snow set. The jersey and hat have patterned bands, with plain trousers, warm mittens and pompon hat.

Knit
Sizes : to fit 24 [26:28:30] inch chest.

22

An eye-catching jersey with a 'Policeman' motif. Fun to make and wear. Or you can make this jersey in one colour only —if you do, allow one extra ball of the main shade.

Knit
Sizes : to fit 26 [28:30: 32:34] inch chest.

23

23

Outdoor set of jersey, trousers, cap and mittens. The jersey is worked in double moss stitch with two interesting pattern panels.

Knit
Sizes: to fit 24 [26:28: 30] inch chest.

24

Chunky jersey, worked in broken basket stitch, with unusual raglan shaping and turn-down buttoned collar.

Knit
Sizes: to fit 24 [26:28: 30:32] inch chest.

25

Classic double-breasted trouser suit. Worked in panels of single rib and stocking stitch the jacket has a neat collar and the trousers flare gently.

Knit
Sizes : to fit 28 [30:32:34] inch chest.

26

Casual trouser suit for the fashion conscious. The long line jersey is worked in panels of mock cable stitch and the flared trousers are in stocking stitch.

Knit
Sizes : to fit 24 [26:28 30:32:34] inch chest.

27

Teenage dress with a bold two-colour motif on the centre front of the bodice. It has wide-ribbed skirt and neat neckline.

Knit
Sizes: to fit 32 [34:36] inch chest.

28

Long-line cardigan with a simple two-colour diamond motif on the front and matching hat.

Knit
Sizes: to fit 30 [32:34] inch chest.

29

There's a wide range of sizes in this elegant lace-panelled jerkin and matching, cleverly-shaped skirt.

Knit
Sizes 34-42 inch bust.

30

A jaunty beret and scarf to cheer you in even the very coldest winter wind.

Knit
Size Average head.

31

A skinny hug-me-tight to make with or without sleeves. The matching pull-on hat completes the outfit.

Knit
Sizes 32-40 inch bust.
Average head.

32

Left Simple to make—great fun to wear. A gay two-piece, with contrasting bib and stripes.

Knit
Sizes 34-38 inch bust.

33

Right Striped maxi or long, sleeveless cardigan—wear it as you will. Finish the edging with a crochet border.

Knit
Sizes 32-40 inch bust.

34

Colourful random stripes, a neat collar and ribbed cuffs—all add up to a bold, well-shaped shirt.

Knit
Sizes 34-42 inch bust.

35

Comfortably casual in a plain jersey, topped with a matching striped jerkin. Gay in contrasting colours; chic in closely related shades as shown here.

Knit
Sizes 32-40 inch bust.

36

Just unfasten the fashionably laced front of this top before you put it on, and even the most elaborate hair-do will survive! The set-in sleeves are delightfully bell-shaped. All in all, the prettiest tunic yet.

Knit
Sizes 32-40 inch bust.

37

Far right Cable and rib panels for a casual, country look, with an interesting saddle-top shoulder. Add two stripes of colour at the neck and cuffs, and you've a smart co-ordinate to match with either skirt or pants.

Knit
Sizes 32-40 inch bust.

38

Summer flattery in
a delightful boat-neck.
Cotton bouclé and a
textured stocking stitch
go to make up this
useful light-weight jersey.

Knit
Sizes 32-42 inch bust.

39

Applied smocking
on bell sleeves is the
outstanding feature of
this eye-catching two-
piece. The dress has a
high ribbed collar, and
the buttoning jacket is
edged with double crochet.

Knit
Sizes 32-38 inch bust.

40

Superb styling for town
or country. A jersey
suit with polo neck top,
and a midi skirt you can
adjust to any length.

Knit
Sizes 34-40 inch bust.

41

Traditional Aran stitches, a shaped waist, and slits front and back make this a tunic with a difference.

Knit
Sizes 34-42 inch bust.

Instructions for designs 1-41

'Patchwork' bell bottoms and epaulette jersey

Sizes
Jersey to fit 18[20:22]in chest
Length at centre back, 10½[11½:12½]in, adjustable
Sleeve seam, 7[8:9]in, adjustable
Trousers length to back waist, 17[18:19]in
Inside leg length, 9[10:11]in
The figures in brackets [] refer to the 20 and 22in sizes respectively
Tension
7½sts and 9½ rows to 1 in over st st worked on No.10 needles
Materials
Sirdar 4 ply Fontein Crepe or Talisman 4 ply 4[4:5] balls main shade, A
1 ball each of contrast colours, B, C, D, E and F
One pair No.10 needles
One pair No.11 needles
4[4:5]in zip fastener
Waist length ¾in wide elastic
Stitch holder
Note
Separate balls of yarn are used for each colour. Always twist yarns at back of work when changing colours. Colour sequence of each patch may be varied if required

Trousers

Patchwork patt is worked over 24[27:30] sts.
1st patch
1st row Using A, K to end.
2nd row Using A, P to end.
Rep these 2 rows 14[15:16] times more, using each colour in turn. 30[32:34] rows.
2nd patch
1st row K12[13:15]D, K12[14:15]E.
2nd row P12[14:15]E, P12[13:15]D.
Rep these 2 rows 6 times more.
15th row Using F, K to end.
16th row Using F, P to end.
Rep last 2 rows 0[1:2] times more.
Next row K12[13:15]A, K12[14:15]B.
Next row P12[14:15]B, P12[13:15]A.
Rep last 2 rows 6 times more. 30[32:34] rows.
3rd patch
1st row Using C, K to end.
2nd row Using C, P to end.
Rep these 2 rows 4 times more.
11th row K8[9:10]D, 8[9:10]E, 8[9:10]F.
12th row P8[9:10]F, 8[9:10]E, 8[9:10]D.
Rep these 2 rows 9[10:11] times more. 30[32: 34] rows.
4th patch
1st row Using A, K to end.
2nd row Using A, P to end.
Rep these 2 rows 14[15:16] times more. 30[32: 34] rows. Work subsequent patches using B, C, D, E and F.
5th patch
1st row K10[11:12]B, 4[5:6]C, 10[11:12]D.
2nd row P10[11:12]D, 4[5:6]C, 10[11:12]B.

Rep these 2 rows 5 times more.
13th row Using C, K to end.
14th row Using C, P to end.
Rep last 2 rows 2[3:4] times more.
Next row K10[11:12]E, 4[5:6]C, 10[11:12]F.
Next row P10[11:12]F, 4[5:6]C, 10[11:12]E.
Rep last 2 rows 5 times more. 30[32:34] rows.

Right leg front

Using No.10 needles and A, cast on 28[31:34] sts. Beg with a K row work 7 rows st st for hem.
Next row K all sts tbl to form hemline.
Work 1st, 2nd, 3rd, 4th and 5th patch patts, dec one st at beg of 9th and every foll 4th row 4 times in all. 24[27:30] sts.
Cont in patt without shaping until 60th[64th: 68th] row has been worked.
Keeping patt correct, inc one st at beg of next and every foll 4th row 6 times in all. 30[33:36] sts.
Cont in patt until 82nd[88th:94th] row has been worked, noting that extra sts are worked in first block of colour.
Shape crutch
Keeping patt correct, cast off 2sts at beg of next row. Work 1 row.
Dec one st at beg of next and foll alt rows 4 times in all. 24[27:30]sts.
Cont in patt without shaping until 142nd [152nd:162nd] row has been worked.
Using A, work 6 rows K1, P1 rib. Cast off loosely in rib.

Right leg side

Using No.10 needles and A, cast on 32[35:38] sts. Work hem as given for front.
Work 4th, 5th, 2nd, 1st and 3rd patch patts, shaping side on 9th row, as foll:
1st dec row K14[15:17] sts, K2 tog, K0[1:0], sl 1, K1, psso, K14[15:17] sts.
Work 3 rows patt without shaping.
2nd dec row K13[14:16] sts, K2 tog, K0[1:0], sl 1, K1, psso, K13[14:16] sts.
Work 3 rows patt without shaping.
3rd dec row K12[13:15] sts, K2 tog, K0[1:0], sl 1, K1, psso, K12[13:15] sts.
Work 3 rows patt without shaping.
4th dec row K11[12:14] sts, K2 tog, K0[1:0], sl 1, K1, psso, K11[12:14] sts. 24[27:30] sts.
Cont in patt without shaping until 143rd [153rd:163rd] row has been worked, ending with a K row.
Shape back
** **Next row** Patt to last 8[9:10] sts, turn.
Next row Patt to end.
Next row Patt to last 16[18:20] sts, turn.
Next row Patt to end.
Next row Patt across all sts.
Using A, work 6 rows K1, P1 rib. Cast off loosely in rib.**

Right leg back

Cast on and work hem as given for front. Work 3rd, 1st, 5th, 2nd and 4th patch patts, dec one st at end of 9th and every foll 4th row 4 times in all, noting that extra sts will be worked in last block of colour. 24[27:30] sts. Cont in patt until 60th[64th:68th] row has been worked.
Keeping patt correct, inc one st at end of next and every alt row 10 times in all. 34[37:40] sts.
Cont in patt until 83rd[89th:95th] row has been worked, noting that extra sts will be worked in last block of colour, ending with a K row.
Shape crutch
Keeping patt correct, cast off 2sts at beg of next row. Work 1 row.
Dec one st at beg of next and every alt row 8 times in all. 24[27:30] sts.
Cont in patt until 149th[159th:169th] row has been worked, ending with a K row.
Shape back
Work as given for side from ** to **, continuing 4th patch.

Left leg

Work 3 sections as given for Right leg, reversing all shaping.

To make up

Press each piece on WS under a damp cloth with a warm iron. Darn in ends. Join 3 Right leg sections tog, including hem and waist ribbing. Join Left leg in same way. Press seams. Join inner leg seams. Join backs and fronts from crutch to waist, including ribbing. Press seams. Turn hem to WS at hemline and sl st in place. Turn waist ribbing to WS and sl st in place. Thread elastic through waistband and secure.

Jersey back

Using No.11 needles and A, cast on 72[80:88] sts.
Work 10[12:14] rows K1, P1 rib. Change to No.10 needles. Beg with a K row cont in st st until work measures 7[7¾:8½]in from beg, or required length to underarm, ending with a P row.
Shape armholes
Cast off 3[4:5] sts at beg of next 2 rows.
Divide for back opening
Next row K2 tog, K31[34:37] sts, turn. Complete right shoulder first.
Dec one st at armhole edge on every alt row until 28[30:32] sts rem.
Cont without shaping until armhole measures 3½[3¾:4]in from beg, ending at armhole edge.
Shape shoulder
Next row Cast off 16[17:18] sts, work to end. Leave sts on holder for back neck.
With RS of work facing, rejoin yarn to rem sts and complete to match first side, reversing shaping.

Jersey front

Work as given for back, omitting back opening, until front measures 6 rows less than back to shoulder, ending with a P row.
Shape neck
Next row K22[23:24] sts, turn. Complete left shoulder first.
Cast off 3sts at neck edge on next and foll alt row. Work until front measures same as back to shoulder, ending at armhole edge.
Shape shoulder
Next row Cast off 16[17:18] sts. Fasten off.
With RS of work facing, sl next 12[14:16] sts onto holder and leave for centre neck. Rejoin yarn to rem sts and complete to match first side, reversing shaping.

Sleeves

Using No.11 needles and A, cast on 38[40:42] sts.
Work 10[12:14] rows K1, P1 rib. Change to No.10 needles.
Work 30[32:34] rows patt as given for 1st patch, then cont in st st using A only, inc one st at each end of 7th and every foll 8th row until there are 46[50:54] sts. Cont without shaping until sleeve measures 7[8:9]in from beg, or required length to underarm, ending with a P row.
Shape top
Cast off 3[4:5] sts at beg of next 2 rows. Dec one st at each end of next and every alt row until 32sts rem. Work 1 row. Dec one st each end of every row until 10sts rem. Work 2¼[2½:2¾]in patt as given for 1st patch on these 10sts. Cast off.

Neckband

Press each piece as given for Trousers. Set sleeves into armholes, joining saddle top of sleeves to back and front shoulders. Using No.11 needles and A and with RS neck facing, K across 12[13:14] sts for left back neck, K up 8sts across left sleeve top, K up 10sts down left side of neck, K across 12[14:16] sts on centre front holder, K up 10sts up right side of neck, K up 8 sts across right sleeve top and K12[13:14] sts from right back neck holder. 72[76:80] sts. Work 1½[1¾:2]in K1, P1 rib. Cast off loosely in rib.

To make up

Join side and sleeve seams. Press seams. Fold neckband in half to WS and sl st in place. Sew in zip to back neck to top of neckband.

2 *Matinée coat decorated with triple spot pattern*

Sizes
To fit 18[19]in chest
Length to centre back, 9½[10¼]in
Sleeve seam, 5¾[6½]in
The figures in brackets [ ] refer to the 19in size
Tension
7½ sts and 9½ rows to 1in over spot patt worked on No.10 needles;
7 sts and 10 rows to 1in over lace patt worked on No.10 needles
Materials
Emu Superlite Bri Nylon 4 ply or Super Crepe 4[5] balls
One pair No.10 needles
One pair No.12 needles
Three small buttons

Coat back

Using No.10 needles cast on 123[135] sts.
K 9 rows g st. Commence patt.
1st row (RS) K to end.
2nd row P to end.
3rd row K7, *yfwd, K2 tog tbl, K10, rep from * to last 8 sts, yfwd, K2 tog tbl, K6.
4th row P to end.
5th row K5, *K2 tog, yfwd, K1, yfwd, K2 tog tbl, K7, rep from * to last 10 sts, K2 tog, yfwd, K1, yfwd, K2 tog tbl, K5.
6th row P to end.
7th row K to end.
8th row P to end.
9th row K13, *yfwd, K2 tog tbl, K10, rep from * to last 2 sts, K2.
10th row P to end.
11th row K11, *K2 tog, yfwd, K1, yfwd, K2 tog tbl, K7, rep from * to last 4 sts, K4.
12th row P to end.
These 12 rows form patt. Cont in patt until work measures 5½[6]in from beg, ending with a WS row.
Next row K5[1] sts, *K2 tog, rep from * 55[63] times more, K6[6] sts. 67[71] sts.
K 3 rows g st.
Shape armholes
Next row Cast off 3[4] sts, K to end.
Next row Cast off 3[4] sts, P to end.
Next row K2 tog, K10[11], *yfwd, K2 tog tbl, K10, rep from * to last 13[14] sts, yfwd, K2 tog tbl, K9[10], K2 tog.
Next row P to end.
Next row K2 tog, K7[8], *K2 tog, yfwd, K1, yfwd, K2 tog tbl, K7, rep from * to last 14[15] sts, K2 tog, yfwd, K1, yfwd, K2 tog tbl, K7[8], K2 tog.
Next row P to end.
Next row K2 tog, K to last 2 sts, K2 tog.
Next row P to end.
Next row K3[4], *yfwd, K2 tog tbl, K10, rep from * to last 4[5] sts, yfwd, K2 tog tbl, K2[3].
Next row P to end.
Next row K1[2], *K2 tog, yfwd, K1, yfwd, K2 tog tbl, K7, rep from * to last 6[7] sts, K2 tog, yfwd, K1, yfwd, K2 tog tbl, K1[2].
Next row P to end.
Keeping patt correct, cont without shaping until armholes measure 3¼[3½]in from beg, ending with a WS row.
Shape shoulders
Cast off 5[5] sts at beg of next 4 rows and 6 [6] sts at beg of foll 2 rows. Cast off rem 23 [25] sts.

Left front

Using No.10 needles cast on 69[69] sts. K9 rows g st. Commence patt.
1st row (RS) K to end.
2nd row K6, P to end.
3rd row K7, *yfwd, K2 tog tbl, K10, rep from * to last 14 sts, yfwd, K2 tog tbl, K12.
4th row K6, P to end.
5th row K5, *K2 tog, yfwd, K1, yfwd, K2 tog tbl, K7, rep from * to last 16 sts, K2 tog, yfwd, K1, yfwd, K2 tog tbl, K11.
6th row K6, P to end.
7th row K to end.
8th row K6, P to end.
9th row K13, *yfwd, K2 tog tbl, K10, rep from * to last 8 sts, K8.
10th row K6, P to end.
11th row K11, *K2 tog, yfwd, K1, yfwd, K2 tog tbl, K7, rep from * to last 10 sts, K10.
12th row K6, P to end.
Keeping patt correct cont until work measures 5½[6]in from beg, ending with a WS row.
Next row *K2 tog, rep from * to last 5[9] sts, K5[9] sts. 37[39] sts.
K3 rows g st.
Shape armhole
Next row Cast off 3[4] sts, K to end.
Next row K6, P to end.
Next row K2 tog, K10[11], yfwd, K2 tog tbl, K10, yfwd, K2 tog tbl, K8.
Next row K6, P to end.
Next row K2 tog, K7[8], K2 tog, yfwd, K1, yfwd, K2 tog tbl, K7, K2 tog, yfwd, K1, yfwd, K2 tog tbl, K7.
Next row K6, P to end.

Next row K2 tog, K to end.
Next row K6, P to end.
Next row K3[4], yfwd, K2 tog tbl, K10, yfwd, K2 tog tbl, K14.
Next row K6, P to end.
Next row K1[2], K2 tog, yfwd, K1, yfwd, K2 tog tbl, K7, K2 tog, yfwd, K1, yfwd, K2 tog tbl, K13.
Next row K6, P to end.
Cont in patt until armhole measures 2¼[2½]in from beg, ending at front edge.
Shape neck
Next row Cast off 10[11] sts, patt to end.
Dec one st at neck edge on next 5 rows. Cont without shaping until armhole measures same as back to shoulder, ending at armhole edge.
Shape shoulder
Cast off 5[5] sts at beg of next and foll alt row. Work 1 row. Cast off rem 6[6] sts.

Right front

Using No.10 needles cast on 69[69] sts. K 9 rows g st. Commence patt.
1st row K to end.
2nd row P to last 6 sts, K6.
3rd row K13, *yfwd, K2 tog tbl, K10, rep from * to last 8 sts, yfwd, K2 tog tbl, K6.
4th row P to last 6 sts, K6.
5th row K11, *K2 tog, yfwd, K1, yfwd, K2 tog tbl, K7, rep from * to last 10 sts, K2 tog, yfwd, K1, yfwd, K2 tog tbl, K5.
6th row P to last 6 sts, K6.
7th row K to end.
8th row P to last 6 sts, K6.
9th row K19, *yfwd, K2 tog tbl, K10, rep from * to last 2 sts, K2.
10th row P to last 6 sts, K6.
11th row K17, *K2 tog, yfwd, K1, yfwd, K2 tog tbl, K7, rep from * to last 4 sts, K4.
12th row P to last 6 sts, K6.
Cont in patt until work measures 5½[6]in from beg, ending with a WS row.
Next row K5[9] sts, *K2 tog, rep from * to end. 37[39] sts.
Next row K to end.
Next row (buttonhole row) K2, cast off 2, K to end.
Next row K to end, casting on 2 sts above those cast off in previous row.
Shape armhole
Next row K to end.
Next row Cast off 3[4] sts, P to last 6 sts, K6.
Next row K9, yfwd, K2 tog tbl, K10, yfwd, K2 tog tbl, K9[10], K2 tog.
Next row P to last 6 sts, K6.
Next row K7, K2 tog, yfwd, K1, yfwd, K2 tog tbl, K7, K2 tog, yfwd, K1, yfwd, K2 tog tbl, K7[8], K2 tog.
Next row P to last 6 sts, K6.
Next row K to last 2 sts, K2 tog.
Next row P to last 6 sts, K6.
Next row K2, cast off 2, K11, yfwd, K2 tog tbl, K10, yfwd, K2 tog tbl, K2[3].
Next row P to last 4 sts, K2, cast on 2, K2.
Next row K13, K2 tog, yfwd, K1, yfwd, K2 tog tbl, K7, K2 tog, yfwd, K1, yfwd, K2 tog tbl, K1[2].
Next row P to last 6 sts, K6.
Complete to match left front, reversing all shapings and making a 3rd buttonhole on 9th row from previous one.

Sleeves

Using No.12 needles cast on 38[38] sts. Work 1in K1, P1 rib, inc one st at end of last row. 39[39] sts. Change to No.10 needles and work in patt as given for back, inc one st at each end of 7th and every foll 6th[5th] row until there are 49[53] sts and working extra sts into patt. Cont without shaping until sleeve measures 5¾

[6½] in from beg, ending with a WS row.
Shape top
Cast off 3[4] sts at beg of next 2 rows. Dec one st at each end of next and every foll alt row until 29[31] sts rem. Dec one st at each end of every row until 7[9] sts rem. Cast off.

Collar

Using No.10 needles cast on 75[77] sts. K9 rows g st. Commence patt.
1st row K to end.
2nd and every alt row K6, P to last 6 sts, K6
3rd row K13[14], *yfwd, K2 tog tbl, K10, rep from * to last 14[15] sts, yfwd, K2 tog tbl, K12[13].
5th row K11[12], *K2 tog, yfwd, K1, yfwd, K2 tog tbl, K7, rep from * to last 16[17] sts. K2 tog, yfwd, K1, yfwd, K2 tog tbl, K11[12].
7th row K to end.
8th row As 2nd.
Change to No.12 needles.
9th row K19[20], *yfwd, K2 tog tbl, K10, rep from * to last 8[9] sts, K8[9].
11th row K17[18], *K2 tog, yfwd, K1, yfwd, K2 tog tbl, K7, rep from * to last 10[11] sts, K10[11].
12th row As 2nd.
Cast off.

To make up

Press each piece under a dry cloth with a cool iron for Bri Nylon or a damp cloth with a warm iron for Super Crepe. Join shoulder, side and sleeve seams. Set in sleeves. Sew collar into position, placing cast off edge to neck, beg and ending at centre of front borders. Neaten buttonholes and sew on buttons.

Matinée coat in arrowhead eyelet pattern

Sizes, tension, and materials
As for triple spot pattern coat (2)

Back

Using No.10 needles cast on 111[121] sts. K9 rows g st.
Commence patt.
1st row K1, *yfwd, sl 1, K1, psso, K5, K2 tog, yfwd, K1, rep from * to end.
2nd and every alt row P to end.
3rd row K2, *yfwd, sl 1, K1, psso, K3, K2 tog, yfwd, K3, rep from * to last 9 sts, yfwd, sl 1, K1, psso, K3, K2 tog, yfwd, K2.
5th row K3, *yfwd, sl 1, K1, psso, K1, K2 tog, yfwd, K5, rep from * to last 8 sts, yfwd, sl 1, K1, psso, K1, K2 tog, yfwd, K3.
7th row K4, *yfwd, sl 1, K2 tog, psso, yfwd, K7, rep from * to last 7 sts, yfwd, sl 1, K2 tog, psso, yfwd, K4.
8th row P to end.
These 8 rows form patt. Cont in patt until 6[7] complete patts have been worked.
Next row K11[10] sts, *K2 tog, rep from * 43[49] times more, K12 [11] sts. 67[71] sts.
K3 rows g st. Beg with a K row cont in st st.
Shape armholes
Cast off 3 sts at beg of next 2 rows. Dec one st at each end of next and every foll alt row until 53[55] sts rem. Cont without shaping until armholes measure 3¼[3½]in from beg, ending with a P row.
Shape shoulders
Cast off 5 sts at beg of next 6 rows. Cast off rem 23[25] sts.

Left front

Using No.10 needles cast on 57[67] sts. K 9 rows g st. Commence patt.
1st row K1, *yfwd, sl 1, K1, psso, K5, K2 tog, yfwd, K1, rep from * to last 6 sts, K6.
2nd and every alt row K6, P to end.
3rd row K2, *yfwd, sl 1, K1, psso, K3, K2 tog, yfwd, K3, rep from * to last 5 sts, K5.
5th row K3, *yfwd, sl 1, K1, psso, K1, K2 tog, yfwd, K5, rep from * to last 4 sts, K4.
7th row K4, *yfwd, sl 1, K2 tog, psso, yfwd, K7, rep from * to last 3 sts, K3.
8th row K6, P to end.
Cont in patt keeping 6 g st border correct until 6[7] complete patts have been worked.
Next row K8[5] sts, *K2 tog, rep from * 19[27] times more, K9[6] sts. 37[39] sts.
K 3 rows g st. Beg with a K row cont in st st keeping g st border correct.
Shape armhole
Cast off 3 sts at beg of next row. Dec one st at armhole edge on every foll alt row until 30[31] sts rem. Cont without shaping until armhole measures 2¼[2½]in from beg, ending at front edge.
Shape neck
Next row Cast off 10[11] sts, P to end.
Dec one st at neck edge on next 5 rows. Cont without shaping until armhole measures same as back to shoulder, ending at armhole edge.
Shape shoulder
Cast off 5 sts at beg of next and foll 2 alt rows.

Right front

Using No.10 needles cast on 57[67] sts. K 9 rows g st. Commence patt.
1st row K7, *yfwd, sl 1, K1, psso, K5, K2 tog, yfwd, K1, rep from * to end.
2nd and every alt row P to last 6 sts, K6.
3rd row K8, *yfwd, sl 1, K1, psso, K3, K2 tog, yfwd, K3, rep from * to last 9 sts, yfwd, sl 1, K1, psso, K3, K2 tog, yfwd, K2.
5th row K9, *yfwd, sl 1, K1, psso, K1, K2 tog, yfwd, K5, rep from * to last 8 sts, yfwd, sl 1, K1, psso, K1, K2 tog, yfwd, K3.
7th row K10, *yfwd, sl 1, K2 tog, psso, yfwd, K7, rep from * to last 7 sts, yfwd, sl 1, K2 tog, psso, yfwd, K4.
8th row P to last 6 sts, K6.
Cont in patt keeping 6 g st border correct until 6[7] complete patts have been worked.
Next row K9[6] sts, *K2 tog, rep from * 19[27] times more, K8[5] sts. 37[39] sts.
Next row K to end.
Next row (buttonhole row) K2 sts, cast off 2 sts, K to end.
Next row K to end casting on 2 sts above those cast off in previous row.
Complete to match left front, reversing all shapings and making 2 more buttonholes at intervals of 1in measured from base of previous buttonhole.

Sleeves

Using No.12 needles cast on 36[38] sts. Work 1in K1, P1 rib, ending with a RS row.
Next row Rib 6[8], *pick up loop that lies between st just worked and next st on left hand needle and K tbl, rib 6[10], rep from * to end. 41[41] sts.
Change to No.10 needles and work in patt as given for back, inc one st at each end of 11th and every foll 12th[10th] row until there are 47[49] sts. Cont without shaping until 6[7] complete patts have been worked.
Shape top
Keeping patt correct, cast off 3 sts at beg of next 2 rows. Dec one st at each end of next and every foll alt row until 25[27] sts rem.

Dec one st at each end of every row until 7[9] sts rem. Cast off.

Collar

Using No.10 needles cast on 74[76] sts. K9 rows g st.
Next row K to end.
Next row K6, P to last 6 sts, K6.
Rep last 2 rows until work measures 1¾in from beg. Change to No.12 needles and work a further ½in. Cast off.

To make up

As given for triple spot pattern coat (2).

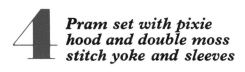

4 *Pram set with pixie hood and double moss stitch yoke and sleeves*

Sizes

To fit an 18[20:22]in chest
Coat length at centre back, 11[12:13]in
Sleeve seam, 6[7½:9]in
The figures in brackets [] refer to the 20 and 22in sizes respectively
Tension
5½ sts and 7½ rows to 1in over st st worked on No.9 needles
Materials
Pingouin Classique Crylor or Multipingouin
Coat 2[3:3] balls
Leggings 2[2:3] balls
Bonnet and mitts 1[1:2] balls
Hood and mitts 1[1:2] balls
One pair No.9 needles
One pair No.11 needles
Stitch holder
Three buttons for coat
One button for bonnet or hood
Waist length of elastic for leggings
1½ yds of ribbon

Coat back

Using No.9 needles cast on 89[95:101] sts.

Commence moss st patt.
1st row K1, *P1, K1, rep from * to end.
2nd row P1, *K1, P1, rep from * to end.
3rd row As 2nd row.
4th row As 1st row.
Beg with a K row cont in st st until work measures 6[6½:7]in from beg, ending with a K row. **
Next row P5[8:11] sts, *P2 tog, rep from * 39 times more, P to end. 49[55:61] sts.
Work 4 rows moss st patt.
Shape raglan
Keeping patt correct dec one st at each end of next and every alt row until 15[17:19] sts rem. Work 1 row. Cast off.

Coat left front

Using No.9 needles cast on 45[49:53] sts and work as given for back to **.
Next row P2[4:6] sts, *P2 tog, rep from * 19 times more, P to end.
Work 4 rows moss st patt.
Shape raglan
Keeping patt correct dec one st at beg of next and every alt row until all sts are worked off, *at the same time* shape neck when work measures 9½[10½:11]in from beg, ending at centre front edge.
Shape neck
Cast off 3[4:5] sts at beg of next row, then dec one st at neck edge on every row 4[5:6] times in all.

Coat right front

Work as given for left front, reversing shaping.

Sleeves

Using No.11 needles cast on 33[35:37] sts. Work 6 rows K1, P1 rib. Change to No. 9 needles and moss st patt as given for back. Keeping patt correct, inc one st at each end of every 4th row until there are 43[47:51] sts. Cont without shaping until sleeve measures 6[7½:9]in from beg, ending with a WS row.
Shape raglan
Work as given for back until 9 sts rem. Work 1 row. Cast off.

Front borders

Using No.11 needles cast on 7 sts. Work 6[6½:7] in K1, P1 rib.
Next row (buttonhole row) Rib 2 sts, cast off 3 sts, rib to end.
Next row Rib to end casting on 3 sts above those cast off in previous row.
Cont in rib making 2 more buttonholes in same way at intervals of 1½[1¾:1¾]in from centre of previous buttonhole. Cont in rib until border measures 9½[10½:11]in from beg. Cast off in rib. Work other border in same way, omitting buttonholes.

To make up

Do not press. Join raglan, side and sleeve seams. Oversew borders to centre front edges, having buttonhole band on right front for a girl or left front for a boy.
Collar Using No.11 needles K up 61[65:73] sts evenly round neck, beg and ending 3 sts from centre front edges. Work 18[20:22] rows K1, P1 rib.
Cast off loosely in rib. Sew on buttons.

Leggings left leg

Using No.11 needles cast on 56[62:68] sts. Work 4 rows K1, P1 rib.
Next row Rib 1 st, *yrn, rib 2 tog, rep from *

to last st, rib 1 st.
Work 5 more rows K1, P1 rib.
Change to No.9 needles and beg with a K row work in st st.
Shape back
1st row K13[15:17] sts, turn.
2nd row P.
3rd row K26[30:34] sts, turn.
4th row P.
5th row K39[45:51] sts, turn.
6th row P.
Beg with a K row cont in st st across all sts, inc one st at each end of 9th[11th:13th] and every foll 6th row until there are 70[76:82] sts. Dec one st at each end of 7th[9th:11th] and every foll alt row until 60[66:72] sts rem and then every foll 4th row until 38[44:50] sts rem. Cont without shaping for a further 1[1½:2]in, ending with a P row.
Next row K1, *yfwd, K2 tog, rep from * to last st, K1.
Next row P to end.
Shape foot
Next row K34[38:42] sts, turn and P12 [14:16] sts. Work 20[22:24] rows st st on these sts.
Next row K up 11[12:13] sts along side of foot, K4 [6:8] sts.
Next row P27 [32:37] sts, P up 11[12:13] sts along side of foot, P22[24:26] sts. 60[68:76] sts. Beg with a K row work 6 rows st st.
Next row K32[34:36] sts, K2 tog tbl, K10 [14:18] sts, K2 tog, K14[16:18] sts.
Next row P to end.
Cont dec in this way above dec on previous row on foll 2 K rows. Cast off.

Leggings right leg

Work as given for left leg, reversing all shaping.

To make up

Do not press. Join back, front and leg seams. Join foot seams. Thread elastic through holes at waist and ribbon through holes at ankles.

Bonnet

Using No.11 needles cast on 67[73:79] sts. Work 6 rows moss st patt as given for coat back. Beg with a K row work 6 rows st st. Work 6 more rows moss st patt. Change to No.9 needles. ***
Beg with a P row to reverse work cont in st st for a further 4½[5:5½]in, ending with a P row.
Shape back
Next row Cast off 22[24:26] sts, K to end.
Next row Cast off 22[24:26] sts, P to end.
Cont in st st on centre 23[25:27] sts for a further 4[4¼:4½]in, ending with a P row.
Next row K2[1:0] sts, *K3 tog, rep from * to end. Cast off rem sts.
Neck edging
Using No.11 needles cast on 4 sts. Work 10[12: 14]in g st.
Next row K1, yfwd, K2 tog, K1.
Next row K to end.
Next row K2 tog twice.
Next row K2 tog. Fasten off.

To make up

Do not press. Join cast off sts to side edges of back. Turn back brim. Oversew neck edging to lower edge of bonnet, stretching to fit and leaving 2[2½:3]in free at shaped end. Sew on button.

Hood

Work as given for bonnet to ***. Beg with a K row cont in st st until work measures 6½[7¼:8]in

from beg, ending with a P row. Cast off.
Neck edging
Work as given for neck edging of bonnet.

To make up

Do not press. Fold cast off edge in half and join tog to form back. Sew on neck edging as given for bonnet.

Mitts

Using No.11 needles cast on 33[37:41] sts. Work 4 rows moss st patt. Change to No.9 needles. Beg with a K row work 6 rows st st.
Next row K1, *K2 tog, yfwd, K2, rep from * to end.
Beg with a P row cont in st st until work measures 2½[3:3½]in from beg, ending with a P row.
Shape top
Next row K1, *K2 tog, rep from * to end.
Next row P to end.
Next row K1, *K2 tog, rep from * to end.
Thread yarn through rem sts, draw up and fasten off.

To make up

Do not press. Join side seams. Thread ribbon through holes at wrist.

5 *Long sleeve rompers and V-neck cardigan in ridge stitch*

Sizes
To fit an 18[20:22:24]in chest
Cardigan length at centre back, 10[11:12½:14]in down Sleeve seam, 6[7:8:10]in
Rompers length at centre back, 15½[16½:18½:19½]in
Sleeve seam, 6[7:8:10]in
The figures in brackets [] refer to the 20, 22 and 24 in sizes respectively
Tension
5 sts and 9 rows to 1in over patt worked on No.8 needles
Materials
5 [6:6:7] balls of Madame Pingouin D.K. for cardigan
7 [8:9:10] balls of Madame Pingouin D.K. for rompers
or
3[4:4:4] balls of Pingouin Super for cardigan
4[5:6:6] balls of Pingouin Super for rompers
One pair of No.8 needles
One pair No.10 needles
Stitch holder
4 buttons for cardigan
5 buttons for rompers
One No.5·00 (ISR) crochet hook

Cardigan back

Using No.10 needles cast on 51[55:59:63] sts. Work 12 rows K1, P1 rib. Change to No.8 needles.
1st row K to end.
2nd row P to end.
3rd row K to end.
4th row *P1, K into st below next st and sl st off needles — called K1B —, rep from * to last st, P1.
5th, 6th and 7th rows As 1st, 2nd and 3rd rows.
8th row P2, *K1B, P1, rep from * to last st, P1.
These 8 rows form patt and are rep throughout. Cont in patt until work measures 5½[6:7:8]in from beg, ending with a 4th or 8th patt row.
Shape raglan
Next row K2 tog, work to last 2 sts, K2 tog.
Work 3 rows without shaping. Rep these 4 rows 3[4:5:6] times more, then dec at each end of every alt row until 17[19:21:23] sts rem. Work 1 row. Cast off.

Cardigan left front

Using No.10 needles cast on 25[27:29:31] sts. Work as given for back until front measures same as back to armhole, ending at armhole edge.
Shape raglan
Next row K2 tog, work to end.
Work 3 rows without shaping. Rep these 4 rows 3[4:5:6] times more, then dec at each end of every alt row until all sts are worked off, *at the same time* when work measures 6½[7:8:9]in from beg, shape neck, ending at centre front edge.
Shape neck
Dec one st at beg of next and every foll 4th row 7[8:9:10] times in all.

Cardigan right front

Work as given for left front, reversing all shaping.

Sleeves

Using No.10 needles cast on 37[39:41:43] sts. Work 1½in K1, P1 rib. Change to No.8 needles. Work in patt as given for back, inc one st at each end of every 12th row until there are 41[43:45:47] sts. Cont without shaping until sleeve measures 6[7:8:10]in from beg, ending with a 4th or 8th patt row.
Shape raglan
Work as given for back raglan shaping until 7 sts rem. Work 1 row. Cast off.

Front border

Using No.10 needles cast on 7 sts. Work ½in K1, P1 rib.
Next row (buttonhole row) Rib 3 sts, cast off 1 st, rib 3 sts.
Next row Rib 3 sts, cast on 1 st, rib 3 sts.
Cont in K1, P1 rib, working 3 more buttonholes in same way at intervals of 2[2:2¼:2¾]in from centre of previous buttonhole, then cont until border is long enough to fit up centre front edges and round neck. Cast off in rib.

To make up

Do not press. Join raglan, side and sleeve seams. Oversew front border to cardigan fronts and round neck, having buttonholes on right front for a girl or left front for a boy. Sew on buttons.

Romper back

Using No.8 needles cast 15[15:17:17] sts. Beg with a K row work in st st, inc one at each end of every row until there are 49[55:61:67] sts. Cast on 6 sts at beg of next 2 rows.
**Dec one st at each end of every foll 6th row until 51[57:63:69] sts rem. Cont without shaping until work measures 7[7½:8½:9]in from beg, ending with a P row.
Waist ribbing
Work 4 rows K1, P1 rib.
Next row Rib 1 st, *yrn, rib 2 tog, rep from * to end.
Work 2 more rows K1, P1 rib.
Next row Rib 3[3:3:1] sts, *rib 2 tog, rib 7[5:4:4] sts, rep from * 4[6:8:10] times more, rib 2 tog, rib to end. 45[49:53:57] sts.
Cont in patt as given for cardigan back, inc one st at each end of every 10th row until there are 51[55:59:63] sts. Cont without shaping until work measures 11[11½:13:13½] in from beg ending with a 4th or 8th patt row. **
Shape raglan
Work as given for cardigan back until 17[19:21:23] sts rem. Work 1 row. Cast off.

Romper front

Using No.8 needles cast on 15[15:17:17] sts. Beg with a K row work 3[4:6:7] rows st st. Cast on 3 sts at beg of next 12[14:14:16] rows and 5[5:7:7] sts at beg of foll 2 rows. Work as given from ** to ** for romper back.
Shape raglan and divide for front opening
Next row K2 tog, work 21[23:25:27] sts, turn. Leave rem sts on holder. Work 3 rows without shaping then dec one st at armhole edge on next row. Dec one st at armhole edge on every foll 4th row 2[3:4:5] times more, then on every alt row until all sts are worked off, *at the same time* shape neck when centre front opening measures 2½[2½:3:3]in from beg.
Shape neck
Dec one st at neck on every row 5[6:7:8] times.
Rejoin yarn to centre edge of sts left on holder, cast off first 5 sts, work to end. Complete to match first side, reversing shaping.

Sleeves

Work as given for sleeves of cardigan.

Front borders

Using No.10 needles cast on 7 sts. Work 1¼[1¼:1¾:1¾]in K1, P1 rib. Work buttonhole rows as given for cardigan front border. Cont until work measures 2½[2½:3:3] in from beg. Cast off in rib. Work another border in same way, omitting buttonhole.

To make up

Do not press. Join raglan, side and sleeve seams. Fold cuffs in half to WS and sl st down. Oversew borders into centre front opening, having buttonhole on right front for a girl or left front for a boy. Sew down at bottom.
Neckband Using No.10 needles K up 67[73:75:81] sts evenly around neck, including borders. Work 6 rows K1, P1 rib working buttonhole as before on 3rd and 4th rows. Cast off in rib.
Legbands Using No.10 needles K up 56[61:65:71] sts evenly round each leg. Work 12 rows K1, P1 rib. Cast off loosely in rib. Fold legbands in half to WS and sl st down.
With RS work facing work 2 rows dc between legs on front. Work 2 rows dc between legs on back, forming 3 buttonholes on 2nd row by working 2ch and missing 2dc.
Using 2 strands of yarn make a crochet chain, thread through holes at waist. Sew on buttons.

6 *Back buttoning cardigan with lace-trimmed neck*

Sizes
To fit 17[20:23]in chest
Length at centre back, 9½[11:12½]in
Sleeve seam, 5½[6½:8]in
The figures in brackets [] refer to the 20 and 23in sizes respectively
Tension
5½ sts and 8 rows to 1in over patt worked on

No.8 needles; 5 sts and 10 rows to 1in over g
st worked on No.8 needles

Materials

5[6:7] balls Pingouin Baby Double Knitting
or 3[4:4] balls Pingouin Super
One pair No.8 needles
One pair No.10 needles
Stitch holder
Six buttons
Lace for trimming

Front

Using No.10 needles cast on 50[58:66] sts. Work
3[3½:4]in K1, P1 rib. Change to No.8 needles.
Commence patt.
1st row K2, *P2, K2, rep from * to end.
2nd row P2, *K2, P2, rep from * to end.
3rd row K to end.
4th row As 1st row.
5th row As 2nd row.
6th row P to end.
These 6 rows form patt and are rep throughout.
Cont in patt until work measures 5[6:7]in from
beg, ending with a WS row.
Shape raglan armholes
Next row K1, K2 tog, patt to last 3 sts, K2 tog
tbl, K1.
Next row K1, patt to last st, K1.
Rep last 2 rows until 28[34:40] sts rem. Work
1 row.
Shape neck
Next row K1, K2 tog, patt 9[10:11] sts, leave
rem sts on holder.
Dec one st at neck edge on every row 4 times,
at the same time cont to work raglan shaping
until 2 sts rem. K2 tog. Fasten off.
With RS of work facing, rejoin yarn to rem sts,
cast off first 4[8:12] sts, then work on rem sts
to match other side of neck, reversing shaping.

Right back

Using No.10 needles cast on 22[26:30] sts.
Work as given for front until work measures
same as front to armhole, ending with a WS row.
Shape raglan armhole
Next row K1, K2 tog, patt to end.
Next row Patt to last st, K1.
Rep last 2 rows until 4[6:8] sts rem. Work 1
row. Cast off.

Left back

Work as given for right back, noting that 1st
raglan shaping row will read: Patt to last 2 sts,
K2 tog tbl, K1.

Sleeves

Using No.10 needles cast on 30[34:34] sts.
Work 1½in K1, P1 rib. Change to No.8 needles.
Work in patt as given for front, inc one st at
each end of every 4th row until there are
42[46:50] sts. Cont without shaping until sleeve
measures 5½[6½:8]in from beg, ending with a
WS row.
Shape top
Work raglan shaping as given for front until
6 sts rem. Work 1 row. Cast off.

Borders

Using No.10 needles cast on 5 sts. Work in g st
throughout. Work ¼[½:¾]in.
Next row (buttonhole row) K2, cast off one, K2.
Next row K2, cast on one, K2.
Work 4 more buttonholes in same way at
intervals of 1¾[2:2¼]in from centre of previous
buttonhole. Cont until border measures 9[10½:12]
in from beg. Cast off. Work other border in
same way, omitting buttonholes.

To make up

Do not press. Join raglan seams. Join side and
sleeve seams. Oversew borders to centre back
edges, stretching slightly.
Neck edge Using No.10 needles and with RS
of work facing, K up 53[61:69] sts evenly round
neck. Work 4 rows K1, P1 rib, making a buttonhole as given for border on 1st row. Cast off in
rib. Sew on buttons. Sew lace to bottom of neck
ribbing.

7 Jersey with lace-trimmed yoke and bootees

Sizes
To fit 17[20:23]in chest
Jersey length at centre back, 9[10:11]in
Sleeve seam, 4½[5:7]in
Bootees to fit the 17 and 20in chest sizes
The figures in brackets [] refer to the 20 and
23in sizes respectively
Tension
As for Back Buttoning Cardigan
Materials
Pingouin Baby Double Knitting
Jersey 4[5:5] balls
Bootees 1[1:1] ball
or Pingouin Super
Jersey 2[3:3] balls
Bootees 1[1:1] ball
One pair No.8 needles, one pair No.10 needles
Stitch holder
Three buttons for jersey
Ribbon for bootees and bow
Lace for trimming

Jersey backs and front

Using No.8 needles cast on 106[122:138] sts.
Work 3 complete patt as given for cardigan
front. Change to g st. Cont until work measures
4½[5:5½]in from beg, ending with a WS row.
Divide for armholes
Next row K24[28:32] sts, K2 tog, turn and
leave rem sts on holder. Complete left back on
these sts. Work 1 row. Dec one st at inside
edge on next and every alt row 7[9:11] times
more. K 1 row. Leave sts on holder.
Break yarn and rejoin to next 54[62:70] sts for
front, work to end.
Next row K2 tog, K to last 2 sts, K2 tog.
Cont dec in this way on every alt row 7[9:11]
times more. K 1 row. Leave sts on holder.
Break yarn and rejoin to rem 26[30:34] sts for
right back and complete as given for left back,
reversing shaping.

Sleeves

Using No.10 needles cast on 30[32:34] sts. Work
1 in K1, P1 rib, inc along last row to 36[40:44]
sts, as folls:
Next row (inc row) Rib 2, *rib twice into next
st, rib 4[3:2], rep from * 4[6:8] times more,
rib twice into next st, rib to end.
Change to No.8 needles. Work in g st. Cont
until sleeve measures 4½[5:7]in from beg.
Shape top
Dec one st at each end of next and every alt
row until 20 sts rem. Leave sts on holder.

Yoke

Using No.8 needles and with WS of work facing,
sl sts from right back holder, sleeve, front,
sleeve and left back on to one needle.

114[122:130] sts.
Next row (RS) K2[2:6], *K2 tog, K10[11:11],
rep from * 8 times more, K2 tog, K to end.
Next row P to end.
Next row P to end.
Next row K to end.
Next row P to end.
Next row K to end.
Next row K 1[1:5], *K2 tog, K9[10:10], rep
from * 8 times more, K2 tog, K to end,
Next row P to end.
Change to No.10 needles. Work 11 rows patt
as for bottom of jersey.
Next row P8[3:7], *P2 tog, P2[3:3], rep from
* 18 times more, P2 tog, P to end.
Next row P to end.
Next row K to end.
Next row P3[7:11], *P2 tog, P1, rep from *
21 times more, P2 tog, P to end.
Work 5 rows K1, P1 rib. Cast off in rib.

To make up

Do not press. Beg at lower edge join backs tog
for 6in. Join sleeve seams. Set in sleeves. Work
2 rows dc along each side of back opening,
working 3 button loops on last row by working
2ch and missing 2dc. Sew on buttons. Sew lace
round beg of yoke. Trim front with ribbon bow.

Bootees

Using No.8 needles cast on 30 sts. Work 3
complete patt as given for cardigan front.
Next row K1, yfwd, K2 tog, rep from * to last
st, K1.
Next row P to end.
Next row K19 sts. Turn and K8 sts.
Work 18 rows g st on these 8 sts.
Next row K8 sts, K up 12 sts along side of
foot, K rem 11 sts.
Next row P31 sts, P up 12 sts along other side
of foot, P rem 11 sts.
Work 8 rows in patt as given for cardigan front.
Next row K2 tog, K23 sts, K2 tog tbl, K2 tog,
K23 sts, K2 tog tbl.
Next row K to end.
Rep these 2 rows once more, working the dec
above previous ones. Cast off.

To make up

Do not press. Join seam along bottom of foot
and back of leg. Thread ribbon through holes
at ankles. Sew lace round top of bootees.

8 Long sleeve, zip fronted jumpsuit with matching hat

Sizes
To fit 18[20:22:24]in chest
Length from centre back to toe, 27½[30:32½:35]in
Sleeve seam, 7[8:9:10]in
The figures in brackets [] refer to the 20, 22 and
24in sizes respectively
Tension
6 sts and 8 rows to 1in over st st worked on
No.8 needles
Materials
Pingouin Baby Double Knitting 10[10:12:13]
balls for Jump Suit
2[2:3:3] balls for Hat
or Pingouin Super
6[6:7:8] balls for Jump Suit
1[1:2:2] balls for Hat
One pair of No.8 needles, one pair No.10 needles
One 10in zip

Jump suit right side

Using No.8 needles, beg at toe and cast on 14[18:24:30] sts. Beg with a K row work in st st. Work 2 rows.
Next row K twice into first st, K5[7:10:13] sts, K twice into each of next 2 sts, K to last 2sts, K twice into next st, K1.
Beg with a P row work 3 rows st st.
Next row K twice into first st, K7[9:12:15] sts, K twice into each of next 2 sts, K to last 2 sts, K twice into next st, K1.
Beg with a P row work 3 rows st st.
Next row K twice into first st, K9[11:14:17] sts, K twice into each of next 2 sts, K to last 2 sts, K twice into next st, K1.
Beg with a P row cont in st st without shaping until work measures 3[4:4½:5]in from beg, ending with a P row.
Next row K3[3:6:9] sts, *K twice into next st, K1, rep from * 9[11:11:11] times more, K twice into next st, K to end. 37[43:49:55] sts.
Change to No.10 needles. Work 13 rows K1, P1 rib. Change to No.8 needles.
Commence patt.
1st row (RS) P1, *K5, P1, rep from * to end.
2nd row P to end.
These 2 rows form patt and are rep throughout.
Cont in patt until work measures 1½[2:2½:3]in from beg of patt. Keeping patt correct. inc one st at each end of next and every foll 4th row 10 times in all, then each end of every foll 3rd row 9 times in all. Dec one st at each end of every foll 3rd row 3 times in all. Cont in patt without shaping for a further 1½[2:2½:3]in, ending with a 2nd row. **
Shape centre front
Next row Patt 14 sts, K2 tog tbl, P1, K2 tog, patt to end.
Next row P to end. Keeping patt correct, work 6 rows without shaping.
Next row Patt 13 sts, K2 tog tbl, P1, K2 tog, patt to end. Keeping patt correct, work 7 rows without shaping.
Next row Patt 14 sts, K up 1, P1, K up 1, patt to end.
Keeping patt correct, work 7 rows without shaping.
Rep last 8 rows once more.
Cont in patt without shaping until work measures 16½[17½:19:20½]in from beg of patt, ending with a 2nd row.
Divide for raglan armhole
Next row Patt 34[37:40:43] sts, cast off one st, patt to end.
Next row Patt 34[37:40:43] sts, turn and leave rem sts on holder for front.
Next row K1, K2 tog, patt to end.
Next row Patt to last st, K1.
Rep last 2 rows until 13[14:15:16] sts rem. Work 1 row. Cast off.
Rejoin yarn at inside edge of rem sts on holder.
Next row K1, patt to end.
Next row Patt to last 3 sts, K2 tog tbl, K1.
Rep last 2 rows until 19[22:25:26] sts rem. Work 1 row.
Shape neck
Cast off 7 sts at beg of next row, then dec one st at neck edge on every row 5[6:7:8] times in all, *at the same time* cont to dec at raglan edge as before until 2 sts rem. K2 tog. Fasten off.

Jump suit left side

Work as given for right side to **.
Shape centre front
Next row Patt to last 19 sts, K2 tog tbl, P1, K2 tog, patt 14 sts.
Rep the dec and inc as given for right side as now set, then cont without shaping until work measures 16½[17½:19:20½]in from beg of patt,

ending with a 2nd row.
Divide for raglan armhole
Next row Patt 34[37:40:43] sts, cast off one st, patt to end.
Next row Patt 34[37:40:43] sts, turn and leave rem sts on holder for back.
Next row K1, K2 tog, patt to end.
Next row Patt to last st, K1.
Cont with raglan shaping and shape neck as given for right side, reversing shaping.
Rejoin yarn at inside edge of rem sts on holder.
Next row K1, patt to end.
Next row Patt to last 3 sts, K2 tog tbl, K1.
Complete as given for back of right side.

Sleeves

Using No.10 needles cast on 38[40:42:44] sts. Work 2in K1, P1 rib.
Change to No.8 needles. Beg with a K row work in st st, inc one st at each end of 5th and every foll 5th row until there are 50[54:58:62] sts.
Cont without shaping until sleeve measures 7[8:9:10]in from beg, ending with a P row.

To make up

Do not press. Join foot and leg seams. Join centre backs tog then join centre fronts, leaving 10in open for zip fastener. Join sleeve seams. Set in sleeves.
Collar Using No.10 needles and with WS of work facing, K up 61[67:73:75] sts evenly round neck, beg and ending 3 sts from centre front edges. Work 20[20:24:24] rows K1, P1 rib. Break off yarn. Pick up and rib 14[14:18:18] sts along side of collar, rib across sts on needle and pick up and rib 14[14:18:18] sts along other side of collar. Work 1 row K1, P1 rib. Cast off in rib. Sew in zip.

Hat

Using No.10 needles cast on 103[103:109:109] sts. Work 17 rows K1, P1 rib. Change to No.8 needles. Work in patt as given for Jump suit until work measures 6[6:6½:6½]in from beg, end with a 2nd row. Change to No.10 needles.
Shape top
Shape raglan
Next row K1, K2 tog, K to last 3sts, K2 tog tbl, K1.
Next row K1, P to last st, K1.
Rep last 2 rows until 8 sts rem. Work 1 row. Cast off.
Next row K2[2:5:5] sts, *K3 tog, K5, rep from * 11 times more, K3 tog, K to end. K 5 rows g st without shaping.
Next row K1[1:4:4] sts, *K3 tog, K3, rep from * 11 times more, K3 tog, K to end. K5 rows g st without shaping.
Next row K1[1:3:3] sts, *K2 tog, rep from * to end. K 1 row.
Next row *K2 tog, rep from * to end.
Thread yarn through rem sts, draw up and fasten off. Join side edges of hat tog.

Short sleeved lacy knit dress

Sizes
To fit 16/18[20/22]in chest

Length to centre back, 14[15]in
Sleeve seam, 1½in
Figures in brackets [] refer to the 20/22in size
Tension
7sts and 9 rows to 1in over st st worked on No.10 needles
Materials
Hayfield Beaulon 4 ply 4[5] balls
One pair No.10 needles
Three small buttons

Back

Using No.10 needles cast on 121[141] sts. Work 4 rows g st. Commence patt.
1st row K2 tog, *K3, yfwd, K1, yfwd, K3, sl 1, K2 tog, psso, rep from * ending last rep K2 tog instead of sl 1, K2 tog, psso.
2nd and every alt row P to end.
3rd row As 1st.
5th row As 1st.
7th row P to end.
8th row P to end.
These 8 rows form patt. Cont in patt until work measures 10[10½]in from beg, ending with a WS row. **
Next row (dec row) K3[7] sts, *K2 tog, rep from * to last 2[6] sts, K to end. 63[77] sts.
Next row P to end.
Beg with a K row, cont in st st.
Shape armhole and divide for back opening
Next row Cast off 2[2] sts, K31[38] sts, turn. Complete right shoulder on these sts.
Next row K3 sts, P to end.
Keeping 3 sts in g st for border at back opening, dec one st at armhole edge on every row until 27[32] sts rem. Cont without shaping until work measures 1½[1¾]in from beg of back opening, ending with a WS row.
Next row (buttonhole row) K to last 3 sts, yfwd, K2 tog, K1.
Make another buttonhole in this way when work measures 1½[1¾]in from previous buttonhole. then cont until work measures 14[15]in from beg, ending with a WS row.
Shape shoulder
Cast off 8[9] sts at beg of next and foll alt row. Cast off rem 11[14] sts.
Rejoin yarn to rem sts and with RS of work facing cast on 3 sts for underwrap. Keeping these 3 sts in g st, complete to match other shoulder, reversing shapings and omitting buttonholes.

Front

Work as given for back to **.
16/18in size only
Next row K2, (K3 tog, K2 tog) 9 times, K3 tog, patt 21 sts, (K3 tog, K2 tog) 9 times, K3 tog, K2. 63 sts.
20/22in size only
Next row (K2 tog) 24 times, (K3 tog) 4 times, patt 21 sts, (K3 tog) 4 times, (K2 tog) 24 times. 77 sts.
Both sizes
Next row P to end.
Keeping patt correct on centre 21 sts, cont in st st on rem sts.
Shape armholes
Cast off 2 sts at beg of next 2 rows. Dec one st at each end of every row until 51[61] sts rem. Cont without shaping until work measures 13[14]in from beg, ending with a WS row.
Shape neck
Next row K20[23] sts, cast off 11[15] sts, K to end.
Cont on these sts for right shoulder, dec one st at neck edge on every row until 16[18] sts rem. Cont without shaping until front measures same as back to shoulder, ending at armhole edge.
Shape shoulder

Cast off 8[9] sts at beg of next and foll alt row. Rejoin yarn to rem sts and work to match first side, reversing shapings.

Sleeves

Using No.10 needles cast on 37[46] sts. Work 4 rows g st.
Next row K4[1] sts, *inc in next st, K1[2] sts rep from * to last 5[0] sts, K5[0]. 51[61] sts.
Next row K to end.
Work 8 patt rows as given for back.
Shape top
Keeping patt correct cast off 2 sts at beg of next 2 rows. Dec one st at each end of next and every alt row until 23[25] sts rem.
Next row P1, (P2 tog) to end. Cast off.

Neckband

Join shoulder seams. Using No.10 needles and with RS of work facing, K up 59[63] sts round neck edge. K3 rows g st making 3rd buttonhole on 2nd row as before. Cast off.

To make up

Press under a dry cloth with a cool iron. Set in sleeves. Join side and sleeve seams. Press seams. Sew on buttons.

10 *Knitted 6-section tinker-ball with bell*

Materials
Oddments of Double Knitting yarn in 12 or less colours, or a total of 2oz
One pair No.8 needles
Kapok for stuffing, small bell
Ball measures 18in circumference
First section
Using No.8 needles and 1st colour cast on 2 sts. K1 row. Work in g st, inc one st at each end of next, then following 3rd row twice, then following 4th row twice, then following 6th row twice and following 7th row twice. 20 sts. Work 10 rows without shaping. Break off 1st colour and join in 2nd colour. Work 10 rows without shaping. Dec one st at each end of next, then following 7th row twice, then following 6th row twice, then following 4th row twice and following 3rd row twice, 2sts. K1 row. Cast off. Work 5 more sections in the same way using colours as required.
To make up
With RS facing join side seams of each section leaving about 2in of last seam open. Stuff with kapok, inserting bell in middle of kapok. Oversew rem seam.

11 *Fair Isle dressing gown with tie belt*

Sizes
To fit 20[22:24]in chest
Length at centre back, 22[24:26]in adjustable
Sleeve seam, 6½[8:9½]in adjustable
The figures in brackets [] refer to the 22 and 24in sizes respectively
Tension
6½ sts and 6½ rows to 1in over Fair Isle patt worked on No.8 needles
Materials
Emu Machine Washable Double Knitting Wool 8[10:12] balls main shade, A
2[2:2] balls each of contrast colours B, C, D and E
One pair No.8 needles
One pair No.10 needles
Stitch holders
Eight small buttons
Note
Weave yarns not in use across back of work

Back and fronts

Using No.8 needles and A, cast on 150[162:174] sts. Beg with a K row work 7 rows st st.
Next row K all sts tbl to form hemline.
Commence Fair Isle patt.
1st row (RS) *K1 A, 1B, rep from * to end.
2nd row *P1 A, 1B, rep from * to end.
3rd row As 1st.
4th row As 2nd. Break off B.
5th row K3 A, *5A, 2C, 5A, rep from * to last 3 sts, K3 A.
6th row P3 A, *4A, 1C, 2A, 1C, 4A, rep from * to last 3 sts, P3 A.
7th row K3 A, *3A, 1C, 1A, 2C, 1A, 1C, 3A, rep from * to last 3 sts, K3 A.
8th row P1 C, 2A, *2A, 1C, 6A, 1C, 2A, rep from * to last 3 sts, P2 A, 1C.
9th row K1 A, 1C, 1A, *1A, 1C, (2A, 1C) 3 times, 1A, rep from * to last 3 sts, K1 A, 1C, 1A.
10th row P1 B, 1C, 1B, *1B, 1C, 1B, 2C, 2B, 2C, 1B, 1C, 1B, rep from * to last 3 sts, P1 B, 1C. 1B.
11th row K as 10th row. Break off B.
12th row P as 9th row.
13th row K as 8th row.
14th row P as 7th row.
15th row K as 6th row.
16th row P as 5th row. Break off C.
17th row *K1 A, 1E, rep from * to end.
18th row *P1 A, 1E, rep from * to end.
19th row As 17th.
20th row As 18th.
21st row K1 D, 2A, *1A, 1D, (3 A, 1D) twice, 2A, rep from * to last 3 sts, K1 A, 1D, 1A.
22nd row P1 D, 1A, 1D, *(1A, 1D) twice, (2A, 1D) twice, 1A, 1D, rep from * to last 3 sts, P1 A, 1D, 1A.
23rd row As 21st.
24th row P3 A, *6A, 1D, 5A, rep from * to last 3 sts, P3 A.
25th row K3 E, *4E, 1D, 1E, 1D, 5E, rep from * to last 3 sts, K3 E.
26th row P3 D, *1E, 4D, 1E, 1D, 1E, 4D, rep from * to last 3 sts, P1 E, 2D.
27th row K2 D, 1E, *4D, 1E, 1D, 1E, 4D, 1E. rep from * to last 3 sts, K3 D.
28th row P3 E, *5E, 1D, 1E, 1D, 4E, rep from * to last 3 sts, P3 E. Break off E.
29th row K3 A, *5A, 1D, 6A, rep from * to last 3 sts, K3 A.
30th row P1 A, 1D, 1A, *2A, 1D, (3A, 1D) twice, 1A, rep from * to last 3 sts, P2 A, 1D.
31st row K1 A, 1D, 1A, *1D, 1A, 1D, (2A, 1D) twice, 1A, 1D, 1A, rep from * to last 3 sts, K1 D, 1A, 1D.
32nd row As 30th. Break off D.
These 32 rows form patt and are rep throughout, noting that in next rep rows 1-4 will be worked with A and C, rows 5-16 will read B for C and C for B, rows 17-20 will be worked with A and D and rows 21-32 will read E for D and D for E. Cont in patt until work measures 12½[13¼:14]in from hemline, or required length to underarm less 4½[5½:6¼]in. Mark beg of next row noting that this row will commence sleeve patt. Cont in patt until work measures 17[18¾:20¼]in from hem line, or required length to underarm ending with a RS row.
Divide for armholes
Next row Keeping patt correct, patt 35[37:39] sts, cast off 4[6:8] sts, patt across 72[76:80] sts, cast off 4[6:8] sts, patt across 35[37:39] sts. Complete right front first. Dec one st at armhole edge on every row 5[6:7] times in all. Cont without shaping until armhole measures 3½[3¾:4]in from beg, ending at front edge.
Shape neck
Cast off 5 sts at beg of next row. Dec one st at neck edge on next 5[6:7] rows. Cont without shaping until armhole measures 4½[4¾:5]in from beg, ending at armhole edge.
Shape shoulder
Cast off 10 sts at beg of next and foll alt row. With RS of work facing rejoin yarn to centre 72[76:80] sts and complete back. Keeping patt correct, dec one st at each end of every row 5[6:7] times in all. Cont without shaping until armholes measure same as front to shoulder, ending with a WS row.
Shape shoulder
Cast off 10 sts at beg of next 4 rows. Cast off rem 22[24:26] sts.
With RS of work facing rejoin yarn to rem sts and complete left front to match right front, reversing shapings.

Sleeves

Using No.10 needles and A, cast on 46[50:56] sts. Work 2[2½:3]in K1, P1 rib, inc 8[4:10]sts evenly across last row. 54[54:66] sts. Adjust length here. Change to No.8 needles.
Work in patt as given for back and fronts, beg with same patt row as marked, until sleeve measures 6½[8:9½]in from beg, ending with same patt row as back and fronts at underarm.
Shape top
Keeping patt correct, cast off 2[3:4] sts at beg of next 2 rows. Dec one st at each end of next and every alt row until 30[32:34] sts rem. Work 1 row. Cast off 3 sts at beg of next 6 rows. Cast off rem 12[14:16] sts.

Front borders

Mark positions for 8 buttons on left front for a girl or right front for a boy, top one to come in neckband with 7 more spaced at 2[2¼:2½]in intervals. Using No.10 needles and A cast on 8 sts. Work in K1, P1 rib until border is long enough to fit from hemline to neck shaping when slightly stretched, making buttonholes as markers are reached as foll:
Next row (buttonhole row) Rib 3 sts, cast off 2 sts, rib to end.
Next row Rib to end, casting on 2 sts above those cast off in previous row.
Leave sts on holder. Make button border in same way, omitting buttonholes.

Neckband

Join shoulder seams. Using No.10 needles, A and with RS of work facing, work in rib across sts on one front border, K up 20[21:22] sts up front neck, K up 22[24:26] sts across back neck, K up 20[21:22] sts down front neck and work in rib across sts for other front border. 78[82:86] sts. Work 7 rows K1, P1 rib, making buttonhole as before on 3rd and 4th rows. Cast off loosely in rib.

Belt

Using No.10 needles and A cast on 8 sts. Work 36in K1, P1 rib, or required length. Cast off in rib.

To make up

Press each piece on WS under a damp cloth with a warm iron. Join sleeve seams. Set in sleeves. Turn hem to WS at hemline and sl st down. Sew on front borders. Press seams. Sew on buttons.

Yoked matinée coat set in eyelet ridge stitch

Sizes

To fit 18[19]in chest
Length at centre back, 10[10½]in
Sleeve seam, 5¼[5¾]in
The figures in brackets [] refer to the 19in size

Tension

6 sts and 10½ rows to 1in over patt worked on No.9 needles

Materials

Emu Scotch 3 ply, Calypso Crepe or Bri Nylon 3 ply
Coat 3[3] balls
Bonnet and mittens 1[1] ball each
One pair No.7 needles
One pair No.9 needles
One pair No.10 needles
One pair long No.10 needles for yoke
¾yd 1in ribbon for coat
1yd 1in ribbon for bonnet
¾yd baby ribbon for mittens

Coat back

Using No.7 needles cast on 72[76] sts. Beg with a K row work 5 rows st st.
Next row (hemline) K all sts.
Beg with a K row work 6 rows st st. Change to No.9 needles. Commence patt.
1st row (RS) K1, *yrn, P2 tog, rep from * to last st, K1.
This row forms patt. Cont in patt until work measures 5¼[5¾]in from hemline. Mark each end of last row with coloured thread. Cont in patt for a further in, ending with WS row. Leave sts on holder.

Coat left front

Using No.7 needles cast on 35[37] sts. Beg with a K row work 5 rows st st.
Next row (hemline) K all sts.
Next row K to end, cast on 11 sts. 46[48] sts.
Next row P to end.
Next row K to last 6 sts, sl 1 p-wise, K5.
Next row P to end.
Rep last 2 rows once more. Change to No.9 needles. Commence patt.
1st row K1, *yrn, P2 tog, rep from * to last 11 sts, K5, sl 1 p-wise, K5.
2nd row P11 sts, *yrn, P2 tog, rep from * to last st, K1.
These 2 rows form patt. Cont in patt until work measures 5¼[5¾]in from hemline. Mark side edge of last row with coloured thread. Cont in patt for a further in, ending with a WS row. Leave sts on holder.

Coat right front

Using No.7 needles cast on 35[37] sts. Beg with a K row work 5 rows st st.
Next row (hemline) K all sts.
Next row Cast on 11 sts, K across these 11 sts, K to end. 46[48] sts.
Next row P to end.
Next row K5, sl 1 p-wise, K to end.
Next row P to end.
Rep last 2 rows once more. Change to No.9 needles. Commence patt.
1st row K5, sl 1 p-wise, K5, *yrn, P2 tog, rep from * to last st, K1.
2nd row K1, *yrn, P2 tog, rep from * to last 11 sts, P11.
Complete to match left front.

Sleeves

Using No.10 needles cast on 42[44] sts. Beg with a K row work 5 rows st st.
Next row (hemline) K all sts.
Beg with a K row work 6 rows st st. Change to No.9 needles. Cont in patt as given for back until sleeve measures 5¼[5¾]in from hemline. Mark each end of last row with coloured thread. Cont in patt for a further in, ending with WS row. Leave sts on holder.

Yoke

Using long No.10 needles, with RS of work facing, beg at right front, K5, sl 1 p-wise, K6, (K2 tog) 17[18] times, K across 42[44] sts of first sleeve, across back K2, (K2 tog) 34[36] times, K2, K across 42[44] sts of 2nd sleeve, across left front (K2 tog) 17[18] times, K6, sl 1 p-wise, K5. 180[188] sts.
Next row P to end.
Next row K5, sl 1 p-wise, K to last 6 sts, sl 1 p-wise, K5.
Next row P to end.
Next row K5, sl 1 p-wise, K17[21], *sl 1, K1, psso, K2 tog, K9, rep from * to last 27[31] sts, sl 1, K1, psso, K2 tog, K17[21], sl 1 p-wise, K5. 158[166] sts.
Next row P to end.
Next row K5, sl 1 p-wise, K to last 6 sts, sl 1 p-wise, K5.
Next row P to end.
Rep last 2 rows once more.
Next row K5, sl 1 p-wise, K16[20], *sl 1, K1, psso, K2 tog, K7, rep from * to last 26[30] sts, sl 1, K1, psso, K2 tog, K16[20], sl 1 p-wise, K5. 136[144] sts.
Next row P to end.
Next row K5, sl 1 p-wise, K5, *yrn, P2 tog, rep from * to last 11 sts, K5, sl 1 p-wise, K5.
Next row P11, *yrn, P2 tog, rep from * to last 11 sts, P11.
Rep last 2 rows twice more.
Next row K5, sl 1 p-wise, K to last 6 sts, sl 1 p-wise, K5.
Next row P to end.
Next row K5, sl 1 p-wise, K15[19], *sl 1, K1, psso, K2 tog, K5, rep from * to last 25[29] sts, sl 1, K1, psso, K2 tog, K15[19], sl 1 p-wise, K5. 114[122] sts.
Next row P to end.
Next row K5, sl 1 p-wise, K to last 6 sts, sl 1 p-wise, K5.
Next row P to end.
Rep last 2 rows once more.
Next row K5, sl 1 p-wise, K14[18], *sl 1, K1, psso, K2 tog, K3, rep from * to last 24[28] sts, sl 1, K1, psso, K2 tog, K14[18], sl 1 p-wise, K5. 92[100] sts.
Next row P to end.
Next row K5, sl 1 p-wise, K6, *yrn, P2 tog, rep from * to last 11 sts, K5, sl 1 p-wise, K5.
Next row P11, *yrn, P2 tog, rep from * to last 11 sts, P11.
Rep last 2 rows twice more.
Next row K5, sl 1 p-wise, K13[13], *K2 tog, K2, rep from * to last 21[21] sts, K2 tog, K13[13] sts, sl 1 p-wise, K5. 78[84] sts.
Next row P to end.
Next row K5, sl 1 p-wise, K5, yfwd, K2 tog to form eyelet hole, K to last 13 sts, K2 tog, yfwd, K5, sl 1 p-wise, K5.
Next row P to end.
Next row Cast off 11 sts, K to last 6 sts, sl 1 p-wise, K5.
Next row Cast off 11 sts, K to end to mark fold line.
Beg with a K row work 4 rows st st. Cast off fairly loosely.

To make up

Press pieces under a damp cloth with a warm iron for wool or dry cloth with a cool iron for Bri Nylon. Join side and sleeve seams as far as coloured threads. Join rem section of sleeve to rem section of armhole. Fold hem, cuffs, front and neck edging to WS at hemline and sl st down.
Thread ribbon through neck, bringing ribbon out at eyelet holes.

Bonnet

Using No.10 needles cast on 90[94] sts. Work hem as given for coat back. Change to No.9 needles. Work in patt as given for coat back until work measures 4[4¼]in from hemline, ending with a WS row.
2nd size only
Next row K12 sts, *K2 tog, K21 sts, rep from * to last 13 sts, K2 tog, K11 sts. 90 sts.
Next row P to end.
Both sizes
Shape back
1st row *K7, K2 tog, rep from * to end. 80 sts.
2nd and every alt row P to end.
3rd row *K6, K2 tog, rep from * to end. 70 sts
5th row *K5, K2 tog, rep from * to end. 60 sts
7th row *K4, K2 tog, rep from * to end. 50 sts
9th row *K3, K2 tog, rep from * to end. 40 sts
11th row *K2, K2 tog, rep from * to end. 30 sts
13th row *K1, K2 tog, rep from * to end. 20 sts
14th row *P2 tog, rep from * to end. 10 sts.
Break yarn, thread through rem sts, draw up and fasten off.

To make up

Press as given for coat. Join back seam as far as shaping. Fold face edging to WS at hemline and sl st down.
Neck edging Using No.10 needles and with RS of work facing, K up 70[74] sts evenly along base of bonnet. Beg with a P row work 4 rows st st.
Next row (hemline) K all sts.
Beg with a K row work 4 rows st st. Cast off fairly loosely.
Fold neck edging to WS at hemline and sl st down.
Thread ribbon through neck hem.

Mittens

Using No.10 needles cast on 40 sts. Beg with a K row work 11 rows st st.
Next row (hemline) K all sts.
Beg with a K row work 12 rows st st.
Make eyelet holes
Next row *K2, yfwd, K2 tog, rep from * to end
Next row P to end.
Change to No.9 needles. Cont in patt as given for coat back until work measures 3¾ [4] in from hemline.
End with a WS row.
Shape top
1st row *K2, K2 tog, rep from * to end. 30 sts.
2nd row K to end.
3rd row *K1, K2 tog, rep from * to end. 20 sts.
4th row *K2 tog, rep from * to end. 10 sts.
Break yarn, thread through rem sts, draw up and fasten off.

To make up

Press as given for coat. Join side seam. Fold cuff to WS at hemline and sl st down. Thread ribbon through eyelet holes at wrist.

13 Bramble stitch layette with shawl

Sizes

To fit an 18[20]in chest
Dress length to centre back, 12[14]in
Sleeve seam, 1½in
Coat length to centre back, 10[11]in
Sleeve seam, 5½[6]in
Shawl 36 by 36in
The figures in brackets [] refer to the 20in size

Tension

7 sts and 10 rows to 1in over patt worked on
No.10 needles

Materials

Robin Soft Bri Nylon or Tricel-Nylon Perle 4 ply
Dress 5[6] balls
Coat 4[5] balls
Bonnet and Bootees 1 ball each
Shawl 14 balls
One pair No.8 needles, one pair No.10 needles,
one pair No.12 needles
Two buttons for dress
Three buttons for coat
¾yd ribbon for bootees
½yd ribbon for bonnet

Dress back

Using No.10 needles cast on 127[139] sts.
1st row (RS) *K1, yfwd, sl 1, K1, psso, K1,
K2 tog, yfwd, rep from * to last st, K1.
2nd row *P2, yrn, P3 tog, yrn, P1, rep from *
to last st, P1.
3rd row *K1, K2 tog, yfwd, K1, yfwd, sl 1,
K1, psso, rep from * to last st, K1.
4th row P2 tog, *yrn, P3, yrn, P3 tog, rep from
* to last 5 sts, yrn, P3, yrn, P2 tog.
These 4 rows form patt. Cont in patt until
work measures 8½[10]in from beg, ending with
a 4th patt row.
Shape raglan
Next row Cast off 6 sts, K to end.
Next row Cast off 6 sts, P3 tog, *P2 tog, rep
from * to last st, P1. 58[64] sts.
Beg with a K row cont in st st, dec one st at
each end of next four rows. **
Divide for back opening
Next row K2 tog, K23[26] sts. Turn. Leave
rem sts on holder.
Next row K3, P to end.
*** Keeping 3 sts at inner edge in g st, dec one
st at raglan edge on every RS row only until
12[13] sts rem, ending with a P row. Cast off.
Rejoin yarn to rem sts at inner edge, K to last
2 sts, K2 tog.
Next row P to last 3 sts, K3.
Complete to match first side, working from ***.

Dress front

Work as given for back to **. Dec one st at
each end of every RS row until 36[40] sts rem,
ending with a P row.
Shape neck
Next row K2 tog, K11[13] sts and leave on
holder, cast off next 10 sts, K to last 2 sts, K2 tog.
Cont dec at raglan edge as before, *at the same
time* dec one st at neck edge on next 2 rows,
then on every RS row until 3 sts rem. Dec at
raglan edge only on next row. K2 tog. Fasten
off. Rejoin yarn to rem sts at inner edge and
complete to match first side.

Sleeves

Using No.10 needles cast on 49[55] sts. Work
4 patt rows as given for back 4 times in all.

Shape raglan

Beg with a K row cont in st st, casting off 6 sts
at beg of next 2 rows. Dec one st at each end of
every RS row until 7[9] sts rem, ending with a
P row. Cast off.

Neck edging

Join raglan seams. Using No.12 needles and with
RS of work facing, K up 68[72] sts evenly around
neck edge. Cast off firmly.

To make up

Press each piece lightly on WS under a dry cloth
using a cool iron. Join side and sleeve seams.
Make 2 button loops at back opening. Press
seams. Sew on buttons.

Coat

Using No.12 needles cast on 187[205] sts and
work in one piece to armholes. Work 8 rows g st.
Change to No.10 needles. Keeping 6 sts at each
end in g st, cont in patt as given for dress until
work measures 6½[7]in from beg, ending with
a 4th patt row.
Divide for armholes
Next row K43[48] sts, cast off 10 sts, K81[89]
sts, cast off 10 sts, K to end.
Complete left front on these sts.
Next row K6, P1, *P2 tog, P2, rep from * to
last 4[5] sts, P to end. 35[39] sts.
** Beg with a K row cont in st st, dec one st
at raglan edge on next 6[8] rows, then on every
RS row until 23[25] sts rem, ending at centre
front edge.
Shape neck
Next row K6 sts and leave on holder, cast off
next 3 sts, work to end.
Cont dec at raglan edge as before, *at the same
time* dec one st at neck edge on the next 4 rows,
then on every alt row until 3 sts rem. Dec at
raglan edge only on next row. K2 tog. Fasten off.
With WS of work facing rejoin yarn to centre sts
and complete back.
Next row P1, *P2 tog, P2, rep from * to end.
61[67] sts.
Beg with a K row cont in st st, dec one st at
each end of next 6[8] rows, then on every RS row
until 25[27] sts rem, ending with a P row.
Cast off.
With WS of work facing rejoin yarn to rem sts
and complete right front on these sts.
Next row P6[7] sts, *P2 tog, P2, rep from * to
last 9 sts, P2 tog, P1, K6.
Next row (buttonhole row) K3 sts, yfwd, K2
tog, K to end.
Complete to match left front working from **
and making 2nd buttonhole on 10th[12th] row
from previous one.

Sleeves

Using No.10 needles cast on 49[55] sts. Work
4 patt rows as given for dress until sleeve
measures 5½[6]in from beg, ending with a 4th
patt row.
Shape raglan
Work as given for dress sleeve.

Neckband

Join raglan seams. Using No.12 needles and
with RS of work facing, K across sts on holder
at right front, K up 60[64] sts evenly all round
neck edge to left front band, K across sts on
holder. 72[76] sts. Work 8 rows g st making 3rd
buttonhole as before on 4th row. Cast off.

To make up

Press as given for dress. Join sleeve seams.
Press seams. Sew on buttons.

Bonnet

Using No.12 needles cast on 85[91] sts. Work
8 rows g st. Change to No.10 needles and cont
in patt as given for dress until work measures 3½
[3¾]in from beg, ending with a 4th patt row.
Shape back
1st row K5[1] sts, *K2 tog, K8 sts, rep from *
to end.
2nd and every alt row P to end.
3rd row K5[1] sts, *K2 tog, K7 sts, rep from
* to end.
5th row K5[1] sts, *K2 tog, K6 sts, rep from
* to end.
Cont dec in this way on every alt row until
21[19] sts rem, ending with a K row.
Next row P1, * P2 tog, rep from * to end.
Break yarn, thread through rem sts, draw up
and fasten off. Join back seam for approx 2½in.

Neck edging

Using No.12 needles and with RS of work facing,
K up 66[70] sts evenly round lower edge of
bonnet. Cast off firmly.

To make up

Press seam as given for dress. Sew on ribbon
at either side to tie under chin.

Bootees

Using No.12 needles cast on 43 sts. Work 8
rows g st. Work 4 patt rows as given for dress
4 times in all.
Divide for instep
Next row K28 sts, turn, K13 sts, turn.
Work 22 rows g st on these 13 sts. Break yarn.
With RS of work facing, rejoin yarn at side of
instep and K up 12 sts evenly from side of
instep, K across instep sts, K up 12 sts from
other side of instep, K to end of row. 67 sts.
Work 15 rows g st across all sts.
Shape sole
1st row K5 sts, K2 tog, K20 sts, K2 tog, K9
sts, K2 tog, K 20 sts, K2 tog, K5 sts.
2nd row K4 sts, K2 tog, K20 sts, K2 tog,
K7 sts, K2 tog, K20 sts, K2 tog, K4 sts.
3rd row K3 sts, K2 tog, K20 sts, K2 tog,
K5 sts, K2 tog, K20 sts, K2 tog, K3 sts.
4th row K2 sts, K2 tog, K20 sts, K2 tog,
K3 sts, K2 tog, K20 sts, K2 tog, K2 sts.
5th row K1 st, K2 tog, K20 sts, K2 tog,
K1st, K2 tog, K20 sts, K2 tog, K1 st.
Cast off.

To make up

Join leg and foot seams. Press seams. Thread
ribbon through last row of patt holes at ankles.

Shawl centre piece

Using No.8 needles cast on 217 sts. Work in
patt as given for dress until work measures
32 in from beg, ending with a 4th patt row.
Cast off.

Shawl border

Using No.10 needles cast on 12 sts.
1st row K5 sts, yrn, P2 tog, K1, (yrn, P2 tog)
twice.
2nd row Yfwd, K7 sts, yrn, P2 tog, K2 sts, sl1.
3rd row K5 sts, yrn, P2 tog, K2 sts, yrn, P2
tog, yfwd, K2 sts.
4th row Yrn, P2 tog, K7 sts, yrn, P2 tog,
K 2sts, sl 1.

5th row K5 sts, yrn, P2 tog, K3 sts, yrn, P2 tog, yfwd, K2 sts.
6th row Yrn, P2 tog, K8 sts, yrn, P2 tog, K2 sts, sl 1.
7th row K5 sts, yrn, P2 tog, K4 sts, yrn, P2 tog, yfwd, K2 sts.
8th row Yrn, P2 tog, K9 sts, yrn, P2 tog, K2 sts, sl 1.
9th row K5 sts, yrn, P2 tog, K9 sts.
10th row K5 sts, pass 1st, 2nd, 3rd and 4th st over 5th st, K6 sts, yrn, P2 tog, K2 sts, sl 1.
These 10 rows form patt. Cont in patt until border fits along cast on edge of centre piece, work a further 1½in to allow for easing round corner, insert a marker, cont and work the same length 3 times more, ending with a 10th patt row. Cast off.

To make up

Join short edges of border. Pin border to centre piece, placing marker at each corner and seam to last corner. Join border to centre piece using a flat seam and easing in fullness at corners. Press seam and edges.

14 All-in-one shorts suit, zip fronted and crochet edged

Sizes
To fit 22 [24:26]in chest
Length to shoulder, 17 [18½:20]in
Sleeve seam, 1 [1¼:1½]in
The figures in brackets [] refer to the 24 and 26in sizes respectively

Tension
5 sts and 6 rows to 1in over st st worked on No.8 needles

Materials
7 [8/:9] balls Paton's Camelot in main shade, A
1 ball of contrast colour, B
One pair No.8 needles
One pair No.10 needles
One No.3·50 (ISR) crochet hook
10 [12:14]in zip fastener

Right half
Using No.10 needles and A, cast on 78[83:88] sts. Beg with a K row work 5 rows st st.
Next row K all sts tbl to form hemline.
Change to No.8 needles. Beg with a K row cont in st st until work measures 1½ [2:2½]in from hemline, ending with a P row.
Shape gusset
Cast off at beg of next and every row 5 sts once, 3 sts once and 2 sts twice. Dec one st at each end of next and foll 2 alt rows. Cont without shaping until work measures 4 [4½:5]in from hemline, ending with a P row. Cast off 3 sts at beg of next row. 57[62:67] sts. Cont without shaping until work measures 13 [14:15]in from hemline, ending with a P row.
Divide for armhole
Next row K23[25:27] sts, cast off 6 sts, K to end.
Complete this side first.
Next row P to end.
Cast off 2 sts at beg of next row, then dec one st at this edge on foll 2 alt rows. 24[27:30] sts. Cont without shaping until armhole measures 4 [4½:5]in from beg, ending with a P row.
Shape shoulder and neck
Next row Cast off 4[4:6] sts, K to end.
Next row Cast off 8[9:10] sts, P to end.
Next row Cast off 4[6:6] sts, K to end.
Next row Cast off 2 sts, P to end.
Cast off rem 6 sts.
With WS of work facing, rejoin yarn to rem sts,

cast off 2 sts, P to end. Dec one st at armhole edge on next and foll alt row. Cont without shaping until armhole measures 2 [2½:3]in from beg, ending with a P row.
Shape neck
Cast off 2 sts at beg of next row. Dec one st at neck edge on foll 3 alt rows. 14[16:18] sts. Cont without shaping until armhole measures same as back to shoulder, ending with a K row.
Shape shoulder
Cast off at beg of next and every alt row 4[4:6] sts once, 4[6:6] sts once and 6 sts once.

Left half
Work as given for right half, reversing all shapings.

Sleeves
Using No.10 needles and A, cast on 42[44:46] sts. Work hem as given for right half. Change to No.8 needles. Beg with a K row cont in st st, inc one st at each end of 3rd[5th:5th] row. Cont without shaping until sleeve measures 1 [1¼:1½]in from hemline, ending with a P row.
Shape top
Cast off at beg of next and every row 4 sts twice and 2 sts twice. Dec one st at each end of next and foll 6[7:8] alt rows, ending with a P row. Cast off 2 sts at beg of next 4 rows. Cast off rem 10 sts.

Pocket
Using No.10 needles and A, cast on 16 sts. Beg with a K row work 2in st st, ending with a K row.
Next row K all sts tbl to mark fold line.
Beg with a K row work 3 rows st st. Cast off.

To make up
Press each piece lightly under a damp cloth with a warm iron. Join shoulder seams. Set in sleeves. Join sleeve and back seams. Join lower part of front seam, leaving 9 [11:13]in open for zip. Turn all hems to WS and sl st down. Using No.3·50 (ISR) hook and A, with RS of work facing, work in dc along front opening, round neck and down other side of front opening. Break off A. Join in B and start again at beg of row, work one ss into each st all round, then work across lower edge of opening. Break off B. Join in A and start again at beg of row, work one dc into each st, working behind the row of B into the loops of first row of A, working 3 dc into each front corner of neck edge, turn and work a 2nd row of dc. Break off A. With RS of work facing and A, beg at corner of neck and work a row of dc round neck to other corner, turn and work a 2nd row of dc. Fasten off. Sew in zip to front opening. Turn hem at top of pocket to WS and sl st down. Make a crochet ch using B and sew on to pocket in the shape of an initial. Sew on pocket. Press all seams.
See overleaf for alphabet trace pattern

15 Practical dungaree and jersey set with big striped pockets

Sizes
to fit 22[24:26]in chest
Jersey length to shoulder, 12½[14½:16½]in
Sleeve seam, 8 [9½:11]in
Trousers inside leg, 12½ [14½:17]in
The figures in brackets [] refer to the 24 and 26in sizes respectively

Tension
7 sts and 9 rows to 1in over st st worked on No.10 needles

Materials
Lister Lavenda 4 ply
Jersey 6 [7:9] balls in main shade, A
Trousers 9 [11:13] balls of contrast colour, B
1 ball of main shade, A
One pair No.10 needles; One pair No.12 needles
Set of 4 No.12 needles pointed at both ends
4 buttons

Jersey back
Using No.12 needles and A, cast on 79 [85:93] sts.
1st row K1, *P1, K1, rep from * to end.
2nd row P1, *K1, P1, rep from * to end.
Rep these 2 rows for 1½in, ending with a 2nd row and inc one st at end of last row on 24in size only. 79 [86:93] sts. Change to No.10 needles.
1st row *P2, K5, rep from * to last 2 sts, P2.
2nd row *K2, P5, rep from * to last 2 sts, K2.
These 2 rows form patt. Cont in patt until work measures 8 [9½:11]in from beg, ending with a WS row.
Shape armholes
Cast off 5 sts at beg of next 2 rows. 69[76:83] sts. Dec one st at each end of next and every alt row until 27[30:33] sts rem, ending with a WS row. Leave sts on holder.

Jersey front
Work as given for back until 45[48:51] sts rem after beg armhole shaping, ending with a WS row.
Shape neck
Next row Dec one st, rib 15 sts, turn and leave rem sts on holder.
Next row Rib to end.
Next row Dec one st, rib to last 2 sts, dec one st.
Rep last 2 rows 5 times more, then cont to dec at raglan edge only on foll 2 alt rows, ending with a RS row.
Next row P2 tog. Fasten off.
With RS of work facing, sl first 11[14:17] sts on holder and leave for centre neck rejoin yarn to rem sts, rib to last 2 sts, dec one st.
Complete to match first side, reversing shaping.

Sleeves
Using No.12 needles and A, cast on 39[43:47] sts. Work in K1, P1 rib as given for back for 1½in, ending with a 2nd row. Change to No.10 needles.
1st row K1[3:5] sts, *P2, K5, rep from * to last 3[5:7] sts, P2, K1[3:5] sts.
2nd row P1[3:5] sts, *K2, P5, rep from * to last 3[5:7] sts, K2, P1[3:5] sts.
Cont in patt as now set, inc one st at each end of 5th and every foll 4th[6th:6th] row until there are 59[63:67] sts, and working extra sts into patt when possible. Cont without shaping until sleeve measures 8 [9½:11]in from beg, ending with a WS row.

Shape raglan
Cast off 5 sts at beg of next 2 rows. Dec one st at each end of next and every alt row until 7 sts rem, ending with a WS row. Leave sts on holder.

Neckband
Join raglan seams. Using set of 4 No.12 needles, A and with RS of work facing, K across sts of back neck and left sleeve, K2 tog at seam, K up 16 sts down side of neck, K across centre front neck sts, K up 16 sts up other side of neck, then K across sts of right sleeve, K last st tog with first st of back neck. 82[88:94] sts. Work in rounds of K1, P1 rib for 3½ [4:4½]in. Cast off loosely in rib.

To make up
Press each piece under a damp cloth with a

A B C D E F
G H I J K L
M N O P Q R
S T U V W X
Y Z

warm iron. Join side and sleeve seams. Press seams.

Trousers right half
Using No.12 needles and B, cast on 70[75:80] sts. Beg with a K row work 10 rows st st. P 1 row to mark hemline. Beg with a P row work 11 rows st st. P 1 row to mark 2nd fold line. Beg with a P row work 6 rows st st. Change to No.10 needles. Beg with a K row to reverse work, cont in st st, inc one st at each end of every 14th [14th:16th] row until there are 82 [89:96] sts. Cont without shaping until work measures 11½ [13½:16]in from 2nd fold line, ending with a P row. Inc one st at each end of next and foll 4 alt rows, ending with a P row. 92[99:106] sts.
Shape gusset
Cast off at beg of next and every row 4 sts once and 2 sts 3 times. Dec one st at each end of next and foll alt row, then on foll 4th rows twice, ending with a P row. 74[81:88] sts. Leave sts on holder for time being.

Trousers left half
Work as given for right half, reversing shaping of gusset and ending with a P row.

Trousers body
Next row K first 73[80:87] sts of left half, K next st tog with first st of right half, K to end. 147[161:175] sts.
Cont in st st until work measures 5½ [6:6½]in from beg of body, ending with a P row.
Shape back
Next row K16[20:24] sts, turn and P to end.
Next row K12[15:18] sts, turn and P to end.
Next row K8[10:12] sts, turn and P to end.
Next row K4[5:6] sts, turn and P to end.
K 1 row across all sts, then shape other side to match first side, reading K for P and P for K.
Next row P to end.
Next row K110[120:131] sts, turn and leave rem 37[41:44] sts on holder.
Next row P73[79:87] sts, turn and leave rem 37[41:44] sts on holder.
Cont in st st until work measures 11 [12:13½]in from gusset, ending with a K row.
Next row K11[12:13] sts, P to last 11[12:13] sts, K to end.
Next row K to end.
Next row Cast off 11[12:13] sts K-wise, P to last 11[12:13] sts, cast off rem sts K-wise. Break off yarn. Rejoin yarn to rem sts and cont in st st, dec one st at each end of next and every alt row until 33[37:41] sts rem, ending with a P row. Change to No.12 needles. K 2 rows g st.
Next row K3 sts, cast off 2 sts, K4 sts, cast off 2 sts, K to last 11 sts, cast off 2 sts, K4 sts, cast off 2 sts, K to end.
Next row K to end, casting on 2 sts above those cast off in previous row.
K3 more rows g st. Cast off K-wise.
With RS of work facing, rejoin yarn to rem sts on holder, K across all sts, K2 tog in centre. 73[81:87] sts. Complete to match first side, omitting buttonholes.

Pockets (make 2)
Using No.12 needles and B, cast on 26[28:30] sts. K 2 rows. Join in A. **K2 rows A, then work 4 rows st st using B. Rep from ** until work measures 4½ [4¾:5]in from beg, ending with K 2 rows A. K3 rows B. Cast off K-wise using B.

Straps (make 2)
Using No.12 needles and B, cast on 16 sts. P 1 row.
2nd row Using B, K to end.
3rd row Using B, K2, yfwd, sl 1 P-wise, P10, sl 1 P-wise, ybk, K2.
4th and 5th rows As 2nd and 3rd rows.
6th and 7th rows Using A, K to end.
Rep rows 2-7 for 8 [8½:9]in. Cast off.

To make up
Press as given for jersey
Join back seam. Join leg seams and gusset. Join side seams. Turn in hem at first fold line to RS and sl st down, then turn up hem to RS again on 2nd fold line and press to form turn up. Using No.12 needles, B and with RS of work facing, K up 66[70:74] sts round armhole. K 6 rows. Cast off K-wise. Turn in edges of straps at sl st line and st down. Sew straps to back, then sew on 2 buttons to other end of each strap to fasten. Sew on pockets. Press all seams.

16 *Fringed and braided bolero*

Sizes
To fit 24 [26:28]in chest
Length to shoulder, 11 [12¼:13½]in
The figures in brackets [] refer to the 26 and 28in sizes respectively
Tension
4½ sts and 6 rows to 1in over st st worked on No.6 needles, using yarn double throughout
Materials
8[10:12] balls Lee Target Motoravia Double Knitting in main shade, A
1 ball each of contrast colours, B and C
One pair No.6 needles
One No.3·50 (ISR) crochet hook

Back
Using No.6 needles and A double throughout, cast on 59[64:69] sts. Beg with a K row work 6½ [7¼:8]in st st, ending with a P row.
Shape armholes
Cast off at beg of next and every row 4 sts twice and 2 sts twice. Dec one st at each end of next and foll 3[4:5] alt rows, then at each end of every 4th row twice. 35[38:41] sts. Cont without shaping until work measures 11 [12¼:13½]in from beg, ending with a K row.
Shape neck and shoulders
Next row P12[13:14] sts, cast off 11[12:13] sts, P to end.
Complete this side first.
Next row Cast off 5 sts, K to last 2 sts, K2 tog.
Next row P to end.
Cast off rem 6[7:8] sts.
With RS of work facing, rejoin yarn to rem 12[13:14] sts and complete to match first side, reversing shaping.

Right front
Using No.6 needles and A double throughout, cast on 23[26:29] sts. Beg with a K row work in st st, inc one st at beg of 3rd and foll 2 alt rows, then at beg of every 4th row twice. 28[31:34] sts. Cont without shaping until work measures same as back to underarm, ending with a K row.
Shape armhole
Cast off at beg of next and foll alt rows 4 sts once and 2 sts once. Dec one st at armhole edge on next and foll 3[4:5] alt rows, then on every 4th row twice, *at the same time* shape front edge when work measures 9 [9¾:10½]in from beg, ending with a P row.
Shape front edge
Dec one st at beg of next and foll 9[10:11] alt rows. Cont without shaping until work measures same as back to shoulder, ending with a K row. Cast off.

Left front
Work as given for right front, reversing all shapings.

To make up
Press each piece under a damp cloth with a warm iron.
Join shoulder and side seams.
Fringe Using No.3·50 (ISR) hook and A single, make a ch long enough to fit round outer edge of bolero, turn and work 1 row dc along ch. Fasten off. Cut a strip of cardboard about 1½in wide. Commence at beg of dc row, rejoin yarn and make 1ch, *loop round card, insert hook into next st and draw up a loop, yrh and draw through 2 loops, 1ch, rep from * all along row, taking card out of loops at intervals. Fasten off. Make 2 more pieces in same way for armholes.
Picot edging Using No.3·50 (ISR) hook and B, make a ch long enough to fit round outer edge of bolero about ½in inside the edge.
Next row Into 2nd ch from hook work 1dc, *work 3dc into next ch, rep from * to end. Fasten off.
Sew fringe to edges of bolero with WS of dc row facing outwards. Sew picot edging ½in inside edge with picots facing towards outer edge. Using No.3·50 (ISR) hook and C, with RS of work facing, work a ch all round about ½in inside picot edging, making loops at each lower corner, also at centre back neck and centre of lower edge of back.
Press all seams.

17 *Cotton dress with narrow contrast bands*

Sizes
To fit 22 [24:26]in chest
Length to shoulder, 15½ [17:18½]in
Sleeve seam, 1½ [2:2½]in
The figures in brackets [] refer to the 24 and 26in sizes respectively
Tension
7½ sts and 10 rows to 1in over st st worked on No.12 needles
Materials
6[7:8] balls Coton du Pingouin in main shade, A
1 ball of contrast colour, B
One pair No.12 needles
One pair No.14 needles
One No.2·00 (ISR) crochet hook
3 buttons

Back
Using No.14 needles and A, cast on 134[142:150] sts. Beg with a K row work 7 rows st st.
Next row K all sts tbl to form hemline.
Change to No.12 needles. Beg with a K row work 12 rows st st. Join in B. (K 2 rows B then work 6 rows st st with A) twice, K 2 rows B. Break off B and cont in st st with A only.
Shape darts
Next row K1, K2 tog, K27[29:31] sts, sl 1, K1, psso, K27(29:31] sts, K2 tog, K12 sts, sl 1, K1, psso, K27(29:31) sts, K2 tog, K27(29:31) sts, sl 1, K1, psso, K1. 128[136:144] sts.
Beg with a P row work 7[9:11] rows st st.
Next row K1, K2 tog, K26[28:30] sts, sl 1, K1, psso, K25[27:29] sts, K2 tog, K12 sts, sl 1, K1, psso, K25[27:29] sts, K2 tog, K26[28:30] sts, sl 1, K1, psso, K1. 122[130:138] sts.
Cont dec in this way on every foll 8th(10th:12th] row until 86[94:102] sts rem. Cont without shaping until work measures 11½ [12½:13½]in from hemline, ending with a P row.

Shape armholes

Cast off at beg of next and every row 5 sts twice and 2 sts twice. Dec one st at each end of next and foll 2[3:4] alt rows, ending with a P row. 66[72:78] sts.

Divide for opening

Next row K31[34:37] sts, turn and cast on 4 sts, leave rem sts on holder.

Next row K4 sts, P to end.

Keeping 4 sts at inside edge in g st, cont without shaping until armhole measures 4 [4½: 5]in from beg, ending with a WS row.

Shape shoulder and neck

Next row Cast off 5[5:6] sts, K to end.

Next row Cast off 11[12:13] sts, P to end.

Next row Cast off 5[5:6] sts, K to end.

Next row Cast off 3 sts, P to end.

Next row Cast off 5[5:6] sts, K to last 2 sts, K2 tog.

Next row P to end.

Cast off rem 5[7:6] sts.

Mark positions for 3 buttons on this side, first to come on 7th row above beg of opening, and last to come 2 rows below neck shaping with one more evenly spaced between.

With RS of work facing, rejoin yarn to rem sts, K to end.

Next row P to last 4 sts, K4.

Rep last 2 rows twice more.

Next row (buttonhole row) K2 sts, cast off 2 sts, K to end.

Next row Patt to end, casting on 2 sts above those cast off in previous row.

Complete to match first side, making buttonholes as before as markers are reached, and reversing all shapings.

Front

Work as given for back until armhole shaping is completed. Cont without shaping until armholes measure 2½ [3:3½]in from beg, ending with a P row.

Shape neck

Next row K28[30:32] sts, turn and leave rem sts on holder.

Cast off 2 sts at beg of next and foll alt row, then dec one st at neck edge on every alt row until 20[22:24] sts rem. Cont without shaping until armhole measures same as back to shoulder, ending at armhole edge.

Shape shoulder

Cast off at beg of next and every alt row 5[5:6] sts 3 times and 5[7:6] sts once.

With RS of work facing, sl first 10[12:14] sts on to holder, rejoin yarn to rem sts and K to end. Complete to match first side, reversing shaping.

Sleeves

Using No.14 needles and A, cast on 54[58:62] sts. Beg with a K row work 7 rows st st.

Next row K all sts tbl to form hemline.

Change to No.12 needles. Beg with a K row cont in st st, inc one st at each end of 7th and foll 4th row. Cont without shaping until sleeve measures 1½ [2:2½]in from hemline, ending with a P row.

Shape top

Cast off 5 sts at beg of next 2 rows. Dec one st at each end of next and foll 9[11:13] alt rows. Cast off at beg of next and every row 2 sts 6 times and 3 sts twice. Cast off rem 10 sts.

Collar

Using No 12 needles and A, cast on 49[51:53] sts.

1st row P1, *K1, P1, rep from * to end.

2nd row K1, *P1, K1, rep from * to end.

Rep these 2 rows twice more.

Next row Rib 5 sts, K to last 5 sts, rib 5.

Next row Rib 5 sts, P to last 5 sts, rib 5.

Rep last 2 rows once more.

Next row Rib 5 sts, K1, K2 tog, K to last 8 sts, sl 1, K1, psso, K1, rib 5.

Cont dec in this way on every 4th row 4 times more. Cont without shaping until work measures 2 [2¼:2½]in from beg, ending with a WS row. Cast off at beg of next and every alt row 12[13: 14] sts once and 5 sts 4 times. Cast off rem sts. Work second piece in same way, reversing shaping.

Edging

Using No.2·00 (ISR) hook, B and with RS of collar facing, crochet a ch along the 3rd st from edge, (the P st), down side of collar along 2nd row of lower edge, then along 3rd st in from other side. Rep along 5th st and 4th row from lower edge. Fasten off.

To make up

Press each piece under a damp cloth with a warm iron. Join shoulder seams. Set in sleeves. Join side and sleeve seams. Turn hems to WS and sl st down. Sew on 2 pieces of collar. Sew down underflap on back opening. Press seams. Sew on buttons. Using 2 strands each of A and B, make a ch 24 [26:28]in long. Tie into a bow and sew to front under collar.

18 Playsuit with short striped sleeves and zip front

Sizes

To fit 22 [24]in chest

Length to shoulder, 26½ [30½]in

Sleeve seam, 4½ [5]in

The figures in brackets [] refer to the 24in size only

Tension

12 sts and 16 rows to 2in over rib patt worked on No.9 needles

Materials

10[12] balls Hayfield Courtier Bri-Nylon Double Knitting in main shade, A

2[2] balls of contrast colour, B

One pair No.9 needles; One pair No.11 needles

4in zip fastener in contrast colour

Right half

Using No.11 needles and A, cast on 86[91] sts.

1st row P1, *K4, P1, rep from * to end.

2nd row K1, *P4, K1, rep from * to end.

These 2 rows form patt. Cont in patt until work measures 1¼in from beg, ending with a 1st row.

Next row K all sts tbl to form hemline.

Change to No.9 needles. Beg with a 1st row, cont in rib until work measures 12 [15]in from hemline, ending with a WS row.

Shape crutch

Cast off at beg of next and every row 3 sts twice and 2 sts twice. Dec one st at each end of next and every foll 4th row 4 times in all. 68[73] sts. Cont without shaping until work measures 22 [25½]in from hemline, ending with a WS row.

Divide for armhole

Next row Rib 31[33] sts, cast off 6[7] sts, rib to end.

Cont on last 31[33] sts for back. Dec one st at armhole edge on foll 3 alt rows. Cont without shaping until armhole measures 3½ [4]in from beg, ending with a WS row.

Shape shoulder

Cast off at beg of next and every alt row 5 sts twice and 4[5] sts once. Leave rem 14[15] sts on holder.

With WS of work facing, rejoin yarn to rem sts

and rib to end. Dec one st at end of next and foll 2 alt rows. Cont without shaping until armhole measures 2½ [3]in from beg, ending with a RS row.

Shape neck

Next row Rib to last 10[11] sts, turn and leave these 10[11] sts on holder.

Dec one st at neck edge on next and foll 3 alt rows. Cont without shaping until armhole measures same as back to shoulder, ending with a RS row.

Shape shoulder

Cast off at beg of next and every alt row 5 sts twice and 4[5] sts once.

Left half

Work as given for right half, reversing all shapings.

Sleeves

Using No.11 needles and A, cast on 50[54] sts. Work 1½in K2, P2 rib, ending with a WS row. Change to No.9 needles.

Next row K2[4] sts, *P1, K4, rep from * to last 3[5] sts, P1, K2[4] sts.

Next row P2[4] sts, *K1, P4, rep from * to last 3[5] sts, K1, P2[4] sts.

Rep last 2 rows once more. Join in B. Cont in rib as now set, working 4 rows B and 4 rows A throughout and K each first row at change of colour, *at the same time* inc one st at each end of next and every foll 6th row until there are 56[60] sts. Cont without shaping until sleeve measures 4½ [5]in from beg, ending with a WS row.

Shape top

Cast off 2 sts at beg of every row until 20 sts rem. Cont on these 20 sts for length of shoulder, ending with a WS row. Leave sts on holder.

Neckband

Sew saddle tops of sleeves to front and back shoulders. Join centre back seam. Using No.11 needles, A and with RS of work facing, K across front neck sts, K up 8 sts up side of neck, K across sts of right sleeve, back neck and left sleeve, K2 tog at each seam and centre back seam, K up 8 sts down other side of neck, then K across front neck sts. 101[105] sts.

Next row K2[4] sts, (P2, K2 tog, K1, P2, K2) 11 times, K0[2] sts. 90[94] sts.

Next row K4[2] sts, (P2, K2) 20[22] times, P2, K4[2] sts.

Next row K2[4] sts, (P2, K2) 21[21] times, P2, K2[4] sts.

Rep last 2 rows for 1½in, ending with a RS row. Cast off in rib.

Pockets (make 2)

Using No.11 needles and A, cast on 18 sts. Beg first row with K2, work 4 rows K2, P2 rib. Change to No.9 needles. Join in B. K 1 row.

Next row K2 sts, *P4, K1, rep from * twice more, K1.

Next row K1, P1, *K4, P1, rep from * twice more, K1.

Rib 1 more row, then work 4 rows A, 4 rows B, 4 rows A, always K first row at change of colour.

Next row Using B, K2 sts, K2 tog, rib to last 4 sts, K2 tog tbl, K2 sts.

Next row K2 sts, P3, K1, P4, K1, P3, K2.

Next row K1, P1, K2 tog, rib to last 4 sts, K2 tog tbl, P1, K1.

Keeping striped patt correct, cont dec in this way at each end of every alt row until 8 sts rem. Cast off.

To make up

Press each piece under a dry cloth with a cool iron. Join centre front seam, leaving top 4in open for zip. Sew in zip. Set in sleeves. Join sleeve seams. Join leg seams. Turn hems to WS and sl st down. Sew on pockets. Press seams.

Jersey with three-colour Jacquard design

Sizes
To fit 26 [28:30:32]in chest
Length to shoulder, 16 [18:20:22]in
Sleeve seam, 11 [12½:14:16]in
The figures in brackets [] refer to the 28, 30 and 32in sizes respectively

Tension
7½ sts and 10 rows to 1in over st st worked on No.11 needles.

Materials
6[7:8:9] balls Patons Purple Heather 4 ply in main shade, A
2[2:3:3] balls each of contrast colours, B and C
One pair No.11 needles; One pair No.13 needles
Set of 4 No.13 needles pointed at both ends

Back
Using No.13 needles and A, cast on 101[109: 117:125] sts.
1st row K1, *P1, K1, rep from * to end.
2nd row P1, *K1, P1, rep from * to end.
Rep these 2 rows for 1½in, ending with a 2nd row and inc one st at end of last row. 102[110: 118:126] sts. Change to No. 11 needles. Commence patt.
1st row Using A, K to end.
2nd row Using A, P to end.
Rep last 2 rows once more.
5th row Using B, K1, *K3 sts, sl 1 noting that when sl st yarn is kept at WS of work, rep from * to last st, K1.
6th row Using B, P1, *sl 1 keeping yarn at front of work, P3, rep from * to last st, P1.
7th row Using A, K1, *sl 1, K3, rep from * to last st, K1.
8th row Using A, P1, *P3, sl 1, rep from * to last st, P1.
9th row Using B, K2, *sl 1, K3, rep from * to end.
10th row Using B, *P3, sl 1, rep from * to last 2 sts, P2.
11th-14th rows Using A, work in st st.
15th and 16th rows Using C, as 5th and 6th rows.
17th and 18th rows As 7th and 8th rows.
19th and 20th rows Using C, as 9th and 10th rows.
These 20 rows form patt. Cont in patt until work measures 11 [12½:14:15½]in from beg, ending with a WS row.
Shape armholes
Keeping patt correct, cast off 3 sts at beg of next 2 rows. Dec one st at each end of next and foll 4[5:6:7] alt rows. 86[92:98:104] sts. Cont without shaping until armholes measure 5 [5½: 6:6½]in from beg, ending with a WS row.
Shape shoulders
Cast off at beg of next and every row 5 sts 6 [6:10:10] times and 6[7:6:8] sts 4[4:2:2] times. Leave rem 32[34:36:38] sts on holder.

Front
Work as given for back until armholes measure 3 [3½:4:4½]in from beg, ending with a WS row.
Shape neck
Keeping patt correct, patt 33[35:37:39] sts, turn and leave rem sts on holder. Cast off 2 sts at neck edge on next row, then dec one st at neck edge on every alt row until 27[29:31:33] sts rem. Cont without shaping until armhole measures same as back to shoulder, ending with a WS row.

Shape shoulder
Cast off at beg of next and every alt row 5 sts 3[3:5:5] times and 6[7:6:8] sts 2[2:1:1] times. With RS of work facing, sl first 20[22:24:26] sts on holder and leave for centre neck, rejoin yarn to rem sts and patt to end. Complete to match first side, reversing all shapings.

Sleeves
Using No.13 needles and A, cast on 53[57:61: 65] sts. Work 2¼in rib as given for back, ending with a 2nd row and inc one st at end of last row on all sizes. 54[58:62:66] sts. Change to No.11 needles. Beg with a K row cont in patt as given for back, inc one st at each end of 5th and every foll 6th row until there are 80[86:92:98] sts. Cont without shaping until sleeve measures 11 [12½:14:16]in from beg, ending with a WS row.
Shape top
Keeping patt correct cast off 3 sts at beg of next 2 rows. Dec one st at each end of next and every alt row until 62[64:70:72] sts rem, ending with a WS row. Cast off at beg of next and every row 2 sts 10[10:12:12] times, 3 sts 6 times and 4 sts 4 times. Cast off rem 8[10:12: 14] sts.

Neckband
Join shoulder seams. Using set of 4 No.13 needles and A, with RS of work facing, K across back neck sts on holder, K up 22 sts down side of neck, K across centre front neck sts and K up 22 sts up other side of neck. Work in rounds of K1, P1 rib for 2 [2:3:3]in. Cast off loosely in rib.

To make up
Press each piece under a damp cloth with a warm iron. Set in sleeves. Join side and sleeve seams. Fold neckband in half to WS and sl st down. Press seams.

Aran jerseys with V or crew neck

Sizes
To fit 20 [22:24]in chest
Length to shoulder, 12 [13½:15]in
Sleeve seam, 8½ [10:11½]in
The figures in brackets [] refer to the 22 and 24in sizes respectively
Tension
9 sts and 12 rows to 2in over st st worked on No.7 needles
Materials
5[6:7] balls Mahony's Blarney Bainin Wool
One pair No.7 needles
One pair No.10 needles
One cable needle
Set of 4 No.10 needles for V-neck jersey
One button for crew neck jersey
Note
For V-neck jersey it is essential to finish with the 4th row of patt st, and length to underarm can only be adjusted by adding or subtracting 8 rows.
For crew neck jersey, length to underarm can be adjusted as required without interfering with the patt.
Crew neck jersey back
Using No.10 needles cast on 48[54:58] sts. Work 9 rows K1, P1 rib.
Next row Rib 4[4:6] sts, *inc in next st, rib 2 sts, rep from * to last 5[5:7] sts, inc in next st,

rib to end. 62[70:74] sts.
Change to No.7 needles. Commence patt.
1st row (K1, P1) 1[3:4] times, K into back of next st – called KB1 –, P2, sl next 2 sts on cable needle and hold at front of work, P2 sts, then K2 sts from cable needle – called T4F –, P3, sl next 2 sts on to cable needle and hold at front of work, K2 sts, then K2 sts from cable needle – called C4F –, P4, (K into front of 2nd st on left-hand needle, then P first st and sl both sts off needle tog – called T2R –, P into back of 2nd st on left-hand needle, then K first st and sl both sts off needle tog – called T2L –, P2) 4 times, P2, sl next 2 sts on cable needle and hold at back of work, K2 sts, then K2 sts from cable needle – called C4B –, P3, sl next 2 sts on cable needle and hold at back of work, K2 sts, then P2 sts from cable needle – called T4B –, P2, KB1, (P1, K1) 1[3:4] times.
2nd row (P1, K1) 1[3:4] times, P1, K4, P2, K3, P4, K4, (P1, K2) 8 times, K2, P4, K3, P2, K4, P1, (K1, P1) 1[3:4] times.
3rd row (K1, P1) 1[3:4] times, KB1, P2, T4B, P1, T4B, T4F, P1, (T2R, P2, T2L) 4 times, P1, T4B, T4F, P1, T4F, P2, KB1, (K1, P1) 1[3:4] times.
4th row (K1, P1) 1[3:4] times, P1, K2, P2, K3, P2, K4, P2, K1, P1, (K4, P 2nd st on left-hand needle then P first st and sl both sts off needle tog – called cross 2P) 3 times, K4, P1, K1, P2, K4, P2, K3, P2, K2, P1, (P1, K1) 1[3:4] times.
5th row (K1, P1) 1[3:4] times, KB1, P1, sl next st on to cable needle and hold at back of work, K2 sts, then P st from cable needle – called T3B –, P3, K2, P4, K2, P1, (T2L, P2, T2R) 4 times, P1, K2, P4, K2, P3, sl next 2 sts on cable needle and hold at front of work, P1 st, then K2 sts from cable needle – called T3F –, P1, KB1, (P1, K1) 1[3:4] times.
6th row (P1, K1) 2[4:5] times, (P2, K4) twice P2, (K2, P1) 8 times, K2, (P2, K4) twice, P2, (K1, P1) 2[4:5] times.
7th row (P1, K1) 1[3:4] times, KB1, P1, T3F, P3, T4F, T4B, (P2, T2L, T2R) 4 times, P2, T4F, T4B, P3, T3B, P1, KB1, (K1, P1) 1[3:4] times.
8th row (K1, P1) 1[3:4] times, P1, K2, P2, K5, P4, K5, (cross 2P, K4) 3 times, cross 2P, K5, P4, K5, P2, K2, P1, (P1, K1) 1[3:4] times.
These 8 rows form patt. Cont in patt until work measures 7 [7¾:8½]in from beg, or required length to underarm ending with a 4th patt row.
Shape raglan armholes
** Cast off 1[2:2] sts at beg of next 2 rows.
3rd row K1, sl 1, K1, psso, patt to last 3 sts, K2 tog, K1.
4th row P2 sts, patt to last 2 sts, P2. **
Rep last 2 rows until 34[36:36] sts rem, ***, ending with a WS row.
Next row K1, sl 1, K2 tog, psso, patt to last 4 sts, K3 tog, K1.
Next row As 4th raglan armhole row.
Rep last 2 rows until 22[24:24] sts rem, ending with a RS row.
Next row P2[3:3] sts, (P2 tog, P2) 4 times, P2 tog, P2[3:3] sts.
Sl rem 17[19:19] sts on holder.

Crew neck jersey front
Work as given for back to ***, ending with a RS row.
Shape neck
Next row Patt 12[13:13] sts, (P2 tog, P2) twice, P2 tog, P1[2:2] sts, sl the last 9[11:11] sts just worked on to a holder for centre neck and patt to end on rem 11 sts.
Complete this side first.
Next row K1, sl 1, K2 tog, psso, patt to last 2 sts, work 2 tog.
Next row Work 2 tog, patt to last 2 sts, P2.

Rep last 2 rows once more. Dec one st at neck edge only on next row. Cast off.
With RS of work facing, rejoin yarn to rem sts and complete to match first side, reversing all shapings.

Sleeves
Using No.10 needles cast on 28[30:32] sts. Work 9 rows K1, P1 rib.
Next row Rib 5[4:3] sts, *inc in next st, rib 1, rep from * to last 7[6:5] sts, inc in next st, rib to end. 37[41:45] sts.
Change to No.7 needles. Commence patt.
1st row (K1, P1) 1[2:3] times, KB1, P2, T4F, P3, C4F, P5, C4B, P3, T4B, P2, KB1, (P1, K1) 1[2:3] times.
2nd row (P1, K1) 1[2:3] times, P1, K4, P2, K3, P4, K5, P4, K3, P2, K4, P1, (K1, P1) 1[2:3] times.
3rd row (P1, K1) 1[2:3] times, KB1, P2, T4B, P1, T4B, T4F, P1, T4B, T4F, P1, T4F, P2, KB1, (K1, P1) 1[2:3] times.
4th row (K1, P1) 1[2:3] times, P1, K2, P2, K3, P2, K4, P2, K1, P2, K4, P2, K3, P2, K2, P1, (P1, K1) 1[2:3] times.
5th row (K1, P1) 1[2:3] times, KB1, P1, T3B, P3, K2, P4, K2, P1, K2, P4, K2, P3, T3F, P1, KB1, (P1, K1) 1[2:3] times.
6th row (P1, K1) 2[3:4] times, P2, (K4, P2) twice, K1, (P2, K4) twice, P2, (K1, P1) 2[3:4] times.
7th row (P1, K1) 1[2:3] times, KB1, P1, T3F, P3, T4F, T4B, P1, T4F, T4B, P3, T3B, P1, KB1, (K1, P1) 1[2:3] times.
8th row (K1, P1) 1[2:3] times, P1, K2, P2, (K5, P4) twice, K5, P2, K2, P1, (P1, K1) 1[2:3] times.
Cont in patt, inc one st at each end of next and every foll 8th[10th:12th] rows, and working extra sts into double moss st, until there are 47[51:55] sts. Cont without shaping until sleeve measures 8½ [10:11½]in from beg, or required length to underarm ending with a WS row.
Shape top
Work as given for back from ** to **. Rep last 2 rows until 19[15:15] sts rem, ending with a WS row.
Next row K1, sl 1, K2 tog, psso, patt to last 4 sts, K3 tog, K1.
Next row P2 sts, patt to last 2 sts, P2.
Rep last 2 rows 2[1:1] times more. Sl rem 7 sts on holder.

Neckband
Join raglan seams leaving left back seam open. Using No.10 needles cast on 3 sts, then with RS of work facing K across sts of left sleeve top, K up 6 sts down left side of neck, K across front neck sts, K up 6 sts up right side of neck, K across sts of right sleeve top and back neck.
1st row *K1, P1, rep from * to last 3 sts, K3.
2nd row K4 sts, *P1, K1, rep from * to last st, P1.
Keeping g st and rib correct, work 1 more row.
Next row (buttonhole row) Patt 2 sts, cast off 2 sts, patt to end.
Next row Patt to end, casting on 2 sts above those cast off in previous row.
Work 2 more rows.
Next row Cast off 3 sts, patt to end.
Work 8 more rows. Sl sts on to holder.

To make up
Press each piece lightly on WS under a damp cloth with a warm iron. Join rem raglan seam, leaving top 1½in open. Fold neckband in half to WS and sl st down taking care to catch every st. Join side and sleeve seams. Press seams. Sew on button.

V-neck jersey back
Work as given for crew neck jersey, casting off sts at end.

V-neck jersey front
Work as given for back to beg of raglan armhole shaping.
Shape raglan armholes and divide for neck
Next row Cast off 1[2:2] sts, patt 28[31:33] sts, K into front of 2nd st on left-hand needle then K first st and sl both sts off needle tog, turn and sl rem 31[35:37] sts on holder.
Next row P2 sts, patt to last 2 sts, P2.
Next row K1, sl 1, K1, psso, patt to last 3 sts, K2 tog, K1.
Rep last 2 rows until 16[19:25] sts rem. Cont to dec one st at raglan edge on every alt row, *at the same time* dec one st at neck edge on every foll 4th row until 7 sts rem, ending with a WS row.
Next row K1, sl 1, K2, tog, psso, patt one st, K2.
Next row P2 sts, patt one st, P2.
Next row K1, K3 tog, K1.
Next row P3 sts.
Next row K2 tog, K1. Cast off.
With RS of work facing, rejoin yarn to rem sts.
1st row K into back of 2nd st on left-hand needle then K first st, work in patt to end.
2nd row Cast off 1[2:2] sts, patt to last 2 sts, P2.
3rd row K1, sl 1, K1, psso, patt to last 3 sts, K2 tog, K1.
Complete to match first side, reversing all shapings.

Sleeves
Work as given for crew neck jersey.

Neckband
Join raglan seams. Using set of 4 No.10 needles and with RS of work facing, K up 17[19:19] sts across back neck, K up 6 sts across sleeve top, K up 34[38:42] sts down left side of neck, make one st at centre neck by lifting loop between 2 centre sts and Ktbl, K up 34[38:42] sts up right side of neck and K up 6 sts across other sleeve top.
1st round P1, *K1, P1, rep from * to 2 sts before made st at centre front, sl 1, K1, psso, K1, K2 tog, **P1, K1, rep from ** to end.
Keeping rib correct, cont to dec one st at each side of centre K st on next 6 rounds. Cast off in rib, still dec at centre front.

To make up
Press as given for crew neck jersey. Join side and sleeve seams. Press seams.

21 Snow set of jersey, trousers, hat and mittens

Sizes
To fit 24 [26:28:30]in chest
Sweater length to shoulder, 13½ [15½:17½:19½]in
Sleeve seam, 10 [11½:13:14½]in
Trousers inside leg, 12 [14:17:21]in
The figures in brackets [] refer to the 26, 28 and 30in sizes respectively

Tension
7½ sts and 10 rows to 2in over st st worked on No.4 needles

Materials
12[13:15:17] balls Lister Prema Bulky Knitting in main shade, A, for complete set
1 ball each of contrast colour, B and C
6[7:7:8] balls of A for sweater and hat only
6[7:8:9] balls of A for trousers and mittens only
One pair No.4 needles
One pair No.6 needles
Waist length of elastic

Sweater back
Using No.6 needles and A, cast on 49[53:57:61] sts.
1st row K1, *P1, K1, rep from * to end.
2nd row P1, *K1, P1, rep from * to end.
Rep these 2 rows once more, then first of them again. Change to No.4 needles. P 1 row.
Commence patt.
1st row K0[0:0:2] C, 0[0:1:1] A, 0[0:1:1] C, 0[1:1:1] A, 5[6:6:6] C, *1A, 1C, 1A, 6C, rep from * 3 times more, 1A, 1C, 1A, 5[6:6:6] C, 0[1:1:1] A, 0[0:1:1] C, 0[0:1:1] A, 0[0:0:2] C.
2nd row P0[0:0:2] A, 0[1:3:3] B, 5[6:6:6] A, *3B, 6A, rep from * 3 times more, 3B, 5[6:6:6] A, 0[1:3:3] B, 0[0:0:2] A.
Cont in this way working in patt from chart, until 20 rows have been completed. Cont in st st using A only until work measures 7½ [9:10½:12]in from beg, ending with a P row.
Shape armholes
Cast off 2 sts at beg of next 2 rows.
Next row K3 sts, K2 tog, K to last 5 sts, sl 1, K1, psso, K3 sts.
Next row P to end.
Rep last 2 rows until 15[17:17:19] sts rem, ending with a P row. Cast off.

Sweater front
Work as given for back until 25[27:27:29] sts rem, ending with a K row
Shape neck
Next row K9 sts, cast off 7[9:9:11]sts, P to end.
Complete this side first. Dec one st at neck edge on next and foll alt row, *at the same time* cont to dec at raglan edge on every alt row as before until 4 sts rem, ending with a P row.
Next row K2 sts, K2 tog.
Next row P3 sts.
Next row K1 st, K2 tog.
Next row P2 tog. Fasten off.
With RS of work facing, rejoin yarn to rem sts and complete to match first side, reversing all shapings.

Sleeves
Using No.6 needles and A, cast on 27[29:29:31] sts. Work 1¼in rib as given for back, ending with a 2nd row. Change to No.4 needles. Beg with a K row cont in st st, inc one st at each end of 5th and every foll 6th row until there are 39[43:47:51] sts. Cont without shaping until sleeve measures 10 [11½:13:14½]in from beg, ending with a P row.
Shape top
Cast off 2 sts at beg of next 2 rows. Dec one st at each end of next and every alt row as given for back until 5[7:7:9] sts rem, ending with a P row. Cast off.

Collar
Join 3 raglan seams, leaving left back seam open. Using No.6 needles, A and with RS of work facing, K up 61[61:69:69] sts evenly round neck. Work 4 rows rib as given for back, inc 4[4:5:5] sts evenly along last row. 65[65:74:74] sts. Change to No.4 needles. Work first 13 rows of patt from chart, beg where indicated. Using A, P 1 row.
Next row Using A, P to end to mark fold line. Using A and beg with a P row work 3 rows st st. Cast off.

To make up
Press each piece under a damp cloth with a warm iron. Join left back raglan and collar seam. Join side and sleeve seams. Turn in hem

of collar to WS and sl st down. Press seams.

Trousers right leg

Using No.6 needles and A, cast on 29[33:37:41] sts. Work 1½in rib as given for sweater back, ending with a 2nd row. Change to No.4 needles. Beg with a K row cont in st st for 1½in.

Shape leg

Next row K2 sts, K up 1, K11[13:15:17] sts, K up 1, K3 sts, K up 1, K11[13:15:17] sts, K up 1, K2 sts.

Beg with a P row work 7[7:9:9] rows without shaping.

Next row K2 sts, K up 1, K13[15:17:19] sts, K up 1, K3 sts, K up 1, K13[15:17:19] sts, K up 1, K2 sts.

Beg with a P row work 7[7:9:9] rows without shaping. Cont inc in this way on next and every foll 8th[8th:10th:10th] row until there are 57[61:65:69] sts. Cont without shaping until work measures 12 [14:17:21]in from beg, ending with a P row. Mark each end of last row with coloured thread.

Shape gusset

Cast off 2 sts at beg of next 3 rows. P 1 row. Dec one st at each end of next row, then work 7 rows without shaping. Dec one st at end only of next row, then work 7 rows without shaping. Rep last 16 rows once more, then dec one st at each end of next row on 28 and 30in sizes only. 45[49:51:55] sts. Cont without shaping until work measures 7½ [8:8½:9]in from marked point, ending with a K row.

Shape back

Next row P36 sts, turn and K to end.

Next row P24 sts, turn and K to end.

Next row P12 sts, turn and K to end.

Next row P to end.

Change to No.6 needles. Work 1in K1, P1 rib. Cast off in rib.

Trousers left leg

Work as given for right leg, reversing all shapings.

To make up

Press as given for sweater. Join back and front seams. Join leg seams. Sew elastic inside waistband using casing st. Press seams.

Hat

Using No.6 needles and A, cast on 65[73] sts. Work 5 rows rib as given for sweater back. Change to No.4 needles. P 1 row, inc one st at end of row on 2nd size only. 65[74] sts. Cont in patt working from chart and beg as indicated, until 14 rows have been completed. Cont in

st st using A only, until work measures 6¼ [7¼]in from beg, ending with a P row.

Shape top

Next row K2 sts, *K2 tog, K1, rep from * to end. 44[50] sts.

Beg with a P row work 5 rows without shaping.

Next row K2 sts, *K2 tog, K1, rep from * to end. 30[34] sts.

Beg with a P row work 3 rows without shaping.

Next row *K2 tog, rep from * to end. 15[17] sts. P 1 row. Break off yarn, thread through rem sts, draw up and fasten off.

Ear flaps (make 2)

Using No.6 needles and A, cast on 17 sts. Work 2in rib as given for sweater back, ending with a 2nd row.

Next row Rib 6 sts, sl 1, K1, psso, K1, K2 tog, rib to end.

Next row Rib 6 sts, P3 sts, rib to end.

Next row Rib 6 sts, sl 1, K2 tog, psso, rib to end.

Next row Rib to end.

Cont to dec in this way in centre of every alt row until 3 sts rem. Cast off.

To make up

Press as given for sweater. Join seam. Sew one ear flap to each side of hat. Make 2 ch cords and sew one to point of each ear flap. Using B and C, make a large pompon and sew to top of hat.

Mittens

Using No.6 needles and A, cast on 25[29] sts. Work 2½ [3]in rib as given for sweater back, ending with a 2nd row. Change to No.4 needles. Beg with a K row work 2[4] rows st. st

Next row K12[14] sts, K up 1, K1, K up 1, K to end.

Next row P to end.

Next row K12[14] sts, K up 1, K3, K up 1, K to end.

Next row P to end.

Cont to inc in this way on next and every alt row until there are 31[37] sts. Work 3[5] rows without shaping.

Shape thumb

Next row K19[23] sts, cast on one st, turn.

Next row P8[10] sts, cast on one st, turn. Beg with a K row work 6[8] rows on these 9[11] sts.

Next row K1, *K2 tog, rep from * to end. Break off yarn, thread through rem sts, draw up and fasten off.

With RS of work facing, rejoin yarn to rem sts, K up 2 sts from cast on sts at base of thumb,

K to end. 26[30] sts. Cont without shaping until work measures 6½ [8]in from beg, ending with a P row.

Shape top

Next row K1[2] sts, *K2 tog, K1, rep from * to last st, K1. 18[21] sts.

Next row P to end.

Next row *K2 tog, K1, rep from * to end. 12[14] sts.

Next row P to end.

Next row *K2 tog, rep from * to end. Break off yarn, thread through rem sts, draw up and fasten off.

To make up

Press as given for sweater. Join seams. Press seams.

See chart at foot of page

22 *Jersey with 'Policeman' motif*

Sizes

To fit 26 [28:30:32:34]in chest
Length to shoulder, 17 [18¼:19½:20¾:22]in
Long sleeve seam, 14½ [14½:15:16:16½]in
Short sleeve seam, 4 [4:4½:5:5]in
The figures in brackets [ ] refer to the 28, 30, 32 and 34in sizes respectively

Tension

7½ sts and 9½ rows to 1in over st st worked on No.10 needles

Materials

Emu Scotch 4 ply
Long sleeved version 7 [8:8:9:9] balls main shade, A
1 ball each contrast colours B, C, D, E and F
Short sleeved version 6 [7:7:8:8] balls main shade, A
1 ball each contrast colours B, C, D, E and F
One pair No.10 needles
One pair No.12 needles
Oddments of yarn and 2 small white beads for features

Note

Wind contrast colours into several small balls and use separate balls of yarn for each colour. Always twist yarns at back of work when changing colours.

Back

Using No.12 needles and A, cast on 102 [110: 118:124:132] sts. Work 2in K1, P1 rib. Change to No.10 needles. ** Beg with a K row cont in st st until work measures 11 [12:13:14:15]in from beg, ending with a P row.

Shape armholes

Cast off 5[6:7:7:8] sts at beg of next 2 rows. Dec one st at each end of next and foll 6[7:8: 9:10] alt rows. 78[82:86:90:94] sts. Cont without shaping until armholes measure 6 [6¼: 6½:6¾:7]in from beg, ending with a P row.

Shape shoulders

Cast off at beg of next and every row 7[8:8:9: 9] sts 4 times and 8[7:8:7:8] sts twice. Leave rem 34[36:38:40:42] sts on holder for back neck.

Front

Work as given for back to **. Beg with a K row work 1 [1½:2:3:4]in st st, ending with a P row. Commence patt.

1st row Using first ball of A, K28[32:36:39:43] sts, using first ball of B, K14 sts, using 2nd ball

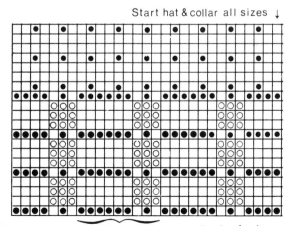

Start hat & collar all sizes ↓

Rep 9 sts

↑   ↑   ↑   ↑
1st 2nd 3rd 4th sizes   Start back & front

NO. 21

Colour Key

☐ = A

◨ = B

◼ = C

of A, K4 sts, using first ball of B, K7 sts, using 2nd ball of A, K to end.

2nd row Using 2nd ball of A, P49[53:57:60:64] sts, using B, P24 sts, using first ball of A, P to end.

Cont working from chart in this way until work measures same as back to underarm, ending with a P row.

Shape armholes

Keeping patt correct, cast off 5[6:7:7:8] sts at beg of next 2 rows. Dec one st at each end of next and foll 6[7:8:9:10] alt rows. 78[82:86: 90:94] sts. Cont without shaping until armholes measure 4 [4¼:4½:4¾:5]in from beg, using A only when motif is completed and ending with a P row.

Shape neck

Next row K29[30:31:32:33] sts, turn and leave rem sts on holder.

Dec one st at neck edge on next 7 rows. 22[23: 24:25:26] sts. Cont without shaping until armhole measures same as back to shoulder, ending at armhole edge.

Shape shoulder

Cast off at beg of next and every alt row 7[8:8: 9:9] sts twice and 8[7:8:7:8] sts once.

With RS of work facing, sl first 20[22:24:26:28] sts on holder and leave for centre neck, rejoin yarn to rem sts and K to end. Complete to match first side, reversing all shapings.

Long sleeves

Using No.12 needles and A, cast on 50[52:56: 58:60] sts. Work 2in K1, P1 rib. Change to No.10 needles. Beg with a K row cont in st st, inc one st at each end of 5th and every foll 8th row until there are 74[78:82:86:90] sts. Cont without shaping until sleeve measures 14½ [14½: 15:16:16½]in from beg, ending with a P row.

Shape top

Cast off 5[6:7:7:8] sts at beg of next 2 rows. Dec one st at each end of next 2[2:4:4:6] rows, then each end of every alt row until 32 sts rem, ending with a P row. Cast off at beg of next and every row 2 sts 6 times and 3 sts 4 times. Cast off rem 8 sts.

Short sleeves

Using No.12 needles and A, cast on 66[70:74: 78:82] sts. Work 1in K1, P1 rib. Change to No.10 needles. Beg with a K row cont in st st, inc one st at each end of 5th and every foll 6th row until there are 74[78:82:86:90] sts. Cont without shaping until sleeve measures 4 [4:4½: 5:5]in from beg, ending with a P row.

Shape top

Work as given for long sleeves.

Neckband

Join left shoulder seam. Using No.12 needles, A and with RS of work facing, K across sts of back neck holder, K up 24 sts down left side of neck, K across 20[22:24:26:28] sts of centre front holder and K up 24 sts up right side of neck. 102[106:110:114:118] sts. Work 2in K1, P1 rib. Cast off loosely in rib.

To make up

Press each piece on WS under a damp cloth with a warm iron. Using black yarn outline glove and fingers with ch st. Using black work eyes in satin st and highlight each eye with small white bead. Using black, outline nose and chin strap with stem st. Using pink, fill in cheeks with satin st. Using brown, work moustache by cutting lengths about 1½in long and with 3 strands tog, knot fringing under outline of nose. Trim ends of fringe. Join right shoulder and neckband seam. Join side and sleeve seams. Set in sleeves. Turn neckband in half to WS and sl st down. Press seams.

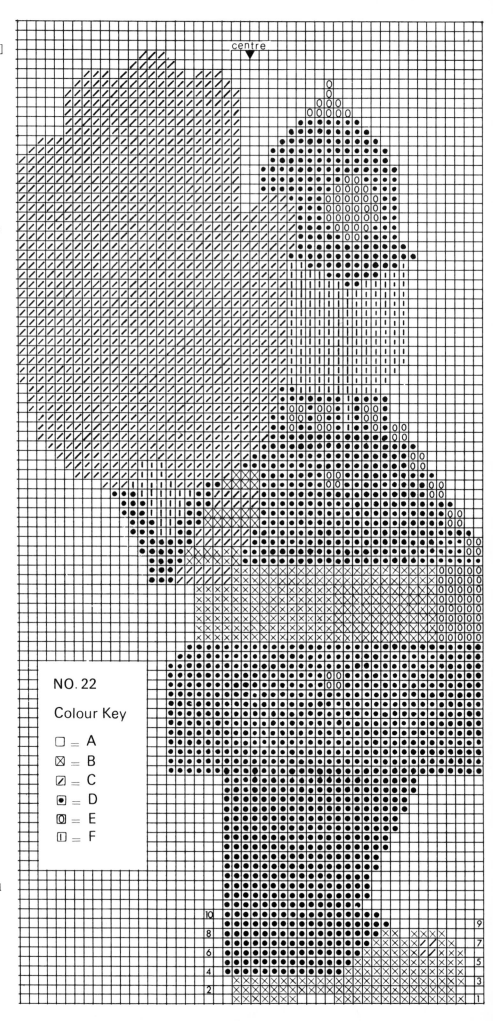

NO. 22

Colour Key

☐ = A
⊠ = B
☑ = C
⊡ = D
◫ = E
⊟ = F

23 *Jersey, trousers, cap and mitts in double moss stitch*

Sizes
To fit 24 [26:28:30]in chest
Jersey length to shoulder, 15½ [17:18½:20]in
Sleeve seam, 10 [11½:13:15]in
Trousers inside leg, 12½ [15:17½:20]in
The figures in brackets [] refer to the 26, 28 and 30in sizes respectively
Tension
5 sts and 6 rows to 1in over double moss st worked on No.5 needles
Materials
24[27:30:33] balls Lister Double Six in main shade, A
1 ball of contrast colour, B
One pair No.5 needles; One pair No.7 needles
Set of 4 No.7 needles pointed at both ends
Waist length of elastic

Jersey back
Using No.7 needles and A, cast on 63[69:75:81] sts.
1st row K1, *P1, K1, rep from * to end.
2nd row P1, *K1, P1, rep from * to end.
Rep these 2 rows 3[4:4:5] times more. Change to No.5 needles. Commence patt.
1st row (P1, K1) 5[6:7:8] times, *(P2, K3) twice, P2, *, K1, (P1, K1) 9[10:11:12] times, rep from * to * once more, (K1, P1) to end.
2nd row (K1, P1) 5[6:7:8] times, *(K2, P3) twice, K2, *, P1, (K1, P1) 9[10:11:12] times, rep from * to * once more, (P1, K1) to end.
3rd row (K1, P1) 5[6:7:8] times, rep from * to * as given for 1st row, P1, (K1, P1) 9[10:11:12] times, rep from * to * as given for 1st row, (P1, K1) to end.
4th row (P1, K1) 5[6:7:8] times, rep from * to * as given for 2nd row, K1, (P1, K1) 9[10:11:12] times, rep from * to * as given for 2nd row, (K1, P1) to end.
5th and 6th rows As 1st and 2nd rows.
7th row (K1, P1) 5[6:7:8] times, *P2, K3, P2, K2, P3, *, P1, (K1, P1) 9[10:11:12] times, rep from * to * once more, (P1, K1) to end.
8th row (P1, K1) 5[6:7:8] times, *K3, P2, K2, P3, K2, *, K1, (P1, K1) 9[10:11:12] times, rep from * to * once more, (K1, P1) to end.
9th row (P1, K1) 5[6:7:8] times, *P3, K3, P1, K1, P4, *, K1, (P1, K1) 9[10:11:12] times, rep from * to * once more, (K1, P1) to end.
10th row (K1, P1) 5[6:7:8] times, *K4, P1, K1, P3, K3, *, P1, (K1, P1) 9[10:11:12] times, rep from * to * once more, (P1, K1) to end.
11th row (K1, P1) 5[6:7:8] times, *P4, K3, P5, *, P1, (K1, P1) 9[10:11:12] times rep from * to * once more, (P1, K1) to end.
12th row (P1, K1) 5[6:7:8] times, *K5, P3, K4, *, K1, (P1, K1) 9[10:11:12] times, rep from * to * once more, (K1, P1) to end.
13th row (P1, K1) 5[6:7:8] times, *P5, K3, P4, *, K1, (P1, K1) 9[10:11:12] times, rep from * to * once more, (K1, P1) to end.
14th row (K1, P1) 5[6:7:8] times, *K4, P3, K5, *, P1, (K1, P1) 9[10:11:12] times, rep from * to * once more, (P1, K1) to end.
15th row (K1, P1) 5[6:7:8] times, *P4, K1, P1, K3, P3, *, P1, (K1, P1) 9[10:11:12] times, rep from * to * once more, (P1, K1) to end.
16th row (P1, K1) 5[6:7:8] times, *K3, P3, K1, P1, K4, *, K1, (P1, K1) 9[10:11:12] times, rep from * to * once more, (K1, P1) to end.
17th row (P1, K1) 5[6:7:8] times, *P3, K2, P2, K3, P2, *, K1, (P1, K1) 9[10:11:12] times, rep from * to * once more, (K1, P1) to end.
18th row (K1, P1) 5[6:7:8] times, *K2, P3, K2, P2, K3, *, P1, (K1, P1) 9[10:11:12] times, rep from * to * once more, (P1, K1) to end.
19th and 20th rows As 3rd and 4th rows.
These 20 rows form patt. Cont in patt until work measures 10½ [11½:12½:13½]in from beg, or required length to underarm, ending with a WS row.
Shape armholes
Keeping patt correct, cast off 4 sts at beg of next 2 rows. Work 2 rows. Dec one st at each end of next and every foll 4th row until 45[49:53:57] sts rem. ** Work 1 row after last dec.
Shape shoulders
Cast off at beg of next and every row 4[5:5:5] sts 4 times and 5[4:5:6] sts twice. Leave rem 19[21:23:25] sts on holder.

Jersey front
Work as given for back to **, ending with a RS row.
Shape neck and shoulders
Next row Patt 16[17:18:19] sts, turn and leave rem sts on holder.
Next row K2 tog, patt to end.
Next row Cast off 4[5:5:5] sts, patt to end.
Rep last 2 rows once more, then first of them again. Cast off rem 5[4:5:6] sts.
With WS of work facing, sl first 13[15:17:19] sts on holder and leave for centre neck, rejoin yarn to rem sts, P2 tog, patt to end.
Next row Cast off 4[5:5:5] sts, patt to end.
Complete to match first side.

Sleeves
Using No.7 needles and A, cast on 39[39:43:43] sts. Work 6[6:8:8] rows rib as given for back. Join in B. K 1 row, then rib 3 rows. Break off B. Cont with A only. K 1 row, then rib 1 row, inc one st at end of last row. 40[40:44:44] sts.
Change to No.5 needles. Commence patt.
1st row (P1, K1) 7[7:8:8] times, rep from * to * as given for 1st row of back, (K1, P1) to end.
2nd row (K1, P1) 7[7:8:8] times, rep from * to * as given for 2nd row of back, (P1, K1) to end.
3rd row (K1, P1) 7[7:8:8] times, rep from * to * as given for 3rd row of back, (P1, K1) to end.
Cont in patt as given for back as now set, inc one st at each end of 5th and every foll 6th row until there are 50[54:58:62] sts and working extra sts into double moss st. Cont without shaping until sleeve measures 10 [11½:13:15]in from beg, or required length to underarm, ending with a WS row.
Shape top
Cast off 4 sts at beg of next 2 rows. Dec one st at each end of next and every alt row until 28[28:26:26] sts rem, then at each end of every row until 16[16:18:18] sts rem. Cont without shaping on these 16[16:18:18] sts for length of shoulder, ending with a WS row. Leave sts on holder.

Neckband
Sew saddle tops of shoulders to front and back shoulders. Using set of 4 No.7 needles, A, and with RS of work facing, K across sts of right sleeve, back neck and left sleeve, K2 tog at each seam, K up 4 sts down side of neck, K across centre front neck sts, then K up 4 sts up other side of neck. 70[74:82:86] sts. Work 1 round K1, P1 rib. Join in B. K 1 round, then rib 3 rounds. Break off B. Using A, K 1 round, then cont in rib until work measures 3[3:4:4]in from beg. Cast off loosely in rib.

To make up
Press each piece under a damp cloth with a warm iron. Set in sleeves. Join side and sleeve seams. Press seams. Fold neckband in half to WS and sl st down.

Trousers right leg
Using No.7 needles and A, cast on 35[39:43:47] sts. Work 1½in rib as given for jersey back, ending with a 2nd row. Change to No.5 needles. Cont in double moss st for 4 rows.
Shape leg
Next row Inc in first st, patt 15[17:19:21] sts, K twice into each of next 2 sts, patt 16[18:20:22] sts, inc in last st.
Work 7[7:9:9] rows double moss st.
Next row Inc in first st, patt 17[19:21:23] sts, K twice into each of next 2 sts, patt 18[20:22:24] sts, inc in last st.
Cont to inc in this way on every foll 8th[8th:10th:10th] row until there are 63[67:71:75] sts.
Cont without shaping until work measures 12½ [15:17½:20]in from beg, or required leg length, ending with a WS row, Mark each end of last row with coloured thread.
Shape crutch
Cast off at beg of next and every row 4 sts twice and 2 sts once. Work 1 row. Dec one st at each end of next and every foll 4th row until 47[51:55:59] sts rem. Cont without shaping until work measures 7½ [8:8½:9]in from marked point, ending with a RS row.
Shape back
Next row Patt to last 7[11:10:14] sts, turn and patt to end.
Next row Patt to last 15[19:19:23] sts, turn and patt to end.
Cont to work 8[8:9:9] sts less on every alt row 3 times more. Work 1 row across all sts. Change to No.7 needles. Work 1in rib as given at beg. Cast off in rib.
Trousers left leg
Work as given for right leg, reversing all shapings.

To make up
Press as given for jersey. Join back and front seams. Join leg seams. Sew elastic inside waistband, using casing st. Press seams.

Cap
Using No.7 needles and A, cast on 79[89] sts. Work 1 row rib as given for jersey back. Join in B. K 1 row, then rib 3 rows. Break off B. Using A only, K 1 row, then cont in rib until work measures 2¾ [3¼]in from beg, ending with a 1st row. Change to No.5 needles. Beg with a 1st patt row, cont in double moss st until work measures 8 [9]in from beg, ending with a WS row.
Shape top
Next row K2[1] sts, (sl 1, K2 tog, psso, K1) 19[22] times, K1[0]. 41[45] sts.
Beg with a P row work 3 rows st st.
Next row K1, *sl 1, K2 tog, psso, K1, rep from * to end. 21[23] sts.
Beg with a P row work 3 rows st st.
Next row K1, *K2 tog, rep from * to end.
Break off yarn, thread through rem sts, draw up and fasten off.

To make up
Press as given for jersey. Join seam. Make a pompon and sew to top.

Mittens
Using No.7 needles and A, cast on 29[33] sts. Work 2 [2½]in rib as given for jersey back, ending with a 2nd row. Change to No.5 needles. Work 4 rows double moss st.
Next row Patt 13[15] sts, K up 1, K3 sts, K up 1, patt to end.
Next row Patt 13[15] sts, P 5 sts, patt to end.
Next row Patt 13[15] sts, K up 1, K 5 sts, K up 1, patt to end.
Cont to inc in this way twice more, then work 1[3] rows after last inc. 37[41] sts.
Next row Patt 14[16] sts, sl next 9 sts on to holder and leave for thumb, cast on 3 sts, patt to end. 31[35] sts.
Cont in patt for 2½ [3]in, ending with a WS row.

Shape top

Next row K1[2] sts, *K2 tog, K1, rep from * to end. 21[24] sts.

Next row P to end.

Next row *K2 tog, K1, rep from * to end. 14[16] sts.

Next row P to end.

Next row *K2 tog, rep from * to end.

Break off yarn, thread through rem sts, draw up and fasten off.

Thumb

Sl 9 sts on holder on to No.5 needle, K up 3 sts from cast on sts at base of thumb. 12 sts. Cont in st st for 1¼ [1¾]in, ending with a P row.

Shape top

Next row *K2 tog, rep from * to end.

Next row P to end.

Break off yarn, thread through rem sts, draw up and fasten off.

To make up

Press as given for jersey. Join side and thumb seams. Press seams.

24 *Chunky jersey in broken basket stitch*

Sizes

To fit 24 [26:28:30:32]in chest

Length to shoulder, 14½ [16½:18½:20½:22½]in

Sleeve seam, 10 [11:12:13½:15]in

The figures in brackets [] refer to the 26, 28, 30 and 32in sizes respectively

Tension

7 sts and 10 rows to 2in over st st worked on No.4 needles

Materials

7[8:8:9:10] balls Templeton's Sestal Chunky Knitting

One pair No.4 needles; One pair No.6 needles

8 buttons

Back

Using No.6 needles cast on 42[50:50:54:54] sts.

1st row K2, *P2, K2, rep from * so end.

2nd row P2, *K2, P2, rep from * to end.

Rep these 2 rows for 2in, ending with a 2nd row and inc one st at each end of last row on 24, 30 and 32in sizes only. 44[50:50:56:56] sts.

Change to No. 4 needles. Commence patt.

1st row K1[4:4:1:1] sts, P6, *K6, P6, rep from * to last 1[4:4:1:1] sts, K to end.

2nd row P1[4:4:1:1] sts, K6, *P6, K6, rep from * to last 1[4:4:1:1] sts, P to end.

3rd row K1[4:4:1:1] sts, P1, K4, P1, *K1, P4, K1, P1, K4, P1, rep from * to last 1[4:4: 1:1] sts, K to end.

4th row P1[4:4:1:1] sts, K1, P4, K1, *P1, K4, P1, K1, P4, K1, rep from * to last 1 [4:4:1:1] sts, P to end.

5th, 6th, 7th and 8th rows. Rep 3rd and 4th rows twice more.

9th row As 1st.

10th row As 2nd.

11th row K7[10:10:7:7] sts, *P6, K6, rep from * to last 1[4:4:1:1] sts, K to end.

12th row P7[10:10:7:7] sts, *K6, P6, rep from * to last 1[4:4:1:1] sts, P to end.

13th row K2[5:5:2:2] sts, P4, K1, *P1, K4, P1, K1, P4, K1, rep from * to last 1[4:4:1:1] sts, K to end.

14th row P2[5:5:2:2] sts, K4, P1, *K1, P4, K1, P1, K4, P1, rep from * to last 1[4:4:1:1] sts, P to end.

15th, 16th, 17th and 18th rows Rep 13th and 14th rows twice more.

19th row As 11th.

20th row As 12th.

These 20 rows form patt. Cont in patt until work measures 8½ [9½:10½:11½:12½]in from beg, ending with a WS row.

Shape armholes

Keeping patt correct, cast off 1[3:1:3:1] sts at beg of next 2 rows. 42[44:48:50:54] sts.

**Next row K2 sts, P2 tog, patt to last 4 sts, P2 tog, K2.

Next row P2 sts, K1, patt to last 3 sts, K1, P2. ******

Rep last 2 rows until 12[12:14:14:16] sts rem, ending with a WS row. Leave sts on holder.

Front

Using No.6 needles cast on 50[50:54:54:62] sts.

Work 2in rib as given for back, ending with a 2nd row and inc one st at each end of last row on 28 and 30in sizes only. 50[50:56:56:62] sts.

Change to No.4 needles. Commence patt.

1st row K4[4:1:1:4] sts, P6, *K6, P6, rep from * to last 4[4:1:1:4] sts, K to end.

2nd row P4[4:1:1:4] sts, K6, *P6, K6, rep from * to last 4[4:1:1:4] sts, P to end.

3rd row K4[4:1:1:4] sts, P1, K4, P1, *K1, P4, K1, P1, K4, P1, rep from * to last 4[4:1:1:4] sts, K to end.

Cont in patt as given for back, keeping 4[4:1: 1:4] sts in st st at each end instead of 1[4:4:1:1] sts as on back, until work measures same as back to underarm, ending with a WS row.

Shape armholes

Cast off 4[3:4:3:4] sts at beg of next 2 rows. 42[44:48:50:54] sts. Rep from ** to ** as given for back until 24[24:26:26:28] sts rem, ending with a WS row.

Shape neck

Next row K2 sts, P2 tog, patt 6 sts, turn and leave rem sts on holder.

Next row Patt to last 3 sts, K1, P2.

Next row K2 sts, P2 tog, patt to last 2 sts, K2 tog.

Rep last 2 rows once more, then first of them again. 5 sts.

Next row K2 sts, P2 tog, K1.

Next row P1, K1, P2.

Next row K2 sts, P2 tog.

Next row K1, P2.

Next row K1, sl 1, K1, psso.

Next row P2 tog. Fasten off.

With RS of work facing, sl first 4[4:6:6:8] sts on holder and leave for centre neck, rejoin yarn to rem sts and patt to last 4 sts, P2 tog, K2.

Next row P2 sts, K1, patt to end.

Next row Sl 1, K1, psso, patt to last 4 sts, P2 tog, K2.

Complete to match first side, reversing shaping as shown.

Sleeves

Using No.6 needles cast on 22[26:26:30:30] sts.

Work 2in rib as given for back, ending with a 2nd row and inc one st at each end of last row on 24, 28 and 32in sizes only. 24[26:28:30:32] sts. Change to No.4 needles. Commence patt.

1st row K3[4:5:6:1] sts, P6, *K6, P6, rep from * to last 3[4:5:6:1] sts, K to end.

2nd row P3[4:5:6:1] sts, K6, *P6, K6, rep from * to last 3[4:5:6:1] sts, P to end.

3rd row P0[0:0:0:1] st, K0[0:0:1:1] st, P2[3:4:4:4] sts, K1, P1, K4, P1, K1, P4, K1, P1, K4, P1, K1, P2[3:4:4:4] sts, K0[0:0:1:1] st, P0[0:0:0:1] st.

Cont in patt as now set, inc one st at each end of every 6th[8th:8th:10th:10th] row until there are 32[34:36:38:40] sts and working extra sts into patt when possible. Cont without shaping until sleeve measures 10 [11:12:13½:15]in from beg, ending with a WS row.

Shape top

Cast off 3 sts at beg of next 2 rows. 26[28:30:32:34] sts. Work 2 rows without shaping, then work from ** to ** as given for back. Rep last 4 rows 5 times more, then rep from ** to ** as given for back until 8 sts rem, ending with a WS row. Leave sts on holder.

Front neckband

Using No.6 needles and with RS of work facing, K up 10[10:11:11:12] sts down side of front neck, K across front neck sts, and K up 10[10:11:11:12] sts up other side of front neck.

Next row K3 sts, P2, *K2, P2, rep from * to last 3 sts, K3.

Next row K1, P2, *K2, P2, rep from * to last st, K1.

Rep last 2 rows for 2¾ [2¾:2¾:3¼:3¼]in, ending with a 2nd row.

Next row K1, K2 tog, yrn, *P2, K2, rep from * to last 5 sts, P2, yon, sl 1, K1, psso, K1.

Cont in rib as before until neckband measures 4½ [4½:4½:5¼:5¼]in from beg, ending with a 2nd row. Rep buttonhole row as before, then work 2 more rows rib. Cast off in rib.

Back neckband

Using No.6 needles cast on 3 sts, with RS of work facing K across sts of right sleeve, back neck and left sleeve, K2 tog on each seam on all sizes and inc 2 sts evenly across back neck on 24, 28 and 32in sizes only, then cast on 3 sts. 32[32:36:36:36] sts.

Next row K3 sts, *P2, K2, rep from * to last 5 sts, P2, K3.

Next row K5 sts, *P2, K2, rep from * to last 3 sts, K3.

Rep these 2 rows until back neckband measures same as front. Cast off in rib.

To make up

Press each piece under a damp cloth with a warm iron. Join raglan seams, leaving front neckband seams open. Sew the 3 cast on sts at each side of back neckband in front of first sts of front neckband so that when collar turns over to the front, these 3 sts for underflap will be under the sts of front. Join side and sleeve seams. Press seams. Sew on 2 buttons to each side of neckband to correspond with buttonholes, then sew 2 more buttons to each front raglan seam.

7½]in from beg, ending with a WS row.
Shape shoulders
Cast off at beg of next and every row 4[4:5:5] sts 6 times and 4[5:3:4] sts twice. Cast off rem 35[37:39:41] sts.

Jacket left front
Using No.11 needles cast on 59[63:67:71] sts. Work in rib as given for back for 1½ [2:2:2½]in, ending with a 2nd row. Change to No.9 needles. Commence patt.
1st row K31[33:35:37] sts, rib to end.
2nd row Rib 28[30:32:34] sts, P to end.
Rep these 2 rows until work measures same as back to underarm, ending with a WS row.
Shape armhole
Cast off at beg of next and foll alt row 5 sts once and 2 sts once. Dec one st at armhole edge on foll 4[5:6:7] alt rows. 48[51:54:57] sts. Cont without shaping until armhole measures 3½ [4:4½:5]in from beg, ending with a RS row.
Shape neck
Next row Cast off 26[28:30:32] sts in rib, P to end.
Dec one st at neck edge on every alt row until 16[17:18:19] sts rem. Cont without shaping until armhole measures same as back to shoulder, ending at armhole edge.
Shape shoulder
Cast off at beg of next and every alt row 4[4:5:5] sts 3 times and 4[5:3:4] sts once.

Right front
Using No.11 needles cast on 59[63:67:71] sts. Work 1½ [2:2:2½]in rib as given for back, ending with a 2nd row. Change to No.9 needles.
Next row Rib 28[30:32:34] sts, K to end.
Next row P31[33:35:37] sts, rib to end.
Rep these 2 rows until work measures 2½ [3:3½: 4]in from beg, ending with a WS row.
Next row (buttonhole row) Rib 3 sts, cast off 3 sts, rib 15[17:19:21] sts, cast off 3 sts, patt to end.
Next row Patt to end, casting on 3 sts above those cast off in previous row.
Complete to match left front, reversing all shapings and making 3 more pairs of button-holes at intervals of 3½in.

Sleeves
Using No.11 needles cast on 41[45:45:49] sts. Work 1½ [2:2:2½]in rib as given for back, ending with a 2nd row. Change to No.9 needles.
Next row K11[13:13:15] sts, rib 19 sts, K to end.
Next row P11(13:13:15) sts, rib 19 sts, P to end.
Keeping centre sts in rib throughout, cont in patt inc one st at each end of every 6th[7th: 7th:8th] row until there are 63[67:71:75] sts. Cont without shaping until sleeve measures 12 [13½:15:16½]in from beg, ending with a WS row.
Shape top
Cast off 5 sts at beg of next 2 rows. Dec one st at each end of next and foll 6[7:8:9] alt rows. Cast off at beg of next and every row 2 sts 10 [10:12:12] times and 3 sts 4 times. Cast off rem 7[9:7:9] sts.

Collar
Using No.11 needles cast on 89[93:97:101] sts. Work 3½ [4:4½:5]in rib as given for back. Cast off in rib.

To make up
Press under a dry cloth with a cool iron. Join shoulder seams. Set in sleeves. Join side and sleeve seams. Sew on collar, beg and ending just inside cast off sts at neck edge of fronts. Press seams. Sew on buttons.

Trousers right half

Using No.11 needles cast on 81[87:93:99] sts. Beg with a K row work 1½in st st, ending with a K row.
Next row K all sts tbl to form hemline. Change to No.9 needles. Beg with a K row cont in st st until work measures 1½ [2:2½:3]in from hemline, ending with a P row.
Shape leg
Dec one st at each end of next and every foll 10th[12th:14th:16th] row until 71[77:83:89] sts rem. Cont without shaping until work measures 14 [16:18:20]in from hemline, ending with a P row. Inc one st at each end of next and every foll 8th[8th:10th:10th] row until there are 79[85:91:97] sts. Cont without shaping until work measures 19 [21:23½:26½]in from hemline, or required leg length, ending with a P row.
Shape crutch
Cast off at beg of next and every row 3 sts twice and 2 sts twice. Work 2 rows without shaping. Dec one st at each end of next and every foll 4th row 4 times in all. Cont without shaping until work measures 7½ [8:8½:9]in from beg of crutch, ending with a K row.
Shape back
Next row P32[36:40:44] sts, turn and K to end.
Next row P24[27:30:33] sts, turn and K to end. Cont to work 8[9:10:11] sts less on every alt row twice more, then P across all sts. Change to No.11 needles. Work 1½in rib as given for jersey back. Cast off in rib.

Trousers left half
Work as given for right half, reversing shaping at top.

To make up
Press as given for jacket. Join back and front seams. Join leg seams. Turn hems to WS and sl st down. Press seams. Sew elastic inside waist band using casing st.

25 *Trouser suit with double-breasted jacket*

Sizes
To fit 28 [30:32:34]in chest/bust
Sleeve seam, 12 [13½:15:16½]in
Trousers inside leg, 19 [21:23½:26½]in
The figures in brackets [] refer to the 30, 32 and 34in sizes respectively
Tension
6 sts and 8 rows to 1in over st st worked on No.9 needles
Materials
24[27:30:34] balls Patons Four Seasons Courtelle
One pair No.9 needles; One pair No.11 needles
8 buttons
Waist length of elastic

Jacket back
Using No.11 needles cast on 89[95:101:107] sts.
1st row K1, *P1, K1, rep from * to end.
2nd row P1, *K1, P1, rep from * to end.
Rep these 2 rows for 1½ [2:2:2½]in, ending with a 2nd row. Change to No.9 needles. Commence patt.
1st row K31[33:35:37] sts, rib 27[29:31:33] sts, K to end.
2nd row P31[33:35:37] sts, rib 27[29:31:33] sts, P to end.
Rep these 2 rows until work measures 14 [15:16: 17]in from beg, ending with a WS row.
Shape armholes
Keeping centre sts in rib throughout, cast off at beg of next and every row 5 sts twice and 2 sts twice. Dec one st at each end of next and foll 3[4:5:6] alt rows. 61[71:75:79] sts. Cont without shaping until armholes measure 6[6½:7:

26 *Girl's trouser suit, with mock cable jersey*

Sizes
To fit 24 [26:28:30:32:34]in chest/bust
26 [28:30:32:34:36]in hips
Jersey length to shoulder, 16 [17½:19:20½:22: 23½]in
Sleeve seam, 10 [11:12:13½:15:16½]in
Trousers inside leg, 15 [17½:20:22:24:26]in
The figures in brackets [] refer to the 26, 28, 30, 32 and 34in sizes respectively
Tension
7 sts and 9 rows to 1in over st st worked on No.11 needles
Materials
18[21:24:27:30:33] balls Templetons Antler 4 ply
One pair No.11 needles
One pair No.12 needles
Set of 4 No.12 needles pointed at both ends
Waist length of elastic

Jersey back
Using No.12 needles cast on 89[95:103:109: 117:123] sts.
1st row K1, *P1, K1, rep from * to end.
2nd row P1, *K1, P1, rep from * to end.
Rep these 2 rows for 1 [1:1¼:1¼:1½:1½]in, ending with a 2nd row and inc one st at end of last row. 90[96:104:110:118:124] sts. Change to No.11 needles. Commence patt.
1st row P5[5:3:3:4:4] sts, K2, *P4, K2, rep

from * to last 5[5:3:3:4:4] sts, P to end.
2nd row K5[5:3:3:4:4] sts, P2, *K4, P2, rep
from * to last 5[5:3:3:4:4] sts, K to end.
3rd row P5[5:3:3:4:4] sts, put needle behind
first st and K 2nd st tbl then K into front of
first st and sl both sts off needle tog – called
Tw2 –, *P4, Tw2, rep from * to last 5[5:3:3:
4:4] sts, P to end.
4th row As 2nd.
These 4 rows form patt. Cont in patt until work
measures 10½ [11½:12½:13½:14½:15½]in from
beg, ending with a WS row.
Shape armholes
Cast off 6 sts at beg of next 2 rows.
**Next row P1, P2 tog, patt to last 3 sts,
P2 tog, P1.
Next row K2 sts, patt to last 2 sts, K2. **
Rep last 2 rows until 28[30:32:34:36:38] sts
rem, ending with a WS row. Leave sts on
holder.

Jersey front
Work as given for back until 42[44:48:50:54:
56] sts rem, ending with a WS row.
Shape neck
Next row P1, P2 tog, patt 11[11:13:13:15:15]
sts, turn and leave rem sts on holder.
Next row Patt to last 2 sts, K2.
Next row P1, P2 tog, patt to last 2 sts, P2 tog.
Rep last 2 rows 4[4:5:5:6:6] times more, then
first of them again. 3 sts.
Next row P1, P2 tog.
Next row K2 tog and fasten off.
With RS of work facing, sl first 14[16:16:18:
18:20] sts on holder and leave for centre neck,
rejoin yarn to rem sts, patt to last 3 sts, P2 tog,
P1.
Next row K2 sts, patt to end.
Next row P2 tog, patt to last 3 sts, P2 tog, P1.
Complete to match first side, reversing shaping.

Sleeves
Using No.12 needles cast on 51[53:57:59:63:65]
sts. Work 1½ [1½:2:2:2½:2½]in rib as given for
back, ending with a 2nd row and inc one st at
end of last row. 52[54:58:60:64:66] sts. Change
to No.11 needles. Commence patt.
1st row P1[2:1:2:1:2] sts, K2, *P4, K2, rep
from * to last 1[2:1:2:1:2] sts, P to end.
2nd row K1[2:1:2:1:2] sts, P2, *K4, P2, rep
from * to last 1[2:1:2:1:2] sts, K to end.
3rd row P1[2:1:2:1:2] sts, Tw2, *P4, Tw2, rep
from * to last 1[2:1:2:1:2] sts, P to end.
4th row As 2nd.
Cont in patt as now set, inc one st at each end
of next and every foll 8th row until there are
70[74:80:84:90:94] sts, working extra sts into
patt when possible. Cont without shaping until
sleeve measures 10 [11:12:13½:15:16½]in from
beg, ending with a WS row.
Shape top
Cast off 6 sts at beg of next 2 rows. Rep from
** to ** as given for back until 8 sts rem,
ending with a WS row. Leave sts on holder.

Neckband
Join raglan seams. Using set of 4 No.12 needles
and with RS of work facing, K across sts of
back neck and left sleeve K2 tog at seam, K up
10[10:12:12:14:14] sts down side of front neck,
K across sts of centre neck, K up 10[10:12:12:
14:14] sts up other side of neck, K across sts of
right sleeve K2 tog last st and first st of back
neck. 76[80:86:90:96:100] sts. Cont in rounds
of K1, P1 rib for ½ [½:¾:¾:1:1]in.
Cast off in rib.

To make up
Do not press. Join side and sleeve seams.

62

Trousers right leg
Using No.12 needles cast on 116[124:134:142:
152:160] sts. Beg with a K row work 1 [1:1¼:
1¼:1½:1½]in st st, ending with a K row.
Next row K all sts tbl to mark hemline.
Change to No.11 needles. Beg with a K row
cont in st st until work measures 1½ [1½:2:2:2½:
2½]in from hemline, ending with a P row.
Shape leg
Next row K2 sts, K2 tog, K51[55:60:64:69:
73] sts, sl 1, K1, psso, K2 sts, K2 tog, K to last
4 sts, sl 1, K1, psso, K2.
Beg with a P row work 9[9:11:11:13:13] rows
without shaping.
Next row K2 sts, K2 tog, K49[53:58:62:67:
71] sts, sl 1, K1, psso, K2 sts, K2 tog, K to last
4 sts, sl 1, K1, psso, K2.
Beg with a P row work 9[9:11:11:13:13] rows
without shaping. Cont dec in this way on next
and every foll 10th[10th:12th:12th:14th:14th]
row until 96[104:110:118:124:132] sts rem.
Cont without shaping until work measures
15 [17½:20:22:24:26]in from hemline, ending
with a P row.
Shape gusset
Next row Cast off 4 sts, K to end.
Next row Cast off 2 sts, P to end.
Next row Cast off 2 sts, K to end.
Next row P to end.
Next row K1, sl 1, K1, psso, K to last 3 sts,
K2 tog, K1.
Rep last 2 rows 4[5:5:6:6:7] times more. Cont
to dec in same way on every foll 8th[8th:8th:
6th:6th:6th] row until 70[74:78:82:86:90] sts
rem. Cont without shaping until work measures
6½ [7:7½:8:8½:9]in from beg of gusset shaping,
ending with a K row.
Shape back
Next row P30[30:36:36:42:42] sts, turn and K
to end.
Next row P24[24:30:30:36:36] sts, turn and
K to end.
Cont to work 6 sts less on every alt row in this
way 3[3:4:4:5:5] times more. P 1 row across
all sts, dec one st at end of row. Change to
No.12 needles. Work 1in rib as given for Jersey
back. Cast off in rib.

Trousers left leg
Work as given for right leg, reversing all
shapings.

To make up
Do not press. Join back and front seams. Join
leg seams. Turn hems at lower edge to WS and
sl st down. Sew elastic inside waistband using
casing st.

27 Girl's dress with two-colour bodice motif

Sizes
To fit 32 [34:36]in bust
34 [36:38]in hips
Length to shoulders, 33 [34:35]in
Sleeve seam, 16½ [17:17½]in
The figures in brackets [] refer to the 34in and
36in sizes respectively
Tension
6 sts and 8 rows to 1in over st st worked on
No.9 needles

Materials
18[19:21] balls Hayfield Gaylon Double Knitting
in main shade, A
1 ball each of contrast colours, B and C
One pair No.9 needles
One pair No.11 needles
Note
When working front fair isle patt, use separate
balls of A. Always twist yarns at back of work
when changing colours.

Back
Using No.11 needles and A, cast on 146[154:
162] sts. Beg with a K row work 1in st st,
ending with a K row.
Next row K all sts tbl to form hemline.
Change to No.9 needles. Commence rib patt.
1st row K to end.
2nd row K2 sts, *P16[17:18] sts, K2, rep from
* to end.
Rep these 2 rows for 3in, ending with a 2nd
row.
Shape skirt
Next row K9[10:10] sts, *K2 tog, K16[17:18]
sts, rep from * 6 times more, K2 tog, K9[10:10]
sts. Keeping rib patt correct as now set, work
23 rows without shaping.
Next row K8[9:9] sts, *K2 tog, K15[16:17]
sts, rep from * 6 times more, K2 tog, K 8[9:9]
sts. Keeping rib patt correct as now set, work
23 rows without shaping. Cont to dec in this
way on next and every foll 24th row 3 times
more. Cont without shaping until work measures
16 [16½:17]in from hemline, ending with a WS
row. 106[114:122] sts.
Cont in st st until work measures 26½ [27:27½]in
from hemline, ending with a P row.
Shape armholes
Cast off at beg of next and every row 5 sts
twice, 4 sts twice and 2 sts twice. Dec one st at
each end of next and foll 0[1:2] alt rows. 82
[88:94] sts. Cont without shaping until armholes
measure 6½ [7:7½]in from beg, ending with a P
row.
Shape shoulders
Cast off at beg of next and every row 12[13:13]
sts twice and 13[13:14] sts twice. Leave rem
32[36:40] sts on holder.

Front
Work as given for back until work measures 16
rows less than back to underarm, ending with a
P row. Commence patt.
Next row Using 1st ball of A, K52[56:60] sts,
using B, K2, using 2nd ball of A, K52[56:60]
sts.
Next row Using 2nd ball of A, P51[55:59] sts,
P4 B, using 1st ball of A, P51[55:59] sts. Cont
to work in patt from chart until 16 rows have
been completed.
Shape armholes
Still working in patt from chart, shape armholes
as given for back. Cont without shaping until
armholes measure 4½ [5:5½]in from beg, ending
with a P row.
Shape neck
Next row K34[35:36] sts, turn and leave rem
sts on holder.
Cast off 2 sts at neck edge on next and foll 2
alt rows, then dec one st at neck edge on foll 3
alt rows. Cont without shaping on rem 25[26:
27] sts until armhole measures same as back to
shoulder, ending with a P row.
Shape shoulder
Cast off at beg of next and foll alt row 12[13:
13] sts once and 13[13:14] sts once.
With RS of work facing, sl first 14[18:22] sts
on holder and leave for centre neck, rejoin yarn
to rem sts and K to end. Complete to match
first side, reversing all shapings.

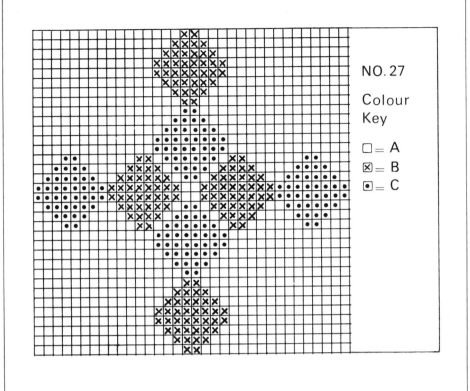

NO. 27

Colour Key

☐ = A
☒ = B
⊡ = C

Sleeves

Using No.11 needles and A, cast on 54[58:62] sts.

1st row K2, *P2, K2, rep from * to end.
2nd row P2, *K2, P2, rep from * to end.
Rep these 2 rows for 2½in, ending with a 2nd row. Change to No.9 needles. Beg with a K row cont in st st, inc one st at each end of 9th and every foll 12th row until there are 72[76:80] sts. Cont without shaping until sleeve measures 16½ [17:17½]in from beg, ending with a P row.

Shape top
Cast off at beg of next and every row 5 sts twice, 4 sts twice and 2 sts twice. Dec one st at each end of next and foll 11[13:15] alt rows. Cast off 2 sts at beg of next 4 rows. Cast off rem 18 sts.

Neckband

Join right shoulder seam. Using No.11 needles, A and with RS of work facing, K up 20 sts down side of neck, K across sts on front neck holder, K up 20 sts up other side of neck, then K across back neck sts. 86[94:102] sts.
1st row P1, *K2, P2, rep from * to last 3 sts, K2, P1.
2nd row K1, *P2, K2, rep from * to last 3 sts, P2, K1.
Rep these 2 rows for 1½in. Cast off loosely in rib.

To make up

Press each piece under a damp cloth with a warm iron. Join left shoulder and neckband seam. Set in sleeves. Join side and sleeve seams. Turn hem at lower edge to WS and sl st down. Fold neckband in half to WS and sl st down. Press seams.

See chart above

28 Cardigan with diamond motif, and matching hat

Sizes

To fit 30 [32:34]in bust
Length to shoulder, 27 [27½:28]in
Sleeve seam, 16½ [17:17½]in
The figures in brackets [] refer to the 32 and 34in sizes respectively

Tension
6 sts and 8 rows to 1in over st st worked on No.9 needles

Materials
20[21:22] balls Lee Target Motoravia Double Knitting in main shade, A
1 ball each of contrast colours, B and C
One pair No.9 needles; One pair No.11 needles
8 buttons

Cardigan back

Using No.11 needles and A, cast on 106[112: 118] sts. Beg with a K row work 1in st st, ending with a K row.
Next row K all sts tbl to form hemline. **
Change to No.9 needles. Beg with a K row cont in st st for 32 rows. Dec one st at each end of next and every foll 20th row until 96[102:108] sts rem. Cont without shaping until work measures 21in from hemline, ending with a P row.

Shape armholes
Cast off at beg of next and every row 4 sts twice, 3 sts twice and 2 sts twice. Dec one st at each end of next and foll 1[2:3] alt rows. 74 [78:82] sts. Cont without shaping until armholes measure 6 [6½:7]in from beg, ending with a P row.

Shape shoulders
Cast off 10[11:12] sts at beg of next 4 rows. 34 sts. Change to No.11 needles. Beg first row with K2, work 9 rows K2, P2 rib. Cast off in rib.

Cardigan left front
Pocket lining
Using No.9 needles and A, cast on 26 sts. Beg with a K row work 46 rows st st. Leave sts on holder.
Using No.11 needles and A, cast on 54[57:60] sts.
Work as given for back to **. Change to No.9 needles. Beg with a K row work 12 rows st st. Commence patt.
Next row K26 [28:29]A, K1 B, K27 [28:30]A.
Next row P25 [27:28]A, P3 B, P26 [27:29]A.
Cont to work in patt from chart 1 until 29 rows have been completed, *at the same time* dec one st at beg of 33rd row from hemline. When 29 rows of patt are completed, work 5 more rows with A, ending with a P row.

NO. 28 **Colour Key**

☐ = A
☒ = B
⊡ = C

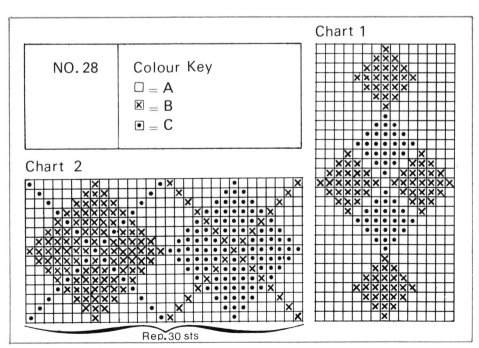

Chart 1

Chart 2

Rep. 30 sts

Place pocket

Next row K13[14:16] sts, sl next 26 sts on to holder, K across pocket lining sts, K to end. Cont in st st, dec one st at side edge on every foll 20th row from last dec until 49[52:55] sts rem. Cont without shaping until work measures 6 rows less than back to underarm, ending with a P row.

Shape front edge

Dec one st at end of next and at the edge on foll 3rd row. Work 2 rows without shaping.

Shape armhole

Cont dec at front edge on every 3rd row, cast off at beg of next and every alt row 4 sts once, 3 sts once and 2 sts once. Dec one st at armhole edge on next and foll 1[2:3] alt rows. Cont dec at front edge only until 20[22:24] sts rem. Cont without shaping until armhole measures same as back to shoulder, ending at armhole edge.

Shape shoulder

Cast off 10[11:12] sts at beg of next and foll alt row.

Right front

Work as given for left front, reversing all shapings.

Sleeves

Using No.11 needles and A, cast on 46[50:54] sts. Beg first row with K2, work 2½in K2, P2 rib, ending with a 2nd row. Change to No.9 needles. Beg with a K row cont in st st, inc one st at each end of 9th and every foll 10th row until there are 68[70:74] sts. Cont without shaping until sleeve measures 16½ [17:17½]in from beg, ending with a P row.

Shape top

Cast off at beg of next and every row 4 sts twice, 3 sts twice and 2 sts twice. Dec one st at each end of next and foll 10[11:13] alt rows. Cast off 2 sts at beg of next 4 rows. Cast off rem 20 sts.

Left front edge

Turn hem to WS and tack in place. Using No.11 needles, A, and with RS of work facing, K up 214[218:222] sts down front edge. Beg first row with P2, work 8 rows K2, P2 rib. Cast off in rib. Mark positions for 8 buttons on left front, first to come on 5th and 6th sts from lower edge and last to come ½in below beg of front shaping, with 6 more evenly spaced between.

Right front edge

Work to match left front edge, making button-holes on 4th row by casting off 2 sts as each marker is reached, and casting on 2 sts above those cast off in 5th row.

Pocket tops

Sl 26 pocket top sts on to No.11 needles, using A and with RS of work facing, beg first row with P2 and work 8 rows K2, P2 rib. Cast off in rib.

To make up

Press each piece under a damp cloth with a warm iron. Join shoulder seams. Set in sleeves. Join side and sleeve seams. Sew down pocket linings. Sl st hem to WS. Fold pocket tops in half to outside and sew down sides. Press seams. Sew on buttons.

Hat

Using No.11 needles and A, cast on 122 sts. Work as given for cardigan back to **. Change to No.9 needles. Cont in st st, working from chart 2 until 15 rows have been completed, keeping one st at each end in A throughout for seam. Cont with A only until work measures 6in from hemline, ending with a P row.

Shape top

Next row K2 sts, *K2 tog, K1, rep from * to end. 82 sts.
Beg with a P row work 5 rows st st.
Next row *K2 tog, rep from * to end. 41 sts.
Beg with a P row work 5 rows st st.
Next row K1, *K2 tog, rep from * to end. 21 sts. Break off yarn, thread through rem sts, draw up and fasten off.

To make up

Press as given for cardigan. Join seam. Turn hem to WS and sl st down. Press seam. Make a pompon using A and sew to top.

See charts on previous page

29 Lace panelled jerkin and plain skirt

Sizes

To fit 34[36:38:40:42]in bust
36[38:40:42:44]in hips
Jerkin length to shoulder, 22½[23:23½:24:24½] adjustable
Skirt length, 20[20½:21:21½:22]in adjustable
The figures in brackets [] refer to the 36, 38, 40 and 42in sizes respectively

Tension

5 sts and 7 rows to 1in over st st worked on No.8 needles

Materials

10[11:12:13:14] balls Mahony Killowen Extra Double Knitting
One pair No.8 needles
One pair No.9 needles
Set of 4 No.9 needles pointed at both ends
Waist length of elastic
One 7in zip fastener

Jerkin back

Using No.9 needles cast on 90[94:98:102:110] sts.
1st row K2, *P2, K2, rep from * to end.
2nd row P2, *K2, P2, rep from * to end.
Rep these 2 rows until work measures 2in from beg, ending with a 2nd row and dec one st at end of last row on 34, 36 and 42in sizes, and inc one st at end of last row on 38 and 40in sizes. 89[93:99:103:109] sts.
Change to No.8 needles. Commence patt.
1st row K11[12:14:15:17] sts, *yfwd, K6, sl 1, K2 tog, psso, K6, yfwd, K11[12:13:14:15] sts, rep from * once more, yfwd, K6, sl 1, K2 tog, psso, K6, yfwd, K11[12:14:15:17] sts.
2nd and every alt row P to end.
3rd row K12[13:15:16:18] sts, *yfwd, K5, sl 1, K2 tog, psso, K5, yfwd, K13[14:15:16:17] sts, rep from * once more, yfwd, K5, sl 1, K2 tog, psso, K5, yfwd, K to end.
5th row K13[14:16:17:19] sts, *yfwd, K4, sl 1, K2 tog, psso, K4, yfwd, K15[16:17:18:19] sts, rep from * once more, yfwd, K4, sl 1, K2 tog, psso, K4, yfwd, K to end.
7th row K14[15:17:18:20] sts, *yfwd, K3, sl 1, K2 tog, psso, K3, yfwd, K17[18:19:20:21] sts, rep from * once more, yfwd, K3, sl 1, K2 tog, psso, K3, yfwd, K to end.
9th row K15[16:18:19:21] sts, *yfwd, K2, sl 1, K2 tog, psso, K2, yfwd, K19[20:21:22:23] sts, rep from * once more, yfwd, K2, sl 1, K2 tog, psso, K2, yfwd, K to end.
11th row K16[17:19:20:22] sts, *yfwd, K1, sl 1, K2 tog, psso, K1, yfwd, K21[22:23:24:25] sts, rep from * once more, yfwd, K1, sl 1, K2 tog, psso, K1, yfwd, K to end.
13th row K17[18:20:21:23] sts, *yfwd, sl 1, K2 tog, psso, yfwd, K23[24:25:26:27] sts, rep from * once more, yfwd, sl 1, K2 tog, psso, yfwd, K to end.
14th row P to end.
These 14 rows form patt. Cont in patt until work measures 14½in from beg, or required length to underarm ending with a P row.

Shape armholes

Cast off at beg of next and every row 3[3:4:4:4] sts twice, 3[3:3:3:4] sts twice and 3 sts twice. 71[75:79:83:87] sts. Cont without shaping until armholes measure 8[8½:9:9½:10]in from beg, ending with a P row.

Shape shoulders

Cast off at beg of next and every row 5[5:6:6:6] sts 6 times and 6[7:5:6:7] sts twice. Leave rem 29[31:33:35:37] sts on holder.

Jerkin front

Work as given for back until work measures 1½in less than back to underarm, ending with a P row.

Divide for neck

Next row Patt 44[46:49:51:54] sts, turn and leave rem sts on holder.
Next row P to end.
Next row Patt to last 3 sts, K2 tog, K1.
Cont to dec at neck edge in this way on every foll 4th row until work measures same as back to underarm, ending at armhole edge.

Shape armhole

Cont dec at neck edge as before, cast off at beg of next and foll alt rows 3[3:4:4:4] sts once, 3[3:3:3:4] sts once and 3 sts once. Cont to dec at neck edge on every 4th row until 21[22:23:24:25] sts rem. Cont without shaping until armhole measures same as back to shoulder, ending at armhole edge.

Shape shoulder

Cast off 5[5:6:6:6] sts at beg of next and foll 2 alt rows. Work 1 row. Cast off rem 6[7:5:6:7] sts. With RS of work facing, leave first st on holder, rejoin yarn to rem sts and patt to end.
Next row P to end.
Next row K1, sl 1, K1, psso, patt to end.
Complete to match first side, reversing shaping,

Neckband

Join shoulder seams. Using set of 4 No.9 needles and with RS of work facing, K across sts of back neck holder, K up 70[73:76:79:82] sts down front neck, K centre front neck st and K up 71[74:77:80:83] sts up other side of front neck. 171[179:187:195:203] sts.
Next round P0[0:1:0:0], K1[2:2:0:1], (P2,K2) 24[25:26:28:29] times, P2 tog, K1, P2 tog, (K2, P2) 17[18:18:19:20] times, K1[0:2:2:1], P0[0:1:0:0]. Work 4 more rounds in rib as set, P2 sts tog at each side of centre st on every round. Cast off in rib still dec at centre front.

Armbands

Using No.9 needles and with RS of work facing, K up 122[126:130:134:138] sts round armhole. Beg with a 2nd row, work 5 rows rib as given for back. Cast off in rib.

To make up

Press each piece under a damp cloth with a warm iron. Join side seams. Press seams.

Skirt back

Using No.9 needles cast on 64[68:74:78:84] sts and beg at waist. Beg with a K row work 1½in st st, ending with a K row.
Next row K all sts tbl to mark foldline.
Change to No.8 needles. Beg with a K row cont in st st until work measures 2in from foldline, ending with a P row.

Shape darts

Next row K21[22:24:26:28] sts, pick up loop lying between sts and K tbl – called inc 1 –, K1, K20[22:24:24:26] sts, inc 1, K1, inc 1,

K21[22:24:26:28] sts.
Beg with a P row work 7 rows st st.
Next row K22[23:25:27:29] sts, inc 1, K1, inc 1, K22[24:26:26:28] sts, inc 1, K1, inc 1, K22[23:25:27:29] sts.
Beg with a P row work 7 rows st st.
Cont inc in this way on next and every foll 8th row until there are 96[100:106:110:116] sts. Cont without shaping until work measures 20[20½:21:21½:22]in from foldline, or required length from waist, ending with a K row.
Next row K all sts tbl to mark hemline.
Change to No.9 needles. Beg with a K row work 1½in st st. Cast off loosely.

Skirt front
Work as given for back.

To make up
Press as given for jerkin. Join side seams, leaving 7in from foldline open on left seam for zip. Turn waistband and hem to WS and sl st down. Press seams. Thread elastic through waistband and secure Sew in zip.

Beret and scarf

Sizes
Beret to fit an average head
Scarf 8in wide by 68in long
Tension
6 sts and 12 rows to 1in over g st worked on No. 9 needles
Materials
Jaeger Celtic-Spun
Beret 1 ball each of 4 colours, A, B, C and D
Scarf 2 balls each of 4 colours, A, B, C and D
One pair No. 9 needles

Beret
Using No. 9 needles and A, cast on 44 sts.
1st row (RS) K to end.
2nd row K40 sts, turn.
3rd row K32 sts, turn.
4th row K28 sts, turn.
5th row K24 sts, turn.
6th row K20 sts, turn.
7th row As 5th.
8th row As 4th.
9th row K36 sts to end.
10th row As 2nd.
11th row K40 sts to end.
12th row K44 sts to end. Do not break yarn.
Rep these 12 rows using B, C and D. These 48 rows form patt and are rep throughout. Work patt rows 6 times more Cast off.

To make up
Darn in all ends. With WS of work facing, join back seam and using running sts, draw up centre crown. Press seam lightly. Using A, B, C and D make a pompon and sew to top.

Scarf
Using No. 9 needles and A, cast on 360 sts. Work in stripes of 12 rows g st using A, B, C and D. Rep these 48 rows once more.
Cast off loosely.

To make up
Darn in all ends. With WS of work facing and using running sts, draw up each short end of scarf and fasten off. Make 2 pompons as given for beret and sew one to each short end.

31 Sleeveless or puff sleeved hug-me-tight and hat

Sizes
To fit a 32[34:36:38:40]in bust
Length at centre back, 19½[19¾:20:20¼:20½]in adjustable
Sleeve seam, 5in adjustable
The figures in brackets [ ] refer to the 34, 36, 38 and 40in sizes respectively

Tension
7½ sts and 8 rows to 1in over patt when pressed worked on No. 8 needles and using 2 ends of yarn
Materials
Twilley's Mohair
Sleeveless version 8[9:9:10:10] balls
Puff sleeved version 12[13:13:14:14] balls
Hat 2 balls
One pair No. 8 needles
One pair No. 10 needles
Six buttons
Note
Yarn is used double throughout. Where an odd number is given in the materials section, wind last ball into 2 separate balls.

Back
Using No. 10 needles and 2 ends of yarn, cast on 117[125:133:141:149] sts.
1st row Sl 1, *P1, K1, rep from * to end.
2nd row Sl 1, *K1, P1, rep from * to last 2 sts, K2.
Rep these 2 rows until work measures 4in from beg, ending with a 2nd row.
Next row Inc in first st, rib to last 2 sts, inc in next st, K1. 119[127:135:143:151] sts.
Change to No. 8 needles. Commence patt. **.
1st row (WS) Sl 1, K1 tbl, *insert needle p-wise into next 3 sts as if to P3 tog but P1, K1 tbl, P1 all into these 3 sts and sl them off left hand needle – called M3 –, K1 tbl, rep from * to last st, K1.
2nd row Sl 1, P to last st, K1.
These 2 rows form patt. Cont in patt until work measures 11in from beg for sleeveless version, or 12in for puff sleeved version, or required length to underarm ending with a WS row.
Shape armholes
Keeping patt correct cast off 7[7:8:8:9] sts loosely at beg of next 2 rows. Dec one st at each end of next 6 rows, then each end of next and every alt row until 83[87:91:95:99] sts rem for sleeveless version, or 91[95:99:103:107] sts for puff sleeved version. Cont without shaping until armholes measure 7¾[8:8¼:8½:8¾]in from beg for sleeveless version, or 6¾[7:7¼:7½:7¾]in for puff sleeved version, ending with a WS row.
Shape shoulders
Cast off loosely at beg of next and every row 6 sts 4 times for sleeveless version, or 8 sts 4 times for puff sleeved version, and 7[8:9:10:11] sts twice for both versions.
Leave rem sts on holder.

Front
Work as given for back to **.
Divide for front
1st row (WS) Sl 1, K1 tbl, *M3, K1 tbl, rep from * 12[13:14:15:16] times more, K1, turn.
Complete right front on these 55[59:63:67:71] sts.
2nd row Sl 1, P to last st, K1.
Cont in patt until work measures same as back to underarm, ending at armhole edge.
Shape armhole
Keeping patt correct cast off 7[7:8:8:9] sts loosely at beg of next row. Work 1 row. Dec one st at armhole edge on next 6 rows, then next and every alt row until 37[39:41:43:45] sts rem for

sleeveless version, or 41[43:45:47:49] sts for puff sleeved version. Cont without shaping until armhole measures 3[3¼:3½:3¾:4]in from beg for sleeveless version, or 2[2¼:2½:2¾:3]in for puff sleeved version, ending at front edge.
Shape neck
Next row Sl 1, patt 7[8:9:10:11] sts and sl these 8[9:10:11:12] sts on to holder and leave for centre neck, patt to last st, K1.
Cont in patt, dec one st at neck edge on every row 10 times in all. 19[20:21:22:23] sts for sleeveless version, or 23[24:25:26:27] sts for puff sleeved version. Cont without shaping until armhole measures same as back to shoulder, ending at armhole edge.
Shape shoulder
Cast off 6 sts loosely at beg of next and foll alt row for sleeveless version, or 8 sts loosely at beg of next and foll alt row for puff sleeved version. Work 1 row. Cast off rem 7[8:9:10:11] sts.
With WS of work facing, sl next 9 sts on to holder and leave for front band. Rejoin yarn to rem sts and complete to match right front, reversing all shapings.

Puff sleeves
Using No. 10 needles and 2 ends of yarn cast on 75[79:83:87:91] sts. Work 1in rib as given for back, ending with a 2nd row.
Next row Rib 2[4:6:8:10] sts, *inc in next st, rib 1, rep from * to last 3[5:7:9:11] sts, inc in next st, rib to end. 111[115:119:123:127] sts. Change to No. 8 needles. Work in patt as given for back until sleeve measures 5in from beg, or required length to underarm ending with a WS row.
Shape top
Keeping patt correct cast off 7[7:8:8:9] sts loosely at beg of next 2 rows. Dec one st at each end of next 6 rows, then each end of next and every alt row until 61 sts rem, then each end of every row until 45 sts rem, ending with a RS row.
32, 36 and 40in sizes only
Next row Sl 1, *K3 tog, K1 tbl, rep from * to end. 23 sts.
34 and 38in sizes only
Next row Sl 1, P1, *K1 tbl, K3 tog, rep from * to last 3 sts, K1 tbl, P1, K1. 25 sts.
All sizes
Next row Sl 1, *P2 tog, rep from * to end.
Cast off loosely.

Buttonhole band
Mark positions for 6 buttons on left front, first to come 1in above waist ribbing and 6th to come in neckband. Using No. 10 needles and with WS of work facing, rejoin 2 ends of yarn to sts on holder and work in rib as given for back, making buttonholes as markers are reached as foll:
Next row (RS row) Rib 3, cast off 2 sts, rib 4.
Next row Rib to end, casting on 2 sts above those cast off in previous row.
Work in rib until band measures same as right front opening to neck shaping, when very slightly stretched. Leave sts on holder.

Button band
Using No. 10 needles and 2 ends of yarn, cast on 9 sts. Work as given for buttonhole band omitting buttonholes.

Neckband
Join shoulder seams. Using No. 10 needles and 2 ends of yarn and with RS of work facing, rib across sts of buttonhole band and centre neck holders, K up 38[40:42:44:46] sts, rib across sts of back neck holder, K up 38[40:42:44:46] sts, rib across sts of centre neck holder and button band holder. 155[163:171:179:187] sts.
Work 1in rib as given for back, making button hole as before on 4th and 5th rows.
Cast off in rib.

Armbands for sleeveless version
Using No. 10 needles and 2 ends of yarn and with
RS of work facing, K up 139[143:147:151:155] sts
round armhole. Work 1in rib as given for back, dec
one st at each end of every alt row.
Cast off in rib.

To make up
Press each piece lightly on WS under a damp cloth
with a warm iron, omitting ribbing. Join side
seams. Join sleeve seams for puff sleeved version and
set in sleeves. Oversew front bands to fronts,
catching down button band at bottom of buttonhole band.
Press seams. Sew on buttons.

Hat
Using No. 10 needles and 2 ends of yarn, cast on
135 sts. Work 1in rib as given for back, ending with
a 2nd row.
Next row Rib 1, *rib 10, inc in next st, rep from *
to last 2 sts, rib 2. 147 sts.
Change to No. 8 needles. Cont in patt as given for
back until work measures 5½in from beg, ending
with a RS row.
Shape top
Next row Sl 1, K1 tbl, *insert needle p-wise into
next 3 sts as if to P3 tog but P1, K1 tbl into them
and sl off left hand needle, K1 tbl, rep from * to
last st, K1. 111 sts.
Next row Sl 1, P to last st, K1.
Next row Sl 1, K1 tbl, *insert needle p-wise into
next 2 sts as if to P2 tog but P1, K1 tbl into them
and sl off left hand needle, K1 tbl, rep from * to
last st, K1.
Rep last 2 rows twice more, then first of these rows
once more.
Next row Sl 1, K1 tbl, *P2 tog, K1 tbl, rep from *
to last st, K1. 75 sts.
Next row Sl 1, *P2 tog, rep from * to end. 38 sts.
Next row Sl 1, *P2 tog, rep from * to last st, K1.
20 sts.
Next row *P2 tog, rep from * to end. 10 sts.
Break yarn and thread through rem sts, draw up
and fasten off.

To make up
Press as given for top. Join back seam. Press seam.

32 *Jumper suit with striped bib*

Sizes
To fit 34[36:38]in bust
36[38:40] hips
Jumper length to shoulder, 25[25½:26]in
Sleeve seam, 8in
Skirt length, 23in adjustable
The figures in brackets [] refer to the 36 and 38in
sizes respectively
Tension
4½ sts and 5½ rows to 1in over st st worked on No.4
needles
Materials
11[12:13] balls Hayfield Croft Thickerknit in
main shade, A
1[1-2] balls in contrast colour, B
One pair No.4 needles
One pair No.6 needles
Set of 4 No.6 needles pointed at both ends
Waist length of elastic
One 8in zip fastener

Jumper back
Using No.6 needles and A, cast on 88[92:96] sts.

Beg with a K row work 1½in st st, ending with a
K row.
Next row K all sts tbl to form hemline.
Change to No.4 needles. Beg with a K row cont in
st st until work measures 14in from hemline.
Dec one st at each end of next and every foll 6th
row until 80[84:88] sts rem. Cont without shaping
until work measures 18in from hemline, ending with
a P row.
Shape armholes
Cast off 5 sts at beg of next 2 rows. Dec one st at
each end of next 3[4:5] alt rows. 64[66:68] sts.
Cont without shaping until armholes measure
7[7½:8]in from beg, ending with a P row.
Shape shoulders
Cast off at beg of next and every row 5 sts 4 times
and 4[5:6] sts twice.
Leave rem 36 sts on holder.

Front
Work as given for back until front measures 7in
from hemline, ending with a P row.
Divide for front opening
Next row K44[46:48] sts, turn and leave rem sts
on holder.
Complete this side first, shaping side edge to match
back and dec one st at centre front edge on every
foll 5th row until work measures same as back to
underarm, ending at armhole edge.
Shape armhole
Cast off 5 sts at beg of next row. Work 1 row. Dec
one st at beg of next and foll 2[3:4] alt rows.
Keeping armhole edge straight, cont to dec at front
edge as before until 14[15:16] sts rem. Cont
without shaping until armhole measures same as
back to shoulder, ending at armhole edge
Shape shoulder
Cast off at beg of next and every alt row 5 sts twice
and 4[5:6] sts once.
With RS of work facing, rejoin yarn to rem sts and
complete to match first side, reversing shaping.

Sleeves
Using No.6 needles and A, cast on 46[48:50] sts.
Beg with a K row 1in st st, ending with a K row.
Next row K all sts tbl to form hemline.
Change to No.4 needles. Beg with a K row cont in
st st, inc one st at each end of 3rd and every foll
4th row until there are 62[64:66] sts. Cont without
shaping until sleeve measures 8in from hemline,
ending with a P row.
Shape top
Cast off 5 sts at beg of next 2 rows. Dec one st at
each end of next and every alt row until 30 sts rem.
Cast off at beg of next and every row 2 sts 8 times
and 3 sts twice. Cast off rem 8 sts.

Neckband
Join shoulder seams. Using set of 4 No.6 needles,
B and with RS of work facing, K across sts on back
neck holder, K up 72[74:76] sts down side of front
neck and K up 72[74:76] sts up other side of front
neck. 180[184:188] sts.
Next round K to 2 sts before centre front, sl 1, K1,
psso, K2 tog, K to end.
Rep this round 5 times more, then P1 round still
dec at centre front.
Next round K to 2 sts before centre front, K twice
into next st, K2, K twice into next st, K to end.
Rep this round 4 times more. Cast off loosely, still
inc at centre front.

Striped bib
Using No.4 needles and A, cast on 4 sts. Beg with
a K row work 8 rows st st, inc one st at each end of
3rd and foll 4th row. Cont in st st, working 6 rows
B, 6 rows A, and inc at each end of every foll 4th
row until there are 50 sts. Cont without shaping
until 5th row of 8th stripe in B has been worked.
97 rows in all. Change to No.6 needles. K 1 row.
Beg with a K row, cont with B and work 5 more
rows. Cast off loosely.

To make up
Press each piece under a damp cloth with a warm
iron. Set in sleeves. Join side and sleeve seams. Turn
all hems to WS and sl st down. Sew in striped bib
to front opening. Press seams.

Skirt back
Using No. 6 needles and A, cast on 90[94:98] sts
and beg at hem. Beg with a K row work 1½in st st,
ending with a K row.
Next row K all sts tbl to form hemline.
Change to No.4 needles. Beg with a K row cont in
st st, working (6 rows A, 6 rows B) twice. Cont in
st st using A only until work measures 14in from
hemline, or required length to waist less 9in, ending
with a P row.
Next row K22[23:24] sts, K2 tog, K42[44:46] sts,
sl 1, K1, psso, K22[23:24] sts.
Beg with a P row work 3 rows st st.
Next row K22[23:24] sts, K2 tog, K40[42:44] sts,
sl 1, K1, psso, K22[23:24] sts.
Beg with a P row work 3 rows st st.
Cont dec in this way on next and every foll 4th row
until 66[70:74] sts rem. Cont without shaping for
further 1in, ending with a K row. Change to No.6
needles.
Next row K all sts tbl to mark fold line.
Beg with a K row cont in st st for 1in. Cast off
loosely.

Skirt front
Work as given for back.

To make up
Press as given for jumper. Join side seams leaving
8in open from fold line on left side for zip. Sew in
zip. Fold hem and waistband to WS and sl st down.
Press seams. Thread elastic through waistband and
secure at each end.

33 *Striped maxi dress*

Sizes
To fit 32[34:36:38:40]in bust
34[36:38:40:42]in hips
Length to shoulder, 46[47:48:49:50]in
The figures in brackets [] refer to the 34, 36, 38
and 40in sizes respectively
Tension
6 sts and 8 rows to 1in over st st worked on No.9
needles
Materials
16[18:20:22:24] balls Emu Scotch Double
Knitting in main shade, A
2[2:3:3:4] balls of contrast colour, B
One pair No.9 needles
One No.3·00 (ISR) crochet hook
20 buttons

Back
Using No.9 needles and A, cast on 158[164:170:
176:182] sts. Beg with a K row work 4in st st,
ending with a P row.
Shape skirt
Next row K19 sts, sl 1, K1, psso, K40[42:44:46:
48] sts, sl 1, K1, psso, K32[34:36:38:40] sts, K2 tog,
K40[42:44:46:48] sts, K2 tog, K19 sts.
Beg with a P row cont in st st until work measures

66

5in from beg, then work 2 rows with B. Cont with A until 17 rows in all have been worked from last dec row.

Next row K19 sts, sl 1, K1, psso, K38[40:42:44:46] sts, sl 1, K1, psso, K32[34:36:38:40] sts, K2 tog, K38[40:42:44:46] sts, K2 tog, K19 sts.
Cont to dec in this way on every foll 18th row until 98[104:110:116:122] sts rem, *at the same time* work in stripes as foll: 4½in A, 2 rows B, 4in A, 2 rows B, 3½in A, 2 rows B, 3in A, 2 rows B, 2½in A, 2 rows B, 2in A, 2 rows B, 1½in A, 2 rows B. Complete back working in 8 rows A and 2 rows B throughout.
Cont without shaping until work measures 38[38½: 39:39½:40]in from beg.
End with a P row.
Shape armholes
Cast off at beg of next and every row 8 sts twice and 2[2:3:3:4] sts twice. Dec one st at each end of next and foll 3[4:4:5:5] alt rows. 70[74:78:82:86] sts.
Cont without shaping until armholes measure 7[7½:8:8½:9]in from beg, ending with a P row.
Shape neck and shoulders
Next row K19[20:21:22:23] sts, turn and leave rem sts on holder.
Next row Cast off 4 sts, P to end.
Next row Cast off 6[6:7:7:8] sts, K to end.
Next row Cast off 4 sts, P to end.
Cast off rem 5[6:6:7:7] sts.
With RS of work facing, rejoin yarn to rem sts and cast off 32[34:36:38:40] sts, K to end. P 1 row.
Complete to match first side reversing shaping.

Left front
Using No.9 needles and A, cast on 79[82:85:88:91] sts. Beg with a K row work 4in st st, ending with a P row.
Shape skirt
Next row K19 sts, sl 1, K1, psso K40[42:44:46:48] sts, sl 1, K1, psso, K to end.
Cont working in striped sequence as given for back, dec in this way on every foll 18th row until 49[52:55:58:61] sts rem. Cont without shaping until work measures same as back to underarm, ending at armhole edge.
Shape armhole
Cast off at beg of next and foll alt row 8 sts once and 2[2:3:3:4] sts once. Dec one st at armhole edge on foll 4[5:5:6:6] alt rows. 35[37:39:41:43] sts. Cont without shaping until armhole measures 3[3½:4: 4½:5]in from beg, ending at front edge.
Shape neck
Cast off at beg of next and foll alt rows 9[9:10:10: 11] sts once, 5[6:6:7:7] sts once, 4 sts once and 2 sts twice. Dec one st at neck edge on foll 2 alt rows. Cont without shaping until armhole measures same as back to shoulder.
End at armhole edge.
Shape shoulder
Cast off at beg of next and foll alt row 6[6:7:7:8] sts once and 5[6:6:7:7] sts once.

Right front
Work as given for left front, reversing shaping.

To make up
Press each piece under a damp cloth with a warm iron. Join shoulder and side seams.
Armbands Using No.3·00 (ISR) hook, A and with RS of work facing, work 1 round dc round armhole. Join with a ss.
Next round 2ch, *1ch, miss 1dc, 1dc into next dc, rep from * to end. Join with ss to 2nd of first 2ch. Rep last round 4 times more. Fasten off.
Borders Mark positions for 20 buttons on left front, first to come 1½in from lower edge and last level with neck shaping with 18 spaced at equal intervals. Work round all edges as given for armbands, working 1dc, 1ch, 1dc into each corner on every row and making buttonholes on 4th row as markers are reached by working 3ch and missing 3 sts, and working 3 sts in to each 3ch sp on 5th row.
Press all seams. Sew on buttons.

34 *Random striped shirt*

Sizes
To fit 34[36:38:40:42]in bust
Length to shoulder, 26½[27:27½:28:28½]in
Sleeve seam, 14[14½:15:15½:16]in
The figures in brackets [] refer to the 36, 38, 40 and 42in sizes respectively
Tension
5½ sts and 7 rows to 1in over st st worked on No.8 needles
Materials
10[11:12:13:14] balls Patons Double Knitting in main shade, A
2 balls each in contrast colours B and D
4 balls in contrast colour, C
One pair No.8 needles
One pair No.10 needles
Four buttons

Back
Using No.10 needles and A, cast on 97[103:109: 115:121] sts. Beg with a K row work 1½in st st, ending with a K row.
Next row K all sts tbl to form hemline.
Change to No.8 needles. Beg with a K row, cont in st st working 2 rows B, 2 rows C, 2 rows A, 2 rows D, then cont in A until work measures 2in from hemline, ending with a P row.
Shape sides
Dec one st at each end of next and every foll 12th row until 85[91:97:103:109] sts rem, *at the same time* work striped patt, as foll: Cont in A until work measures 7¼in from hemline, **2 rows D, 2 A, 2 D, 2 A, 2 C, 2 A, 4 B, 2 A, 2 D, 2 A, 8 C, 2 A, 4 D, **, then cont in A only until work measures 17in from hemline, ending with a P row. Work 4 rows B, 6 A.
Shape armholes
Using C, cast off 3 sts at beg of next 2 rows. 79[85:91:97:103] sts.
3rd row Using A, K1, K2 tog, K to last 3 sts, K2 tog tbl, K1.
4th row Using A, P to end.
5th and 6th rows Using B, work 2 rows without shaping.
7th and 8th rows Using A, as 3rd and 4th rows.
9th and 10th rows Using A, as 5th and 6th rows.
11th and 12th rows Using A, as 3rd and 4th rows.
13th and 14th rows Using D, as 5th and 6th rows.
15th and 16th rows Using D, as 3rd and 4th rows.
Rep 3rd and 4th rows until 27[29:31:33:35] sts rem, working 2 rows B, 2 A, 16 C, 2 D, then cont in A only, ending with a P row.
Cast off.

Front
Work as given for back until work measures 17in from beg, ending with a K row and 1 row less of stripe in A.
Divide for front opening
Next row Using A, P40[43:46:49:52] sts, cast off 5 sts, P to end.
Complete this side first. Cont in striped patt until work measures same as back to underarm, ending at armhole edge.
Shape armhole
Keeping striped patt correct, cast off 3 sts at beg of next row. Work 1 row.
Next row K1, K2 tog, K to end.
Beg with a P row work 3 rows st st.
Rep last 4 rows twice more, then cont to dec at beg of every alt row until 18[19:20:21:22] sts rem, ending at front edge.
Shape neck
Next row Cast off 4[5:6:7:8] sts, P to end.
Next row K1, K2 tog, K to last 2 sts, K2 tog.
Next row P to end.

Rep last 2 rows 4 times more. Cont to dec at armhole edge only on every alt row until 2 sts rem, ending with a K row.
Next row P2 tog. Fasten off.
With RS of work facing, rejoin yarn to rem sts and complete to match first side, reversing shaping.

Sleeves
Using No.10 needles and A, cast on 45[45:47:47: 49] sts.
1st row K1, *P1, K1, rep from * to end.
2nd row P1, *K1, P1, rep from * to end.
Rep these 2 rows for 2in, ending with a 2nd row and inc 4 sts evenly across last row. 49[49:51:51:53] sts. Change to No.8 needles. Beg with a K row, cont in st st inc one st at each end of 7th and every foll 8th row until there are 69[71:73:75:77] sts, *at the same time* working in stripes: Cont in A until work measures 3¼[3½:3¾:4:4¼]in, work as given for back from ** to **, then cont in A until sleeve measures 12½[13:13½:14:14½]in from beg, ending with a P row. Work 4 rows B, 6 A.
Shape top
Working in stripes to match back, cast off 3 sts at beg of next 2 rows.
Next row K1, K2 tog, K to last 3 sts, K2 tog tbl, K1.
Beg with a P row work 3 rows st st. Cont to dec on every 4th row 1[2:3:4:5] times more. 59 sts. P 1 row. Dec one st at each end of next and every alt row until 7 sts rem, ending with a P row. Cast off.

Buttonhole band
Using No.10 needles and A, cast on 55[57:61:63: 67] sts. Beg with a 2nd row work 3 rows rib as given for sleeves.
Next row Rib 4[6:7:9:10] sts, *cast off 2 sts, rib 13[13:14:14:15] sts, rep from * twice more, cast off 2 sts, rib to end.
Next row Rib to end, casting on 2 sts above those cast off in previous row.
Work 3 more rows in rib. Cast off in rib.

Button band
Work as given for buttonhole band, omitting buttonholes.

Collar
Using No.10 needles and C, cast on 35[37:39:41: 43] sts. Work 1 row K1, P1 rib. Cont in rib, casting on at beg of next and every row 8 sts 6 times and 10 sts 4 times. 123[125:127:129:131] sts. Cont in rib until work measures 3[3:3¼:3¼:3½]in from beg. Break off C. Join in B and K 1 row, then rib 1 row. Break off B. Join in A and K 1 row, then rib 3 rows. Cast off loosely in rib.

To make up
Press each piece under a damp cloth with a warm iron. Join raglan seams. Join side and sleeve seams. Sew on front bands. Sew on collar. Turn hem to WS at hemline and sl st down. Press all seams. Sew on buttons.

35 *Jersey and striped sleeveless jacket*

Sizes
To fit 32[34:36:38:40]in bust
Jersey length to shoulder, 24[24½:25:25½:26]in
Sleeve seam, 17in
Jacket length to shoulder, 29[29½:30:30½:31]in
The figures in brackets [] refer to the 34, 36, 38 and 40in sizes respectively

Tension

6 sts and 8 rows to 1in over st st worked on No.9 needles

Materials

Jersey 13[14:15:16:17] balls Patons Fiona in main shade, A

Jacket 8[9:9:10:10] balls main shade, A

4[4:5:5:5] balls in contrast colour, B

One pair No.9 needles

One pair No.11 needles

Set of 4 No.11 needles pointed at both ends

Jersey back

Using No.9 needles cast on 98[104:110:116:122] sts.

1st row K14[17:20:23:26] sts, P14, (K14, P14) twice, K14[17:20:23:26] sts.

2nd row P14[17:20:23:26] sts, K14, (P14, K14) twice, P14[17:20:23:26] sts.

These 2 rows form patt. Cont in patt until work measures 4in from beg, ending with a 2nd row. Keeping patt correct, dec one st at each end of next and every foll 12th row until 88[94:100:106:112] sts rem. Cont without shaping until work measures 17½in from beg, ending with a WS row.

Shape armholes

Cast off 4 sts at beg of next 2 rows. Dec one st at each end of next and foll 5[6:7:8:9] alt rows. 68[72:76:80:84] sts. Cont without shaping until armholes measure 6½[7:7½:8:8½]in from beg, ending with a WS row.

Shape shoulders

Cast off at beg of next and every row 6[6:7:7:7] sts 4 times and 6[7:6:7:8] sts twice. Leave rem sts on holder.

Front

Work as given for back until armhole shaping is completed. Cont without shaping until armholes measure 4½[5:5½:6:6½]in from beg, ending with a WS row.

Shape neck

Next row Patt 26[27:28:29:30] sts, turn and leave rem sts on holder.

Complete this side first. Cast off 2 sts at beg of next and foll alt row, then dec one st at neck edge on every alt row until 18[19:20:21:22] sts rem. Cont without shaping until armhole measures same as back to shoulder, ending at armhole edge.

Shape shoulder

Cast off at beg of next and every alt row 6[6:7:7:7] sts twice and 6[7:6:7:8] sts once.

With RS of work facing, sl first 16[18:20:22:24] sts on holder and leave for centre neck, rejoin yarn to rem sts and patt to end. Complete to match first side, reversing shaping.

Sleeves

Using No.11 needles cast on 42[44:46:48:50] sts.

1st row K0[1:2:3:4] sts, P14, K14, P14, K0[1:2:3:4] sts.

2nd row P0[1:2:3:4] sts, K14, P14, K14, P0[1:2:3:4] sts.

Cont in patt as now set until sleeve measures 1½in from beg. Change to No.9 needles. Cont in patt, inc one st at each end of next and every foll 8th row until there are 70[72:74:76:78] sts. Cont without shaping until sleeve measures 17in from beg, or required length to underarm, ending with a WS row.

Shape top

Cast off 4 sts at beg of next 2 rows. Dec one st at each end of next and every alt row until 48 sts rem. Cast off at beg of next and every row 2 sts 10 times, 3 sts 4 times and 4 sts twice. Cast off rem 8 sts.

Neckband

Join shoulder seams. Using set of 4 No.11 needles, K across sts on back neck holder, K up 20 sts down side of front neck, K across sts on centre front neck holder and K up 20 sts up other side of neck. 88[92:96:100:104] sts. Work 1½in in rounds of K1, P1 rib. Cast off in rib.

To make up

Press each piece under a damp cloth with a warm iron. Set in sleeves. Join side and sleeve seams. Press seams.

Jacket back

Using No.11 needles and A, cast on 106[112:118:124:130] sts. Beg with a K row work 1½in st st, ending with a K row.

Next row K all sts tbl to mark hemline.

Change to No.9 needles. Beg with a K row cont in st st working throughout in stripes of 20 rows A and 4 rows B. Cont in patt until work measures 4in from hemline, ending with a P row. Dec one st at each end of next and every foll 10th row until 90[96:102:108:114] sts rem. Cont without shaping until work measures 22in from hemline, ending with a P row.

Shape armholes

Cast off 5 sts at beg of next 2 rows. Dec one st at each end of next and foll 5[6:7:8:9] alt rows. 68[72:76:80:84] sts. Cont without shaping until armholes measure 7[7½:8:8½:9]in from beg, ending with a P row.

Shape shoulders

Work as given for jersey back. Cast off rem 32 [34:36:38:40] sts.

Jacket left front

Using No.11 needles and A, cast on 57[60:63:66:69] sts. Work as given for back until work measures 4in from hemline, ending with a P row. Dec one st at beg of next and every foll 10th row until 49[52:55:58:61] sts rem. Cont without shaping until work measures same as back to underarm, less 3in, ending with a P row.

Shape front edge

Dec one st at end of next and every foll 4th row until work measures same as back to underarm, ending at armhole edge.

Shape armhole

Cont to dec at front edge as before, cast off 5 sts at beg of next row. Work 1 row. Dec one st at armhole edge at beg of next and foll 5[6:7:8:9] alt rows. Cont dec at front edge only as before until 18[19:20:21:22] sts rem. Cont without shaping until armhole measures same as back to shoulder, ending at armhole edge.

Shape shoulder

Cast off at beg of next and every alt row 6[6:7:7:7] sts twice and 6[7:6:7:8] sts once.

Jacket right front

Work as given for left front, reversing shaping.

Armbands

Join shoulder seams. Using No.11 needles, A and with RS of work facing, K up 85[91:97:103:109] sts round armhole. Beg 1st row with P1, work in K1, P1 rib for ¾in. Cast off in rib.

Front band

Using No.11 needles and B, cast on 11 sts. Work in K1, P1 rib until band is long enough to fit up right front, round back neck and down left front. Cast off in rib.

To make up

Press as given for jersey. Join side seams. Turn hem to WS and sl st down. Sew on front band. Press seams.

36 *Tunic with front lacing*

Sizes

To fit 32[34:36:38:40]in bust

Length to shoulder, 25½[26:26½:27:27½]in

Sleeve seam, 17[17:17½:17½:18]in

The figures in brackets [] refer to the 34, 36, 38 and 40in sizes respectively

Tension

6 sts and 8 rows to 1in over st st worked on No.9 needles

Materials

16[17:18:19:20] balls Jaeger Celtic-Spun

One pair No.9 needles

One pair No.11 needles

Back

Using No.11 needles cast on 114[120:126:132:138] sts. Beg with a K row work 1½in st st, ending with a K row.

Next row K all sts tbl to mark hemline.

Change to No.9 needles. Beg with a K row cont in st st until work measures 4in from hemline, ending with a P row.

Shape darts

Next row K1, K2 tog, K36[38:40:42:44] sts, K2 tog, K32[34:36:38:40] sts, sl 1, K1, psso, K36[38:40:42:44] sts, sl 1, K1, psso, K1. Beg with a P row work 9 rows st st.

Next row K1, K2 tog, K35[37:39:41:43] sts, K2 tog, K30[32:34:36:38] sts, sl 1, K1, psso, K35[37:39:41:43] sts, sl 1, K1, psso, K1. Dec in same way on foll 10th row. 102[108:114:120:126] sts. Cont without shaping until work measures 18½in from hemline, ending with a P row.

Shape armholes

Cast off 6 sts at beg of next 2 rows.

Next row K1, K2 tog, K to last 3 sts, sl 1, K1, psso, K1.

Next row P to end.

Rep last 2 rows 3[4:5:6:7] times more. 82[86:90:94:98] sts. Cont without shaping until armholes measure 7[7½:8:8½:9]in from beg, ending with a P row

Shape neck and shoulders

Next row Cast off 4[5:5:5:6] sts, K17[17:18:19:19] sts, turn and leave rem sts on holder.

Next row Cast off 2 sts, P to end.

Next row Cast off 4 sts, K to end.

Rep last 2 rows once more, then first of these 2 rows once. Cast off rem 3[3:4:5:5] sts.

With RS of work facing, sl first 40[42:44:46:48] sts

on holder and leave for back neck, rejoin yarn to rem sts and K to end. Complete to match first side, reversing shaping.

Front
Work as given for back until front measures 7[7:6½:6½:6]in less than back to underarm, ending with a K row.
Divide for front opening
Next row P50[53:56:59:62] sts, cast off 2 sts, P to end.
Next row K to end, turn and cast on 4 sts. 54[57:60:63:66] sts.
Next row P to end.
Next row K to last 4 sts, sl 1, K3.
Rep last 2 rows for 1½in, ending with a P row.
Next row (eyelet hole) K to last 8 sts, yfwd, K2 tog, K2, sl 1, K3.
Keeping sl st correct on every K row, cont to make eyelet holes in this way at intervals of 1½in from the previous hole, until work measures same as back to underarm ending at armhole edge.
Shape armhole
Cast off 6 sts at beg of next row. Work 1 row.
Next row K1, K2 tog, patt to end.
Next row Patt to end.
Rep last 2 rows 3[4:5:6:7] times more. Cont without shaping, working eyelet holes as before until 7 in all have been made, then cont for a further 1½in, ending at neck edge. 44[46:48:50:52] sts.
Shape neck
Cast off 3 sts, P to end.
Next row K21[22:23:24:25] sts, turn and leave rem 20[21:22:23:24] sts on holder.
Cast off 2 sts at beg of next and foll 2 alt rows, then cont without shaping until armhole measures same as back to shoulder, ending at armhole edge.
Shape shoulder
Cast off at beg of next and every alt row 4[5:5:5:6] sts once, 4 sts twice and 3[3:4:5:5] sts once.
With RS of work facing rejoin yarn to rem sts, cast on 4 sts, K3, sl 1, K to end. Complete to match first side, reversing shaping and noting that eyelet hole row will be worked as foll: K3, sl 1, K2, sl 1, K1, psso, yfwd, K to end.

Sleeves
Using No.11 needles cast on 49[51:53:55:57] sts.
1st row K1, *P1, K1, rep from * to end.
2nd row P1, *K1, P1, rep from * to end.
Rep these 2 rows for 1¼in, ending with a 2nd row.
Change to No.9 needles and cont in st st.
1st row K1[2:3:4:5] sts, (K twice into next st, K4) 9 times, K twice into next st, K2[3:4:5:6] sts. 59[61:63:65:67] sts.
Beg with a P row work 3 rows st st.
5th row K2[3:4:5:6] sts, (K twice into next st, K5) 9 times, K twice into next st, K2[3:4:5:6] sts. 69[71:73:75:77] sts.
Beg with a P row work 3 rows st st.
9th row K2[3:4:5:6] sts, (K twice into next st, K6) 9 times, K twice into next st, K3[4:5:6:7] sts. 79[81:83:85:87] sts.
Beg with a P row work 3 rows st st.
13th row K0[1:2:3:4] sts, (K twice into next st, K6) 11 times, K twice into next st, K1[2:3:4:5] sts. 91[93:95:97:99] sts.
Beg with a P row cont without shaping until sleeve measures 7in from beg, ending with a P row.
Next row K12[13:14:15:16] sts, (K2 tog, K14) 4 times, K2 tog, K to end.
Beg with a P row work 11 rows st st. Cont to dec 5 sts evenly in this way on next and every foll 12th row until 71[73:75:77:79] sts rem. Cont without shaping until sleeve measures 17[17:17½:17½:18]in from beg, ending with a P row.
Shape top
Cast off 6 sts at beg of next 2 rows. Dec at each end of next and every alt row as given for back until 31[33:35:37:39] sts rem. Cast off at beg of next and every row 2 sts 4[4:6:6:6] times and 3 sts 4 times. Cast off rem 11[13:11:13:15] sts.

Neckband
Join shoulder seams. Using No 11 needles and with RS of work facing K across sts of right front neck, K up 18[20:20:22:22] sts up side of front neck, K up 9 sts down back neck, K across sts of back neck, dec one st in centre, K up 9 sts up back neck, K up 18[20:20:22:22] sts down side of front neck and K across sts of left front neck. 133[141:145:153:157] sts. Beg with a 2nd row work 1in rib as given for sleeves.
Cast off in rib.

To make up
Press each piece under a damp cloth with a warm iron. Set in sleeves. Join side and sleeve seams. Turn hem to WS and sl st down. Fold front facings to WS at sl st line and sl st down. Press seams. Make a twisted cord 60in long and thread through eyelet holes to tie at neck edge.

37 *Jersey with cable panels and saddle-top sleeves*

Sizes
To fit 32[34:36:38:40]in bust
Length to shoulder, 22[22½:23:23½:24]in
Sleeve seam, 16½[17:17:17½:18]in
The figures in brackets [] refer to the 34, 36, 38 and 40in sizes respectively
Tension
5¾ sts and 7½ rows to 1in over st st worked on No.8 needles
Materials
12[13:14:15:16] balls Patons Fiona in main shade, A
1 ball each in contrast colours, B and C
One pair No.8 needles
One pair No.11 needles
Set of 4 No.11 needles pointed at both ends
Cable needle

Back
Using No.11 needles and A, cast on 102[106:114:118:126] sts.
1st row K2, *P2, K2, rep from * to end.
2nd row P2, *K2, P2, rep from * to end.
Rep these 2 rows 5 times more, inc one st at each end of last row on 34 and 38in sizes only. 102[108:114:120:126] sts. Change to No.8 needles.
Commence patt.
1st row P4[5:6:7:8] sts, *K6, P6, K4[5:6:7:8] sts, P6, rep from * 3 times more, K6, P4[5:6:7:8] sts.
2nd row K4[5:6:7:8] sts, *P6, K6, P4[5:6:7:8] sts, K6, rep from * 3 times more, P6, K4[5:6:7:8] sts.
3rd row As 1st.
4th row As 2nd.
5th row P4[5:6:7:8] sts, *sl next 3 sts on to cable needle and hold at front of work, K3 sts, then K3 sts from cable needle – called C6F –, P6, K4[5:6:7:8] sts, P6, rep from * 3 times more, C6F, P4[5:6:7:8] sts.
6th row As 2nd.
7th row As 1st.
8th row As 2nd.
These 8 rows form patt. Cont in patt until work measures 14½in from beg, ending with a WS row.
Shape armholes
Cast off 2 sts at beg of next 2 rows. Dec one st at each end of next and every foll 4th row until 76[80:84:88:92] sts rem, then work 2 rows after last dec ending with a WS row.
Shape shoulders
Cast off 25[25:27:27:29] sts, patt 26[30:30:34:34] sts, cast off rem 25[25:27:27:29] sts. Leave sts on holder for centre neck.

Front
Work as given for back.

Sleeves
Using No.11 needles and B, cast on 50[54:54:58:58] sts. Work 2 rows rib as given for back. Break off B. Join in A, K 1 row, then rib 2 rows. Break off A. Join in C, P 1 row, then rib 1 row. Break off C. Using A only, P 1 row, then cont in rib until sleeve measures 3¼in from beg, ending with a 2nd row and inc one st at each end of last row on 32, 36 and 40in sizes only. 52[54:56:58:60] sts. Change to No.8 needles. Beg with a K row cont in st st, inc one st at each end of 5th and every foll 8th row until there are 72[74:78:80:84] sts. Cont without shaping until sleeve measures 16½[17:17:17½:18]in from beg, ending with a P row.
Shape top
Cast off 2 sts at beg of next 2 rows. 68[70:74:76:80] sts.
Next row K3 sts, K2 tog, K to last 5 sts, sl 1, K1, psso, K3 sts.
Beg with a P row work 3 rows st st.
Cont to dec in this way on next and every foll 4th row 0[1:1:2:2] times more, then on every alt row until 24 sts rem.
Saddle top
Cont in st st without shaping until saddle top measures same as top of shoulder on back and front, ending with a P row. Leave sts on holder.

Neckband
Sew saddle top of sleeves to shoulders of back and front. Using set of 4 No.11 needles, A and with RS of work facing, K across all sts on holders, K2 tog at each seam. Cont in rounds of K2, P2 rib, as foll: Work 2 rounds A. With C, K 1 round, then rib 1 round. With A, K 1 round, then rib 2 rounds. With B, K 1 round, then rib 1 round. Cast off in rib with B.

To make up
Press each piece lightly on WS under a damp cloth with a cool iron. Set in sleeves. Join side and sleeve seams. Press seams.

38 *Cotton bouclé jersey*

Sizes
To fit 32[34:36:38:40:42]in bust
Length to shoulder, 20½[21:21½:22:22½:23]in
Sleeve seam, 12in
The figures in brackets [] refer to the 34, 36, 38, 40 and 42in sizes respectively
Tension
9 sts and 14 rows to 2in over st st worked on No.8 needles
Materials
15[15:16:17:17:18] balls Jaeger Sunlin-Spun
One pair No.8 needles
One pair No.10 needles

Back
Using No.10 needles cast on 76[80:86:90:96:100] sts. Beg with a K row work 9 rows st st.
Next row K all sts tbl to mark hemline.
Change to No.8 needles. Beg with a K row cont in st st until work measures 14in from hemline, ending with a P row.
Shape armholes
Cast off at beg of next and every row 4 sts twice and 2 sts twice. K2 tog at each end of next and foll

1[1:2:2:3:3] alt rows. 60[64:68:72:76:80] sts.
Cont without shaping until armholes measure
6½[7:7½:8:8½:9]in from beg, ending with a P row.

Shape shoulders
Cast off 4 sts at beg of next 3 rows.
Next row (neckline) Cast off 4 sts, K to end.
Change to No.10 needles Beg with a K row work
5 rows st st, inc one st at each end of every row.
Cast off.

Front
Work as given for back.

Sleeves
Using No.10 needles cast on 44[46:48:50:52:54]
sts. Work hem as given for back. Change to No.8
needles. Beg with a K row cont in st st, inc one st at
each end of 5th and every foll 8th row until there
are 58[60:62:64:66:68] sts. Cont without shaping
until sleeve measures 12in from hemline, ending
with a P row.

Shape top
Cast off 4 sts at beg of next 2 rows. K2 tog at each
end of next and every alt row until 28 sts rem. Cast
off at beg of next and every row 2 sts 6 times and
3 sts twice.
Cast off rem 10 sts.

To make up
Press each piece under a damp cloth with a warm
iron. Join shoulder, side and sleeve seams. Set in
sleeves. Fold hems at lower edge and neck edge to
WS and sl st down. Press seams.

Dress with smocked sleeves and sleeveless jacket

Sizes
To fit 32[34:36:38]in bust
34[36:38:40]in hips
Dress length to shoulder, 40[40½:41:41½]in
Sleeve seam, 17[17:17½:17½]in
Jacket length to shoulder, 20[20½:21:21½]in
The figures in brackets [] refer to the 34, 36 and
38in sizes respectively

Tension
7 sts and 9 rows to 1in over st st worked on No.10
needles

Materials
Dress 20[22:24:26] balls Emu Crochet Wool 4 ply
Jacket 6[7:8:9] balls
One pair No.10 needles
One pair No.12 needles
Set of 4 No.12 needles pointed at both ends
One No.2·00 (ISR) crochet hook
Six buttons

Dress back
Using No.12 needles cast on 158[164:172:178] sts.
Beg with a K row work 1½in st st, ending with a K
row.
Next row K all sts tbl to mark hemline.
Change to No.10 needles. Beg with a K row cont in
st st until work measures 5in from hemline, ending
with a P row.

Shape darts
Next row K38[40:42:44] sts, sl 1, K1, psso, K to
last 40[42:44:46] sts, K2 tog, K to end.
Beg with a P row work 7 rows st st.
Cont to dec in this way on next and every foll 8th
row until 110[116:124:130] sts rem. Cont without
shaping until work measures 33in from hemline,
ending with a P row.

Shape armholes

Cast off at beg of next and every row 5 sts twice and
3[3:4:4] sts twice. Dec one st at each end of next
and foll 2[3:4:5] alt rows. 88[92:96:100] sts. Cont
without shaping until armholes measure 7[7½:8:
8½]in from beg.
End with a P row.

Shape shoulders
Cast off at beg of next and every row 8 sts 4 times
and 6[7:8:9] sts twice. Leave rem 44[46:48:50] sts
on holder.

Dress front
Work as given for back until armhole shaping is
completed. Cont without shaping until armholes
measure 5[5½:6:6½]in from beg, ending with a P
row.

Shape neck
Next row K30[31:32:33] sts, turn and leave rem
sts on holder.
Cast off at beg of next and foll alt row 3 sts once
and 2 sts once. Dec one st at neck edge on every alt
row until 22[23:24:25] sts rem. Cont without
shaping until armhole measures same as back to
shoulder.
End at armhole edge.

Shape shoulder
Cast off at beg of next and every alt row 8 sts twice
and 6[7:8:9] sts once.
With RS of work facing, sl first 28[30:32:34] sts on
holder and leave for centre neck, rejoin yarn to rem
sts and K to end. Complete to match first side,
reversing shaping.

Sleeves
Using No.10 needles cast on 94[96:98:100] sts.
1st row P1[2:3:4] sts, (K1, P6) 13 times, K1,
P1[2:3:4] sts.
2nd row K1[2:3:4] sts, (P1, K6) 13 times, P1,
K1[2:3:4] sts.
Rep these 2 rows until sleeve measures 2in from beg,
ending with a 2nd row. Cont in patt, inc one st at
each end of next and every foll 10th row until there
are 104[106:108:110] sts. Cont without shaping
until work measures 10in from beg, ending with a
WS row. Dec one st at each end of next and every
alt row until 84[86:88:90] sts rem. Cont without
shaping until sleeve measures 17[17:17½:17½]in
from beg, ending with a WS row.

Shape top
Cast off 2 sts at beg of every row until 8 sts rem.
Cast off.

Neckband
Join shoulder seams. Using set of 4 No.12 needles
and with RS of work facing, K across back neck sts,
K up 20 sts down side of neck, K across front neck
sts and K up 20 sts up other side of neck. Work in
rounds of K1, P1 rib for 8in.
Cast off loosely in rib.

To make up
Press each piece under a damp cloth with a warm
iron.
Sleeve smocking Beg above cast on edge using
blunt ended wool needle and one strand of yarn,
join 1st and 2nd K sts tog, take yarn behind work
and join 2nd and 3rd K sts tog approx 1in above
2 sts already joined, take yarn behind work again
and join 3rd and 4th K sts tog at cast on edge, cont
in this way across sleeve. Fasten off. Beg again with
1st and 2nd K ridges 2in from beg and 2nd and 3rd
K ridges 3in from beg. Cont in this way until 8 lines
of smocking have been worked.
Join side and sleeve seams. Set in sleeves. Turn hem
to WS and sl st down. Press seams.

Jacket back
Using No.12 needles cast on 120[126:134:140] sts.
Work hem as given for dress back. Change to No.10
needles. Beg with a K row cont in st st until work
measures 12in from hemline, ending with a P row.

Shape armholes

Cast off at beg of next and every row 5 sts twice,
4 sts twice and 2[2:3:3] sts twice.
Dec one st at each end of next and foll 4[5:6:7] alt
rows. 88[92:96:100] sts. Cont without shaping until
armholes measure 8[8½:9:9½]in from beg, ending
with a P row.

Shape shoulders
Cast off at beg of next and every row 7 sts 4 times
and 6[7:8:9] sts twice. Cast off rem 48[50:52:54]
sts.

Jacket left front
Using No.12 needles cast on 62[65:69:72] sts. Work
as given for back until front measures same as back
to underarm, ending at armhole edge.

Shape armhole and front edge
Next row Cast off 5 sts, K to last 3 sts, K2 tog, K1.
Next row P to end.
Next row Cast off 4 sts, K to end.
Next row P1, P2 tog, P to end.
Next row Cast off 2[2:3:3] sts, K to end.
Next row P to end.
Dec one st at armhole edge on next and foll 4[5:6:
7] alt rows, *at the same time* cont to dec at front edge
on every 3rd row until 20[21:22:23] sts rem. Cont
without shaping until armhole measures same as
back to shoulder, ending at armhole edge.

Shape shoulder
Cast off at beg of next and every alt row 7 sts twice
and 6[7:8:9] sts once.

Jacket right front
Work as given for left front, reversing all shaping.

To make up
Press as given for dress. Join shoulder and side
seams. Turn hem to WS and sl st down. Using
No.2·00 (ISR) hook and with RS of work facing,
work 2 rounds dc around armholes. Work 2 rows dc
up right front edge, round neck and down left front
edge, making 6 button loops on right front on 2nd
row by working 4ch and missing 4 sts, the first to
come 5in above lower edge and the last just below
beg of neck shaping, with 4 more evenly spaced
between. Press seams. Sew on buttons.

40 Jersey suit with midi skirt

Sizes
To fit 34[36:38:40]in bust
36[38:40:42]in hips
Jersey length to shoulder, 23[23½:24:24½]in
Sleeve seam, 16½[17:17½:18]in
Skirt length, 27½[28:28½:29]in, adjustable
The figures in brackets [] refer to the 36, 38 and
40in sizes respectively

Tension
6 sts and 7½ rows to 1in over st st worked on No.9
needles

Materials
34[36:38:40] balls Lee Target Motoravia Double
Knitting
One pair No.9 needles
One pair No.11 needles
Set of 4 No.11 needles pointed at both ends
Waist length of elastic
One 7in zip fastener

Skirt back
Using No.11 needles cast on 77[83:89:95] sts and
beg at waist.
1st row K1, *P1, K1, rep from * to end.
2nd row P1, *K1, P1, rep from * to end.

Rep these 2 rows for 1½in, ending with a 2nd row and inc one st at end of last row. 78[84:90:96] sts. Change to No.9 needles. Beg with a K row work 4 rows st st.

Shape darts
Next row K3 sts, K up 1, K20[22:24:26] sts, K up 1, K32[34:36:38] sts, K up 1, K20[22:24:26] sts, K up 1, K3 sts.
Beg with a P row work 7 rows st st.
Next row K3 sts, K up 1, K21[23:25:27] sts, K up 1, K34[36:38:40] sts, K up 1, K21[23:25:27] sts, K up 1, K3 sts.
Beg with a P row work 7 rows st st.
Cont inc in this way on next and every foll 8th row until there are 110[116:122:128] sts, then on every foll 20th row until work measures 27½[28:28½:29]in from beg, or required length to hem, ending with a K row. Change to No.11 needles.
Next row K all sts tbl to form hemline.
Beg with a K row work 1in st st. Cast off loosely.

Skirt front
Work as given for back.

To make up
Press each piece under a damp cloth with a warm iron. Join side seams leaving 7in open at top of left seam for zip. Sew in zip. Sew elastic inside waist edge with casing st. Turn hem to WS at hemline and sl st down. Press seams.

Jersey back
Using No.11 needles cast on 106[110:118:122] sts.
1st row K2, *P2, K2, rep from * to end.
2nd row P2, *K2, P2, rep from * to end.
Rep these 2 rows for 1½in, ending with a 2nd row and inc one st at each end of last row on 36 and 40in sizes only. 106[112:118:124] sts. Change to No.9 needles. Commence patt.
1st row K13[16:19:22] sts, P2, K4, P2, (K10, P2, K4, P2) 4 times, K13[16:19:22] sts.
2nd row P13[16:19:22] sts, K2, P4, K2, (P10, K2, P4, K2) 4 times, P13[16:19:22] sts.
These 2 rows form patt. Cont in patt until work measures 16in from beg, ending with a WS row.
Shape armholes
Keeping patt correct, cast off at beg of next and every row 6 sts twice and 2 sts twice. Dec one st at each end of next and foll 5[6:7:8] alt rows. 78[82:86:90] sts. Cont without shaping until armholes measure 7[7½:8:8½]in from beg, ending with a WS row.
Shape neck and shoulders
Next row Patt 25[26:27:28] sts, turn and leave rem sts on holder.
Next row Cast off 2 sts, patt to end.
Next row Cast off 5 sts, patt to end.
Rep last 2 rows twice more. Work 1 row. Cast off rem 4[5:6:7] sts.
With RS of work facing, sl first 28[30:32:34] sts on holder, rejoin yarn to rem sts and patt to end. Complete to match first side, reversing shaping.

Jersey front
Work as given for back until armhole shaping is completed. Cont without shaping until armholes measure 4½[5:5½:6]in from beg. End with a WS row.
Shape neck
Next row Patt 31[32:33:34] sts, turn and leave rem sts on holder.
Cast off 2 sts at beg of next and foll 2 alt rows. Dec one st at neck edge on every alt row until 19[20:21:22] sts rem. Cont without shaping until armhole measures same as back to shoulder, ending at armhole edge.
Shape shoulder
Cast off at beg of next and every alt row 5 sts 3 times and 4[5:6:7] sts once.
With RS of work facing, sl first 16[18:20:22] sts on holder and leave for centre neck, rejoin yarn to rem sts, patt to end. Complete to match first side, reversing shaping.

Sleeves
Using No.11 needles cast on 50[50:54:54] sts. Work 3in K2, P2 rib as given for back. Change to No.9 needles. Cont in K2, P2 rib, inc one st at each end of next and every foll 8th row until there are 74[76:78:80] sts. Cont without shaping until sleeve measures 16½[17:17½:18]in from beg, ending with a WS row.
Shape top
Cast off 6 sts at beg of next 2 rows. Dec one st at each end of next and foll 11[12:13:14] alt rows. 38 sts. Cast off at beg of next and every row 2 sts 8 times and 3 sts 4 times. Cast off rem 10 sts.

Collar
Join shoulder seams. Using set of 4 No.11 needles and with RS of work facing, K across back neck sts on holder, K up 10 sts up side of back neck and 30 sts down side of front neck, K across front neck sts on holder, K up 30 sts up front of neck and 10 sts down back neck. 124[128:132:136] sts. Work in rounds of K2, P2 rib for 8in. Cast off loosely in rib.

To make up
Press as given for skirt. Set in sleeves. Join sides and sleeve seams. Press seams.

Tension
4 sts and 6 rows to 1in over st st worked on No.6 needles
Materials
9[10:11:11:12] balls Mahony Blarney Bainin Quicker Knitting
One pair No.6 needles
One pair No.8 needles
Cable needle
12 small wooden beads for belt

Front panel
Using No.6 needles cast on 55[57:59:61:63] sts.
Work 4 rows K1, P1 rib. Commence patt.
1st row (RS) (K1, P1) twice, P2[3:4:5:6] sts, sl next 2 sts on to cable needle and hold at back of work, K2 sts from left hand needle then K 2 from cable needle – called C4B –, P1, K into front then into back of next st – called M2 –, P1, M2, (P1, K1, P1, K1) all into next st, turn and K4, turn and P4, lift 2nd, 3rd and 4th sts over 1st st and off needle – called B1 –, P1, M2, P1, M2, P6, sl next 3 sts on to cable needle and hold at front of work, K2 sts from left hand needle, sl 1st st on cable needle on to left hand needle and P it, then K2 sts from cable needle – called Cr5 –, P6, M2, P1, M2, P1, B1, M2, P1, M2, P1, sl next 2 sts on to cable needle and hold at front of work, K2 sts from left hand needle then K2 sts from cable needle – called C4F –, P2[3:4:5:6] sts, (P1, K1) twice.
2nd row (P1, K1) twice, K2[3:4:5:6] sts, P4, K1, P2 tog, K1, P2 tog, K2, P2 tog, K1, P2 tog, K6, P2, K1, P2, K6, P2 tog, K1, P2 tog, K2, P2 tog, K1, P2 tog, K1, P4, K2[3:4:5:6] sts, (K1, P1) twice.
3rd row (K1, P1) twice, P2[3:4:5:6] sts, K4, P1, M2, P1, M2, P2, M2, P1, M2, P5, sl next st on to cable needle and hold at back of work, K2 sts from left hand needle then P1 from cable needle – called C3B –, P1, sl next 2 sts on to cable needle and hold at front of work, P1 from left hand needle then K2 sts from cable needle – called C3F –, P5, M2, P1, M2, P2, M2, P1, M2, P1, K4, P2[3:4:5:6] sts, (P1, K1) twice.
4th row (P1, K1) twice, K2[3:4:5:6] sts, P4, K1, P2 tog, K1, P2 tog, K2, P2 tog, K1, P2 tog, K5, P2, K3, P2, K5, P2 tog, K1, P2 tog, K2, P2 tog, K1, P2 tog, K1, P4, K2[3:4:5:6] sts, (K1, P1) twice.
5th row (K1, P1) twice, P2[3:4:5:6] sts, K4, P1, M2, P1, M2, P2, M2, P1, M2, P4, C3B, P3, C3F, P4, M2, P1, M2, P2, M2, P1, M2, P1, K4, P2[3:4:5:6] sts, (P1, K1) twice.
6th row (P1, K1) twice, K2[3:4:5:6] sts, P4, K1, P2 tog, K1, P2 tog, K2, P2 tog, K1, P2 tog, K4, P2, K5, P2, K4, P2 tog, K1, P2 tog, K2, P2 tog, K1, P2 tog, K1, P4, K2[3:4:5:6] sts, (K1, P1) twice.
7th row (K1, P1) twice, P2[3:4:5:6] sts, C4B, P1, M2, P1, M2, P1, B1, M2, P1, M2, P3, C3B, P2, K into front, then into back, then into front, then into back of next st – called M4 –, P2, C3F, P3, M2, P1, M2, B1, P1, M2, P1, M2, P1, C4F, P2[3:4:5:6] sts, (P1, K1) twice.
8th row (P1, K1) twice, K2[3:4:5:6] sts, P4, K1, P2 tog, K1, P2 tog, K2, P2 tog, K1, P2 tog, K3, P2, K3, P4, K3, P2, K3, P2 tog, K1, P2 tog, K2, P2 tog, K1, P2 tog, K1, P4, K2[3:4:5:6] sts, (K1, P1) twice.
9th row (K1, P1) twice, P2[3:4:5:6] sts, K4, P1, M2, P1, M2, P2, M2, P1, M2, P2, C3B, P3, K4, P3, C3F, P2, M2, P1, M2, P2, M2, P1, M2, P1, K4, P2[3:4:5:6] sts, (P1, K1) twice.
10th row (P1, K1) twice, K2[3:4:5:6] sts, P4, K1, P2 tog, K1, P2 tog, K2, P2 tog, K1, P2 tog, K2, P2, K4, P4 tog, K4, P2, K2, P2 tog, K1, P2 tog, K2, P2 tog, K1, P2 tog, K1, P4, K2[3:4:5:6] sts, (K1, P1) twice.
11th row (K1, P1) twice, P2[3:4:5:6] sts, K4, P1, M2, P1, M2, P2, M2, P1, M2, P1, C3B, P1, M4, P5, M4, P1, C3F, P1, M2, P1, M2, P2, M2, P1, M2, P1, K4, P2[3:4:5:6] sts, (P1, K1) twice.
12th row (P1, K1) twice, K2[3:4:5:6] sts, P4, K1, P2 tog, K1, P2 tog, K2, P2 tog, K1, P2 tog, K1, P2, K2, P4, K5, P4, K2, P2, K1, P2 tog, K1, P2

41 Aran tunic with slit sides

Sizes
To fit 34[36:38:40:42]in bust
Length to shoulder, 27[27¼:27½:27¾:28]in
The figures in brackets [] refer to the 36, 38, 40 and 42in sizes respectively

tog, K2, P2 tog, K1, P2 tog, K1, P4, K2[3:4:5:6] sts, (K1, P1) twice.

13th row (K1, P1) twice, P2[3:4:5:6] sts, C4B, P1, M2, P1, M2, B1, P1, M2, P1, M2, P1, C3F, P1, K4, P5, K4, P1, C3B, P1, M2, P1, M2, P1, B1, M2, P1, M2, P1, C4F, P2[3:4:5:6] sts, (P1, K1) twice.

14th row (P1, K1) twice, K2[3:4:5:6] sts, P4, K1, P2 tog, K1, P2 tog, K2, P2 tog, K1, P2 tog, K2, P2, K1, P4 tog, K5, P4 tog, K1, P2, K2, P2 tog, K1, P2 tog, K2, P2 tog, K1, P2 tog, K1, P4, K2[3:4:5:6] sts, (K1, P1) twice.

15th row (K1, P1) twice, P2[3:4:5:6] sts, K4, P1, M2, P1, M2, P2, M2, P1, M2, P3, C3F, P3, M4, P3, C3B, P2, M2, P1, M2, P2, M2, P1, M2, P1, K4, P2[3:4:5:6] sts, (P1, K1) twice.

16th row As 8th.

17th row (K1, P1) twice, P2[3:4:5:6] sts, K4, P1, M2, P1, M2, P2, M2, P1, M2, P3, C3F, P2, K4, P2, C3B, P3, M2, P1, M2, P2, M2, P1, M2, P1, K4, P2[3:4:5:6] sts, (P1, K1) twice.

18th row (P1, K1) twice, K2[3:4:5:6] sts, P4, K1, P2 tog, K1, P2 tog, K2, P2 tog, K1, P2 tog, K4, P2, K2, P4 tog, K2, P2, K4, P2 tog, K1, P2 tog, K2, P2 tog, K1, P2 tog, K1, P4, K2[3:4:5:6] sts, (K1, P1) twice.

19th row (K1, P1) twice, P2[3:4:5:6] sts, C4B, P1, M2, P1, M2, P1, B1, M2, P1, M2, P4, C3F, P3, C3B, P4, M2, P1, M2, B1, P1, M2, P1, M2, P1, C4F, P2[3:4:5:6] sts, (P1, K1) twice.

20th row As 4th.

21st row (K1, P1) twice, P2[3:4:5:6] sts, K4, P1, M2, P1, M2, P2, M2, P1, M2, P5, C3F, P1, C3B, P5, M2, P1, M2, P2, M2, P1, M2, P1, K4, P2[3:4:5:6] sts, (P1, K1) twice.

22nd row As 2nd.

23rd row (K1, P1) twice, P2[3:4:5:6] sts, K4, P1, M2, P1, M2, P2, M2, P1, M2, P6, K2, P1, K2, P6, M2, P1, M2, P2, M2, P1, M2, P1, K4, P2[3:4: 5:6] sts, (P1, K1) twice.

24th row (P1, K1) twice, K2[3:4:5:6] sts, P4, K1, P2 tog, K1, P2 tog, K2, P2 tog, K1, P2 tog, K6, P5, K6, P2 tog, K1, P2 tog, K2, P2 tog, K1, P2 tog, K1, P4, K2[3:4:5:6] sts, (K1, P1) twice.
These 24 rows form patt. Cont in patt until work measures 6in from beg, ending with a WS row.

Next row Inc in first st, P5[6:7:8:9] sts, patt to last 6[7:8:9:10] sts, P5[6:7:8:9] sts, inc in last st. 57[59:61:63:65] sts.
Keeping 7[8:9:10:11] sts at each end in reversed st st, cont in patt until work measures 24¾[25:25¼: 25½:25¾]in from beg, ending with a WS row.**

Shape neck
Next row Patt 20[21:22:23:24] sts, turn and leave rem sts on holder.
Dec one st at neck edge on next 3 rows, then dec one st at same edge on every alt row until 14[15:16: 17:18] sts rem. Cont without shaping until work measures 27[27¼:27½:27¾:28]in from beg, ending at armhole edge.

Shape shoulder
Cast off 7 sts at beg of next row. Work 1 row. Cast off rem 7[8:9:10:11] sts.
With RS of work facing, sl next 17 sts on to holder, rejoin yarn to rem sts and patt to end. Complete to match first side, reversing shaping.

Back panel
Work as given for front panel to **. Cont in patt until work measures same as front to shoulder, ending with a WS row.

Shape shoulders
Cast off at beg of next and every row 7 sts twice and 7[8:9:10:11] sts twice. Leave rem 29 sts on holder.

Side panel (make 2)
Using No.6 needles cast on 29[31:33:35:37] sts.
Work 4 rows K1, P1 rib, dec one st in centre of last row. 28[30:32:34:36] sts. Commence patt.
1st row (RS) (K1, P1) twice, P6[7:8:9:10] sts, M2, P1, M2, B1, P1, M2, P1, M2, P6[7:8:9:10] sts, (P1, K1) twice.

2nd row (P1, K1) twice, K6[7:8:9:10] sts, P2 tog, K1, P2 tog, K2, P2 tog, K1, P2 tog, K6[7:8:9:10] sts, (K1, P1) twice.

3rd row (K1, P1) twice, P6[7:8:9:10] sts, M2, P1, M2, P2, M2, P1, M2, P6[7:8:9:10] sts, (P1, K1) twice.
Rep 2nd and 3rd rows once more, then 2nd row once.

7th row (K1, P1) twice, P6[7:8:9:10] sts, M2, P1, M2, P1, B1, M2, P1, M2, P6[7:8:9:10] sts, (P1, K1) twice.
Rep 2nd and 3rd rows twice more, then 2nd row once.
These 12 rows form patt. Cont in patt until work measures 6in from beg, ending with a WS row.
Next row Inc in first st, P9[10:11:12:13] sts, patt 8, P9[10:11:12:13] sts, inc in last st. 30[32:34:36: 38] sts.
Keeping 11[12:13:14:15] sts in reversed st st at each end, cont in patt until work measures 8in from beg, ending with a RS row.

Shape sides
Next row K9[10:11:12:13] sts, sl 1, K1, psso, patt 8, K2 tog, K to end.
Work 1 row.
Next row K8[9:10:11:12] sts, sl 1, K1, psso, patt 8, K2 tog, K to end.
Work 1 row.
Cont dec in this way on next and every alt row until 12[14:16:18:20] sts rem. Cont without shaping until work measures 12½in from beg, ending with a RS row.
Next row K2[3:4:5:6] sts, pick up loop lying between sts and K tbl – called inc 1 –, patt 8, inc 1, K to end.
Work 3 rows.
Next row K3[4:5:6:7] sts, inc 1, patt 8, inc 1, K to end.
Work 3 rows.
Cont inc in this way on next and every 4th row until there are 26[28:30:32:34] sts. Cont without shaping until work measures 19in from beg, ending with a WS row.

Shape underarm
Next row Patt 9[10:10:11:11] sts, turn and leave rem sts on holder.
Dec one st at beg of next and at same edge on every row until all sts are worked off.
With RS of work facing, sl first 8[8:10:10:12] sts on holder, rejoin yarn to rem sts and patt to end.
Dec one st at end of next and at same edge on every row until all sts are worked off.

Armbands
Press pieces under a damp cloth with a warm iron.
Join side panels to back and front panels from top of ribbing of slits. Using No.8 needles and with RS of work facing, beg at shoulder and K up 43[45:47: 49:51] sts down armhole, K across sts on holder, dec one st in centre, and K up 43[45:47:49:51] sts to shoulder. 93[97:103:107:113] sts. Work 4 rows K1, P1 rib, working 3 sts tog in centre of every alt row. Cast off in rib, still dec at centre.

Neckband
Join right shoulder and armband seam. Using No.8 needles and with RS of work facing K across 29 sts at centre back neck inc in first st, K up 18[20:22: 24:26] sts down front neck, K17 sts on holder and K up 19[21:23:25:27] sts up front neck. 84[88:92: 96:100] sts. Work 4 rows K1, P1 rib. Cast off in rib.

To make up
Join left shoulder and armband seam. Press seams.

Make belt
Cut 12 lengths of yarn 90in long. (Take 2 ends tog and knot at one end, thread on bead) 6 times. Tie tog 10in from beaded end. Form into 3 strands and plait to within 16in of other end. Knot tog at end of plait, (take 2 ends tog, thread on bead and knot at end) 6 times. Trim ends.

42,43

A button-to-the-neck cardigan and pull-on jersey, both featuring a traditional Fair Isle yoke. Make them up in soft Shetland yarn, in a host of colourways.

Knit
Sizes 34-40 inch bust.

44

*A casual
car coat, with
comfortable raglan
sleeves and roomy
pockets. Contrasting
bands of colour on all
edgings make it
come alive!*

*Knit
Sizes 34-42 inch bust.*

45

*A casual classic that's
easy to wear.
This charming cardigan
suit has a wide-ribbed
button-through jacket
and plain stocking
stitch skirt.*

*Knit
Sizes 34-40 inch bust.*

46

Right Soft and feminine—that's how you'll feel in this mohair sleeveless top with face-flattering cowl neck.

Knit Sizes 32-40 inch bust.

47

Centre A delightful diagonal-patterned classic with short sleeves. Wear it under a suit, or as a top over a skirt or slacks.

Knit Sizes 32-40 inch bust.

48

Far right A neatly fitting jersey worked in double rib. The v-neck insert and high warm polo collar are worked separately and then sewn into place.

Knit Sizes 32-38 inch bust.

49

Elegant evenings in this delicate lacy cardigan with high polo collar. Wear it to button either at the front or back.

*Knit
Sizes 34-38 inch bust.*

50

Sparkle all through the evening in this glamorous two-piece cocktail suit, worked in glitter yarn in simple stocking stitch.

*Knit
Sizes 34-42 inch bust.*

51

Two versions of an Aran cardigan for father and son. The boy's version has saddle top shoulders and the man's has raglan sleeves

Knit
Boy's to fit 26 [28:30] inch chest
Man's to fit 38 [40:42] inch chest

52

Cardigan worked in an unusual arrowhead pattern with a zip fastening and bands of two contrast colours on the welt, cuffs and collar

Knit
Sizes to fit 36 [38 : 40 : 42] inch chest

53

Family jerseys using variations of cables and moss stitch.
Jersey A is shown on the smaller child, jersey B on the woman and jersey C on the man and the older child
Knit
Sizes to fit 24 [26 : 28 : 30 : 32 : 34 : 36 : 38 : 40 : 42 : 44]. inch chest

54

Chunky Aran cardigan with deep pockets and raglan sleeves

*Knit
Sizes to fit 34 [36:38: 40:42:44] inch chest*

55

Cardigan with neatly fitting shawl collar, worked in an unusual check pattern in two colours. The collar and all edges are worked in single rib

*Knit
Sizes to fit 38 [40:42:44: 46] inch chest*

56

*Crisply textured
Sleeveless cardigans
for either a man
or woman*

*Knit
Sizes to fit 32 [34:36:
38, 40, 42, 44] inch chest.*

57

*Cardigans, buttoned to
the neck with picot-
trimmed mandarin collar,
for mother and daughter.
Simple crossed basket
weave stitch gives an
interesting finish.*

*Knit
Sizes: to fit 24 [27:30:
33:36] inch chest.*

58

Snug ribbed playsuit and matching hat. Wear it on its own or under trousers or pinafore dress for extra warmth.

Knit
Sizes: to fit 22 [24] inch chest.

59

Warm and practical suit teamed with matching beret and socks worked in distinctive lobster claw stitch.

Knit
Sizes: to fit 28 [31:34] inch chest.

60

Cool, short sleeved
summer dress. The skirt
is in stocking stitch
and the bodice is worked
in cable panels.

Knit
Sizes: to fit 22 [24:26:
28] inch chest.

61

Casual wrapover judo
dressing gown, suitable
for a boy or girl. This
is worked in a simple
broken rib stitch and
edges are in a contrasting
colour.

Knit
Sizes: to fit 24 [26:28]
inch chest.

Ideas for the home

62

For knitters in a hurry—
a plaid blanket to make
in record time with one
inch knitting pins and a
jumbo hook.

Knit and crochet
Size: 72 × 71 inches.

63

*Spherical lampshade
shows off the decorative
quality of an intricate
stitch. You may prefer
to cover the frame with
muslin to diffuse the
light before drawing on
the knitted cover.*

*Knit
Shade diameter: 22
inches.*

64

Big bold bunny makes
a jolly nightdress case
or soft washable toy—
(remember to unstitch
the felt features before
washing).

Knit
Length : 15 inches.

65

Choose chevron stripes
to give a hot water
bottle cover a bright,
fashionable look.

Knit and crochet
Size : $11\frac{1}{2} \times 10\frac{1}{2}$
inches.

66

This dog's jacket is
definitely not designed
for Great Danes, so
check his chest
measurement before you
start knitting!

Knit
Chest : $13\frac{1}{2}$ ($17\frac{3}{4}$: $21\frac{1}{4}$)
inches.

67

Brighten up the
bathroom with a
facecloth, embroidered
with the owner's initial.

Knit
Size : 12 inches square.

68

Left: bright, Mexican pinks and alternating rib direction give this bedspread made in easy ribbed squares a glamorous look. Try it in a mixture of oak brown, camel and beige for a cooler effect.

Knit
Size: 30 × 40 inches, or as required.

69

This time, a bedspread in boldly contrasting patches, trimmed with pierrot pompons at every alternate join.

Knit
Size: 50 × 80 inches.

70,71

A 'Fair Isle' toaster cover (to keep the dust out) and matching pot holder in washable cotton yarn.

Knit
Toaster cover:
9 × 7 × 5 inches.
Pot holder: 30 inches long.

72,73

Patchwork cosies for coffee pots (left) and the traditional tea pot (right). The joining trim on both is crocheted.

Knit and crochet
Coffee cosy: 8 inches high.
Tea cosy: 6½ inches high.

74,75

Two covers, designed to fit over square foam rubber cushions and be used as floor cushions or footstools.

Knit
Size: 18 inches square, 3½ inches deep.

Instructions for designs 42-75

42 Cardigan with Fair Isle yoke

Sizes
To fit 34[36:38:40]in bust
Length to shoulder, 21½[22:22½:23]in
Sleeve seam, 16½[17½:18½:19½]in
The figures in brackets [] refer to the 36, 38 and 40in sizes respectively

Tension
6½ sts and 8½ rows to 1in over st st worked on No.10 needles

Materials
H & O Shetland Fleece distributed by Templetons 10[11:12:13] balls main shade, A
1 ball each contrast colours B, C, D, E and F
1 ball of additional contrast colour, if required, instead of A as background colour of yoke
One pair No.10 needles, one pair No.12 needles
Five stitch holders
Ten buttons

Back
Using No.12 needles and A, cast on 109[113:117: 121] sts. Work in K1, P1 rib for 4in. Change to No.10 needles. Beg with a K row cont in st st, inc one st at each end of 7th and every foll 8th row until there are 115[121:127:133] sts. Cont without shaping until work measures 15in from beg, ending with a P row.

Shape armholes
Cast off 6 sts at beg of next 2 rows. 103[109:115: 121] sts.

36, 38 and 40in sizes only
Dec one st at each end of next and every alt row until 103 sts rem, ending with a P row.

All sizes
Next row K2 tog, K33 sts, K2 tog, turn and leave rem 66 sts on holder.
Complete this side first. Dec one st at each end of every K row until 3 sts rem, ending with a P row.
Next row K2 tog, K1.
Next row P2 sts.
Next row K2 tog and fasten off.
With RS of work facing, sl first 29 sts on to holder and leave for yoke, rejoin yarn to rem 37 sts, K2 tog, K33 sts, K2 tog. Complete to match first side.

Left front
Using No.12 needles and A, cast on 50[52:54:56] sts. Work 4in K1, P1 rib. Change to No.10 needles. Beg with a K row cont in st st, inc one st at beg of 7th and every foll 8th row until there are 57[60:63: 66] sts. Cont without shaping until work measures same as back to underarm, ending at armhole edge.

Shape armhole
Cast off 6 sts at beg of next row. 51[54:57:60] sts.

36, 38 and 40in sizes only
Next row P to end.
Next row K2 tog, K to end.
Rep last 2 rows until 51 sts rem for front yoke.

All sizes
Next row P14 sts and leave on holder, P37 sts.
Next row K2 tog, K to last 2 sts, K2 tog.
Next row P to end.
Rep last 2 rows until 3 sts rem. Complete as given for back.

Right front
Work as given for left front, reversing all shaping.

Sleeves
Using No.12 needles and A, cast on 58[60:62:64] sts. Work 4½in K1, P1 rib. Change to No.10 needles. Beg with a K row cont in st st, inc one st at

each end of 5th and every foll 6th row until there are 84[90:96:102] sts. Cont in st st without shaping until sleeve measures 18½[19½:20½:21½]in from beg, or required length to underarm allowing 2in for turn back cuff, ending with a P row.

Shape top
Cast off 6 sts at beg of next 2 rows. 72[78:84:90] sts.
Next row K2 tog, K to last 2 sts, K2 tog.
Next row P to end.
Rep last 2 rows until 36 sts rem. Leave sts on holder for yoke.

Yoke
Join raglan seams. Using No.10 needles, A and with RS of work facing, K14 sts from right front holder, K up 28[31:34:37] sts up right neck edge, K36 sts from sleeve holder, K up 28[31:34:37] sts down right back neck, K29 sts from centre back holder, K up 28[31:34:37] sts up left back neck, K36 sts from sleeve holder, K up 28[31:34:37] sts down left front neck and K14 sts from left front holder. 241[253:265:277] sts.
Next row P to end, inc one st at centre back. 242[254:266:278] sts.
Next row Work from Chart 1 as foll, *K2 B, K2 A, rep from * to last 2 sts, K2 B.
Next row *P2 A, P2 B, rep from * to last 2 sts, P2 A.
Using A and beg with a K row work 2 rows st st, dec one st at centre back. 241[253:265:277] sts.
Cont in Fair Isle patt, working from charts as foll:

34, 36 and 38in sizes only
Omit first 18[12:6] sts of Chart 2 and beg on 19th [13th:7th] st of Chart 2, K rem 7[13:19] sts of Chart 2, K full patt of 42 sts of Charts 3 and 2 five times, then K17 sts of Chart 3 once, then K first 7[13:19] sts of Chart 2.
Cont working rem 24 rows of Charts, taking care to beg K rows on the 19th[13th:7th] sts and all P rows on the 7th[13th:19th] sts at front edge.

40in size only
Working from Charts, K 1st row of Chart 2, foll by 1st row of Chart 3 right across work, ending with 25 sts of Chart 2.

All sizes
Note that the dec on Chart 3 on 9th and foll alt rows are made by K first 2 sts tbl.
When 25 rows of Charts have been worked, break off all colours except A and the colour used for Chart 1.
Next row Using A, P to end.
Next row Using A, K10[7:4:1] sts, *K2 tog, K1, rep from * to last 9[6:3:0] sts, K2 tog, K7[K2 tog, K4: K2 tog, K1: K0]. 102[108:114:120] sts.
Beg with a P row work 2 rows of Chart 1. Cont using A only.
Next row P to end.
Next row K1[2:2:2] sts, *K2 tog, K3, rep from * to last 1[1:2:3] sts, K1[1:2:3]. 82[87:92:97] sts.
Change to No.12 needles. Work 2in K1, P1 rib. Cast off loosely in rib. Fold ribbing in half to WS and sl st cast off edge to 1st row of ribbing.

Button band
Using No.12 needles and A, cast on 11 sts.
1st row *K1, P1, rep from * to last st, K1.
Rep this row until band is same length as front edge when slightly stretched. Cast off. Sew on button band and mark positions for 10 buttons, first to come ½in above cast on edge and last to come ½in below cast off edge.

Buttonhole band
Work as given for button band, making buttonholes as markers are reached, as foll:
Next row Moss st 4, cast off 3 sts, moss st 4.
Next row Work in moss st to end, casting on 3 sts above those cast off in previous row.

To make up
Press each piece under a damp cloth with a warm iron. Join side and sleeve seams.
Press seams.
Sew on buttons.

43 Jersey with Fair Isle yoke

Sizes
To fit 34[36:38:40]in bust
Length to shoulder, 21½[22:22½:23]in
Long sleeve seam, 16½[17½:18½:19½]in
Short sleeve seam, 4½[5:5½:6]in
The figures in brackets [] refer to the 36, 38 and 40in sizes respectively

Tension
As given for cardigan (design 42)

Materials
H & O Shetland Fleece distributed by Templetons
Long sleeved version 10[11:11:12] balls main shade, A
Short sleeved version 6[7:8:9] balls main shade, A
See materials for cardigan for contrast colours
One pair No.10 needles
One pair No.12 needles
One set of 4 No.10 needles pointed at both ends
One 4½in zip fastener

Front
Work as given for back of cardigan.

Back
Using No.12 needles and A, cast on 108[112:116: 120] sts and work as given for cardigan back until there are 114[120:126:132] sts. Cont without shaping until work measures 15in from beg, ending with a P row.

Shape armholes
Work as given for cardigan back until 102 sts rem. Work shaping as given for cardigan back, leaving 28 sts for yoke.

Short sleeves
Using No.12 needles and A, cast on 78[80:82:84] sts. Work 1in K1, P1 rib. Change to No.10 needles. Beg with a K row cont in st st, inc one st at each end of 3rd and every foll 4th row until there are 84[90:96:102] sts. Cont without shaping until sleeve measures 4½[5:5½:6]in from beg, ending with a P row.

Shape top
Work as given for top of cardigan sleeve.

Long sleeves
Work as given for sleeves of cardigan.

Yoke
Join raglan seams. With RS of work facing leave first 14 sts of back on holder. Using first needle of set of 4 No.10 needles, A, beg at centre back and K rem 14 sts of back, K up 28[31:34:37] sts up left back neck, K36 sts from sleeve, using 2nd needle K up 28[31:34:37] sts down left front neck, K29 sts from centre front holder, K up 28[31:34:37] sts up right neck, using 3rd needle K36 sts from other sleeve, K up 28[31:34:37] sts down right back neck, then K rem 14 sts from centre back neck. 241[253:265:277] sts.
Work as given for cardigan yoke until neckband is reached. Change to No.12 needles. Work 8 rows K1, P1 rib.
Cast off loosely in rib.

To make up
Press as given for cardigan. Join side and sleeve seams. Press seams. Sew back opening leaving 4½in open for zip. Sew in zip.

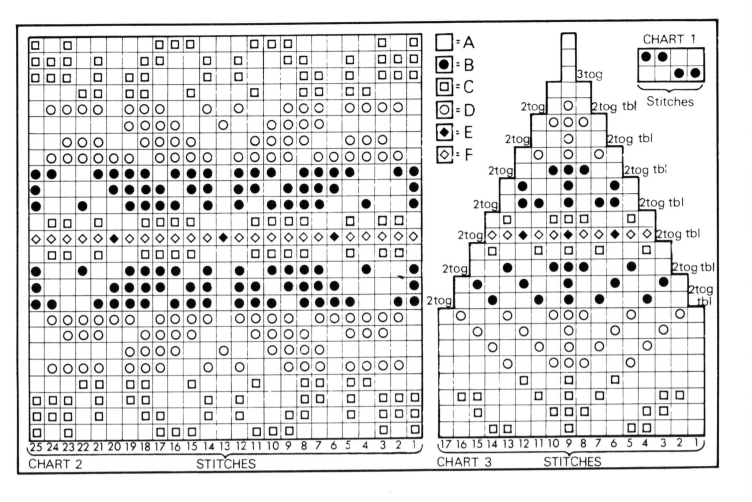

CHART 1 — Stitches

□ = A
● = B
◨ = C
◉ = D
◆ = E
◇ = F

CHART 2 STITCHES
25 24 23 22 21 20 19 18 17 16 15 14 13 12 11 10 9 8 7 6 5 4 3 2 1

CHART 3 STITCHES
17 16 15 14 13 12 11 10 9 8 7 6 5 4 3 2 1

(Chart 3 decrease markings: 3tog; 2tog / 2tog tbl; 2tog / 2tog tbl; 2tog / 2tog tbl; 2tog / 2tog tbl; 2tog / 2tog tbl; 2tog / 2tog tbl; 2tog / 2tog tbl)

Casual car coat

Sizes
To fit 34[36:38:40:42]in bust
36[38:40:42:44]in hips
Length to shoulder, 33[33½:34:34½:35]in, adjustable.

Sleeve seam, 16½[17:17:17½:18]in, adjustable
The figures in brackets [] refer to the 36, 38, 40 and 42in sizes respectively

Tension
4 sts and 5 rows to 1in over st st worked on No.5 needles

Materials
18 [19:20:21:22] balls Listers Prema Bulky
Knitting in main shade, A
1 ball of contrast colour, B
One pair No.5 needles
One pair No.7 needles
7 buttons

Back
Using No.7 needles and A, cast on 107[111:115:119:123] sts.
1st row K1, *P1, K1, rep from * to end.
2nd row P1, *K1, P1, rep from * to end.
Rep these 2 rows twice more. Change to No.5 needles. Beg with a K row cont in st st for 2½in, ending with a P row.
Shape darts
Next row K1, K2 tog, K19[20:21:22:23] sts, sl 1, K1, psso, K59[61:63:65:67] sts, K2 tog, K19[20:21:22:23] sts, sl 1, K1, psso, K1.
Beg with a P row work 11 rows st st.
Next row K1, K2 tog, K18[19:20:21:22] sts, sl 1, K1, psso, K57[59:61:63:65] sts, K2 tog, K18[19:20:21:22] sts, sl 1, K1, psso, K1.
Beg with a P row work 11 rows st st.
Cont dec in this way on next and every foll 12th row until 75[79:83:87:91] sts rem. Cont without shaping until work measures 25in from beg, or required length to underarm.
End with a P row.
Shape armholes
Cast off 3 sts at beg of next 2 rows.
Next row K3 sts, K2 tog, K to last 5 sts, sl 1, K1, psso, K3 sts.

Next row P to end.
Rep last 2 rows until 29[29:31:31:33] sts rem, ending with a K row. **Join in B and change to No.7 needles. P 1 row, then work 1st row of rib. Join in A. P 1 row, then rib 6 rows. Join in B. K 1 row.
Cast off loosely in rib. **

Left front
Using No.5 needles and A, cast on 23 sts for pocket lining. Beg with a K row work 4in st st, ending with a P row. Leave sts on holder. Using No.7 needles and A, cast on 53[55:57:59:61] sts. Work 6 rows rib as given for back. Change to No.5 needles. Beg with a K row cont in st st for 2½in.
End with a P row.
Shape darts
Next row K1, K2 tog, K19[20:21:22:23] sts, sl 1, K1, psso, K to end
Beg with a P row work 11 rows st st.
Next row K1, K2 tog, K18[19:20:21:22] sts, sl 1, K1, psso, K to end.
Beg with a P row work 11 rows st st.
Cont dec in this way on next and every foll 12th row until work measures 8in from beg, ending with a P row.
Place pocket
Next row K to last 33[33:34:34:35] sts, sl next 23 sts on to holder, K across pocket lining sts, K to end.
Cont to dec on every foll 12th row as before until 37[39:41:43:45] sts rem. Cont without shaping until work measures 10 rows less than back to underarm.
End with a P row.
Shape front edge
Next row K to last 3 sts, K2 tog, K1.
Beg with a P row work 5 rows st st.
Next row K to last 3 sts, K2 tog, K1.
Beg with a P row work 3 rows st st.

Shape armhole
Next row Cast off 3 sts, K to end.
Next row P to end.
Next row K3 sts, K2 tog, K to last 3 sts, K2 tog, K1.
Cont to dec at front edge on every foll 6th row 7[7:8:8:9] times more, *at the same time* dec at raglan edge on every alt row until 4 sts rem, ending with a P row.
Next row K2 sts, K2 tog.
Next row P3 sts.
Next row K1 st, K2 tog.
Next row P2 tog. Fasten off.

Right front
Work as given for left front, reversing position of pocket and all shaping.

Sleeves
Using No.7 needles and A, cast on 33[35:37:39:41] sts. Work 4in rib as given for back, ending with a 2nd row. Change to No.5 needles. Beg with a K row cont in st st, inc one st at each end of first and every foll 6th row until there are 53[57:59:63:65] sts. Cont without shaping until sleeve measures 16½[17:17:17½:18]in from beg, or required length to underarm ending with a P row. Mark each end of last row with coloured thread. Work 4 more rows.
Shape top
Next row K3 sts, K2 tog, K to last 5 sts, sl 1, K1, psso, K3 sts.
Next row P to end.
Rep last 2 rows until 7 sts rem, ending with a K row. Work as given for back from ** to **

Left front band
Using No.7 needles and A, with RS of work facing K up 125[127:129:131:133] sts along front edge. Work as given for back from ** to **.
Mark positions for 7 buttons, first to come 1½in from lower edge and last to come ½in below beg of front shaping, with 5 more evenly spaced between.

Right front band
Work as given for left front band, making buttonholes on 3rd row of rib in A as foll: Rib to first marker, (cast off 2 sts, rib to next marker) 6 times, cast off 2 sts, rib to end.
Next row Rib to end, casting on 2 sts above those cast off in previous row.

Pocket tops
Using No.7 needles and with WS of work facing, sl 23 sts from holder on to needle and work as given for back from ** to **, inc one st at each end of first row.

To make up
Press each piece under a damp cloth with a warm iron. Join raglan seams, sewing last 4 rows of sleeves to cast off sts at underarm. Join side and sleeve seams. Sew down pocket tops and pocket linings. Press all seams. Sew on buttons.

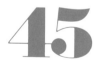

45 *Casual suit*

Sizes
To fit 34[36:38:40]in bust
36[38:40:42]in hips
Jacket length to shoulder, 21[21½:22:22½]in
Sleeve seam, 16½[17:17½:18]in
Skirt length, 19½[20:20½:21]in
The figures in brackets [] refer to the 36, 38 and 40in sizes respectively
Tension
5 sts and 7 rows to 1in over rib worked on No.9 needles

Materials
18[19:21:23] balls Patons Camelot
One pair No.9 needles
One pair No.11 needles
Five buttons
Waist length of elastic
One 7in zip fastener

Jacket back
Using No.11 needles cast on 87[92:97:102] sts.
1st row P2, *K3, P2, rep from * to end.
2nd row K2, *P3, K2, rep from * to end.
These 2 rows form patt. Cont in patt until work measures 1½in from beg. Change to No.9 needles and cont in patt until work measures 14in from beg, ending with a 2nd row.
Shape armholes
Cast off 5 sts at beg of next 2 rows. Dec one st at each end of next and foll 4[5:6:7] alt rows. 67[70:73:76] sts. Cont without shaping until armholes measure 7[7½:8:8½]in from beg, ending with a WS row.
Shape shoulders
Cast off at beg of next and every row 7 sts 4 times and 5[6:7:8] sts twice. Cast off rem 29[30:31:32] sts.

Jacket left front
Using No.9 needles cast on 21 sts for pocket lining. Beg with a K row work 4in st st, ending with a K row.
Next row P3 sts, *P twice into next st, P2, rep from * to end. 27 sts. Leave sts on holder.
Using No.11 needles cast on 51[54:56:59] sts.
1st row *P2, K3, rep from * to last 11[9:11:9] sts, P2[0:2:0] sts, K4, sl 1, K4.
2nd row P9 sts, K2[0:2:0] sts, *P3, K2, rep from * to end.
Rep these 2 rows for 1½in. Change to No.9 needles and cont in patt until work measures 5in from beg, ending with a WS row.
Place pocket
Next row Rib 10 sts, sl next 27 sts on to holder for pocket top, rib across sts of pocket lining, rib to end. Cont in patt until work measures same as back to underarm, ending with a WS row.
Shape armhole and front edge
Next row Cast off 5 sts, patt to last 11 sts, K2 tog, K4, sl 1, K4.
Next row Patt to end.
Next row K2 tog, patt to end.
Next row P9 sts, P2 tog, patt to end.
Cont dec at armhole edge on every alt row 4[5:6:7] times more, *at the same time* cont to dec at front edge on every 3rd row until 28[29:30:31] sts rem. Cont without shaping until armhole measures same as back to shoulder, ending at armhole edge.
Shape shoulder
Cast off at beg of next and every alt row 7 sts twice and 5[6:7:8] sts once. Cont on rem 9 sts until strip is long enough to reach centre back neck. Cast off.

Right front
Work pocket lining as given for left front.
Using No.11 needles cast on 51[54:56:59] sts.
1st row K4, sl 1, K4, P2[0:2:0] sts, *K3, P2, rep from * to end.
2nd row *K2, P3, rep from * to last 11[9:11:9] sts, K2[0:2:0] sts, P9.
Cont as given for left front until work measures 2½in from beg, ending with a WS row.
Next row (buttonhole row) K1, cast off 2 sts, K1, sl 1, K1, cast off 2 sts, patt to end.
Next row Patt to end, casting on 2 sts above those cast off in previous row.
Complete to match left front, reversing position of pocket and all shaping and making 4 more buttonholes in same way at intervals of 2½in from previous one.

Sleeves
Using No.11 needles cast on 32[37:37:42] sts. Work in rib as given for back for 1½in. Change to No.9 needles and cont in rib, inc one st at each end of next and every foll 6th row until there are 62[67:71:74] sts. Cont without shaping until sleeve measures 16½[17:17½:18]in from beg, ending with a WS row.
Shape top
Cast off 5 sts at beg of next 2 rows. Dec one st at each end of next and foll 6[8:10:11] alt rows. Cast off at beg of next and every row 2 sts 8 times and 3 sts 4 times. Cast off rem 10[11:11:12] sts.

Pocket tops
Using No.11 needles and with RS of work facing, work across pocket top sts, as foll: K3 sts, *K2 tog, K2, rep from * to end. 21 sts. Beg with a P row work 4 rows st st.
Next row K all sts tbl to mark fold line.
Beg with a K row work 4 rows st st. Cast off.

To make up
Do not press. Join shoulder seams. Set in sleeves. Join side and sleeve seams. Join ends of front band. Fold front bands in half to WS and sl st down and sew to back neck. Neaten buttonholes. Sew down pocket tops and pocket linings. Sew on buttons.

Skirt back
Using No.11 needles cast on 66[70:74:78] sts and beg at waist.
1st row K2, *P2, K2, rep from * to end.
2nd row P2, *K2, P2, rep from * to end.
Rep these 2 rows for 1¼in, ending with a 2nd row. Change to No.9 needles. Beg with a K row cont in st st for 4 rows.
Shape darts
Next row K21[22:23:24] sts, K twice into next st, K24[26:26:28] sts, K twice into next st, K21[22:23:24] sts.
Beg with a P row work 3 rows st st.
Next row K21[22:23:24] sts, K twice into next st, K24[26:28:30] sts, K twice into next st, K21[22:23:24] sts.
Beg with a P row work 3 rows st st.
Cont to inc in this way on next and every foll 4th row until there are 96[100:104:108] sts, then on every foll 8th row until work measures 19½[20:20½:21]in from beg, ending with a K row. Change to No.11 needles.
Next row K all sts tbl to form hemline.
Beg with a K row work 1¼in st st. Cast off loosely.

Skirt front
Work as given for back.

To make up
Do not press. Join side seams leaving 7in open at top of left seam for zip. Sew in zip. Sew elastic inside waist edge with casing st. Turn hem to WS and sl st down.

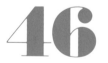

46 *Sleeveless mohair jersey with cowl neck*

Sizes
To fit 32[34:36:38:40]in bust
Length to shoulder, 20½[21:21½:22:22½]in adjustable
The figures in brackets [] refer to the 34, 36, 38 and 40in sizes respectively
Tension
4 sts and 5 rows to 1in over rib worked on No.2 needles
Materials
7[8:9:9:10] balls Jaeger Mohair-Spun
One pair No.2 needles
One pair No.9 needles
One No.4·50 (ISR) crochet hook

Back

Using No.9 needles cast on 67[71:75:79:83] sts.
1st row K1, *P1, K1, rep from * to end.
2nd row P1, *K1, P1, rep from * to end.
Rep these 2 rows twice more.
Change to No.2 needles. Cont in rib until work measures 14in from beg, or required length to underarm ending with a WS row.

Shape armholes

Cast off 5 sts at beg of next 2 rows. Dec one st at each end of next and foll 2[2:3:3:4] alt rows. 51[55:57:61:63] sts. Cont without shaping until armholes measure 6[6½:7:7½:8]in from beg, ending with a WS row.

Shape neck

Next row Rib 17[18:19:20:21] sts, cast off 17[19:19:21:21] sts, rib to end.
Complete this side first. Dec one st at neck edge on next and foll 2 alt rows. Cast off rem sts.
With WS of work facing, rejoin yarn to rem sts and complete to match first side, reversing shaping.

Front

Work as given for back.

Collar

Using No.9 needles cast on 99[101:103:105:107] sts. Work 6 rows rib as given for back. Change to No.2 needles and cont in rib until work measures 6½in from beg. Cast off very loosely in rib.

To make up

Do not press. Join shoulder and side seams. Join collar seam, then sew round neck with seam to centre back. Using No.4·50 (ISR) hook work a row of dc round each armhole.

47 Diagonal patterned jersey

Sizes

To fit 32[34:36:38:40]in bust
Length to shoulder, 22[22½:23:23½:24]in
Sleeve seam, 6in
The figures in brackets [] refer to the 34, 36, 38 and 40in sizes respectively

Tension

7 sts and 9 rows to 1in over st st worked on No.10 needles

Materials

9[10:11:12:13] balls Robin Casino Crepe 4 ply
One pair No.10 needles
One pair No.12 needles
Set of 4 No.12 needles pointed at both ends

Back

Using No.12 needles cast on 110[118:126:134:142] sts.
1st row K2, *P2, K2, rep from * to end.
2nd row P2, *K2, P2, rep from * to end.
Rep these 2 rows until work measures 2in from beg, ending with a 1st row. Change to No.10 needles. Beg with a P row cont in st st until work measures 15½in from beg, ending with a P row.

Shape armholes

Cast off at beg of next and every row 6 sts twice and 2[3:3:4:4] sts twice. Dec one st at each end of next and foll 3[4:5:6:7] alt rows. 86[90:96:100:106] sts. Cont without shaping until armholes measure 6½[7:7½:8:8½]in from beg, ending with a P row.

Shape shoulders

Cast off at beg of next and every row 6[6:7:8:8] sts 6 times and 6[8:7:6:8] sts twice. Leave rem 38[38:40:40:42] sts on holder.

Front

Using No.12 needles cast on 110[118:126:134:142]

---

sts. Work in rib as given for back for 2in, ending with a 1st row and inc 10[10:11:11:9] sts evenly across last row. 120[128:137:145:151] sts.
Change to No.10 needles. Commence patt.
1st row (WS) P18[22:16:20:23] sts, *(P1, K1) 7 times, P1, K6, rep from * 3[3:4:4:4] times more, P to end.
2nd row K18[22:16:20:23] sts, *P5, yrn, P1, (K1, P1) 6 times, K first and 3rd sts on left hand needle tog and let first st drop off needle, P 2nd st then let 2nd and 3rd sts drop off needle – called Tw3 –, rep from * 3[3:4:4:4] times more, K to end.
3rd row P18[22:16:20:23] sts, K1, *rib 15, K6, rep from * 2[2:3:3:3] times more, rib 15, K5, P to end.
4th row K18[22:16:20:23] sts, P4, yrn, P1, *rib 12, Tw3, P5, yrn, P1, rep from * 2[2:3:3:3] times more, rib 12, Tw3, P1, K to end.
5th row P18[22:16:20:23] sts, K2, *rib 15, K6, rep from * 2[2:3:3:3] times more, rib 15, K4, P to end.
6th row K18[22:16:20:23] sts, P3, yrn, P1, *rib 12, Tw3, P5, yrn, P1, rep from * 2[2:3:3:3] times more, rib 12, Tw3, P2, K to end.
7th row P18[22:16:20:23] sts, K3, *rib 15, K6, rep from * 2[2:3:3:3] times more, rib 15, K3, P to end.
8th row K18[22:16:20:23] sts, P2, yrn, P1, *rib 12, Tw3, P5, yrn, P1, rep from * 2[2:3:3:3] times more, rib 12, Tw3, P3, K to end.
9th row P18[22:16:20:23] sts, K4, *rib 15, K6, rep from * 2[2:3:3:3] times more, rib 15, K2, P to end.
10th row K18[22:16:20:23] sts, P1, yrn, P1, *rib 12, Tw3, P5, yrn, P1, rep from * 2[2:3:3:3] times more, rib 12, Tw3, P4, K to end.
11th row P18[22:16:20:23] sts, K5, *rib 15, K6, rep from * 2[2:3:3:3] times more, rib 15, K1, P to end.
12th row K18[22:16:20:23] sts, yrn, P1, *rib 12, Tw3, P5, yrn, P1, rep from * 2[2:3:3:3] times more, rib 12, Tw3, P5, yon, K to end.
13th row P19[23:17:21:24] sts, *K6, rib 15, rep from * 3[3:4:4:4] times more, K to end.
14th row K18[22:16:20:23] sts, *rib 12, Tw3, P5, yrn, P1, rep from * 3[3:4:4:4] times more, K to end.
15th row P19[23:17:21:24] sts, K1, P1, *K6, rib 15, rep from * 2[2:3:3:3] times more, K6, rib 13, P to end.
16th row K18[22:16:20:23] sts, rib 10, Tw3, *P5, yrn, P1, rib 12, Tw3, rep from * 2[2:3:3:3] times more, P5, yrn, P1, K1, P1, K to end.
17th row P19[23:17:21:24]sts, (K1, P1) twice, *K6, rib 15, rep from * 2[2:3:3:3] times more, K6, rib 11, P to end.
18th row K18[22:16:20:23] sts, rib 8, Tw3, *P5, yrn, P1, rib 12, Tw3, rep from * 2[2:3:3:3] times more, P5, yrn, P1, rib 4, K to end.
19th row P19[23:17:21:24] sts, rib 6, *K6, rib 15, rep from * 2[2:3:3:3] times more, K6, rib 9, P to end.
20th row K18[22:16:20:23] sts, rib 6, Tw3, *P5, yrn, P1, rib 12, Tw3, rep from * 2[2:3:3:3] times more, P5, yrn, P1, rib 6, K to end.
21st row P19[23:17:21:24] sts, rib 8, *K6, rib 15, rep from * 2[2:3:3:3] times more, K6, rib 7, P to end.
22nd row K18[22:16:20:23] sts, rib 4, Tw3, *P5, yrn, P1, rib 12, Tw3, rep from * 2[2:3:3:3] times more, P5, yrn, P1, rib 8, K to end.
23rd row P19[23:17:21:24] sts, rib 10, *K6, rib 15, rep from * 2[2:3:3:3] times more, K6, rib 5, P to end.
24th row K18[22:16:20:23] sts, rib 2, Tw3, *P5, yrn, P1, rib 12, Tw3, rep from * 2[2:3:3:3] times more, P5, yrn, P1, rib 10, K to end.
25th row P19[23:17:21:24] sts, rib 12, *K6, rib 15, rep from * 2[2:3:3:3] times more, K6, rib 3, P to end.
26th row K18[22:16:20:23] sts, Tw3, *P5, yrn, P1, rib 12, Tw3, rep from * 2[2:3:3:3] times more, P5, yrn, P1, rib 12, K to end.

27th row P19[23:17:21:24] sts, rib 14, *K6, rib 15, rep from * 2[2:3:3:3] times more, K6, P1, P to end.
28th row K18[22:16:20:23] sts, P2 tog, P4, yrn, P1, *rib 12, Tw3, P5, yrn, P1, rep from * 2[2:3:3:3] times more, rib 12, Tw3, K to end.
Rows 3 to 28 form patt. Cont in patt until work measures same as back to underarm, ending with a WS row.

Shape armholes

Keeping patt correct, cast off at each end of next and every row 6 sts twice and 2[3:3:4:4] sts twice. Dec one st at each end of next and foll 3[4:5:6:7] alt rows. 96[100:107:111:115] sts. Note that when working patt between 12th and 27th rows there will be one more st. Cont without shaping until armholes measure 4½[5:5½:6:6½]in from beg, ending with a WS row.

Shape neck

Next row Patt 37[39:41:43:45] sts, turn and leave rem sts on holder.
Cast off 2 sts at beg of next and foll 2 alt rows, then dec one st at neck edge on next 4 alt rows. Cont without shaping until armhole measures same as back to shoulder, ending at armhole edge.

Shape shoulder

Cast off 6[7:7:8:9] sts at beg of next and foll 2 alt rows. Work 1 row. Cast off rem 9[8:10:9:8] sts.
With RS of work facing, sl first 22[22:25:25:27] sts on holder, rejoin yarn to rem sts and patt to end, noting that when working patt between 12th and 27th rows there will be one more st. Complete to match first side, reversing shaping.

Sleeves

Using No.12 needles cast on 66[66:70:70:74] sts. Work 2½in rib as given for back, ending with a 2nd row and inc one st at each end of last row on 34 and 38in sizes only. 66[68:70:72:74] sts. Change to No.10 needles. Beg with a K row cont in st st, inc one st at each end of 5th and every foll 6th row until there are 72[74:76:78:80] sts. Cont without shaping until sleeve measures 6in from beg, ending with a P row.

Shape top

Cast off 6 sts at beg of next 2 rows. Dec one st at each end of next and every alt row until 34 sts rem. Cast off at beg of next and every row 2 sts 6 times, 3 sts twice and 4 sts twice. Cast off rem 8 sts.

Neckband

Join shoulder seams. Using set of 4 No.12 needles and with RS of work facing, K across sts on back neck holder, K up 22 sts down side of neck, K across sts on front neck holder dec one st in centre on 36, 38 and 40in sizes only, then K up 22 sts up other side of neck. 104[104:108:108:112] sts. Note that if sts were left on holder for front neck between 12th and 27th patt rows, dec one more st. Work 1in in rounds of K2, P2 rib. Cast off in rib.

To make up

Press each piece under a damp cloth with a warm iron Join side and sleeve seams. Set in sleeves. Press seams.

48 Ribbed polo neck jersey

Sizes

To fit 32[34:36:38]in bust
Length to shoulder, 24[25:26:27]in
Sleeve seam, 17[17½:18:18½]in
The figures in brackets [] refer to the 34, 36 and 38in sizes respectively

Tension

6 sts and 7½ rows to 1in over rib patt worked on No.8 needles

Materials

Lee Target Motoravia Double Knitting
24[25.26:27] balls
One pair No. 8 needles
One pair No. 10 needles

Back

Using No. 10 needles cast on 102[106:114:118] sts.
1st row K2, *P2, K2, rep from * to end.
2nd row P2, *K2, P2, rep from * to end.
Rep these 2 rows until work measures 4in from beg,
ending with a 2nd row and inc one st in centre of
last row on 34 and 38in sizes and dec one st in
centre of last row on 32 and 36in sizes. 101
[107:113:119] sts. Change to No. 8 needles.
Next row K2, *P1, K2, rep from * to end.
Next row P2, *K1, P2, rep from * to end.
Rep last 2 rows until work measures
16½[17:17½:18]in from beg, ending with a WS row.
Shape armholes
Cast off 3 sts at beg of next 8 rows. 77[83:89:95] sts.
Cont without shaping until armholes measure
7½[8:8½:9]in from beg, ending with a WS row.
Shape shoulders
Cast off at beg of next and every row 5[6:6:7] sts
6 times and 6[5:7:6] sts twice. Cast off rem
35[37:39:41] sts.

Front

Work as given for back until 12 rows less than back
to armholes, ending with a WS row.
Divide for neck
Next row Patt 50[53:56:59] sts, turn and leave
rem sts on holder.
Next row Patt to end.
Next row Patt to last 4 sts, P2 tog, K2.
Next row P2, K1, patt to end.
Next row Patt to last 3 sts, P1, K2.
Next row P2, K1, patt to end.
Rep last 4 rows once more, then first 2 of these last
4 rows once.
Shape armhole
Cast off 3 sts at beg of next and foll 3 alt rows,
at the same time cont to dec at neck edge on every
4th row until 21[23:25:27] sts rem. Cont without
shaping until work measures same as back to
shoulder, ending at armhole edge.
Shape shoulder
Cast off 5[6:6:7] sts at beg of next and foll 2 alt
rows. Work 1 row. Cast off rem 6[5:7:6] sts. With
RS of work facing, rejoin yarn to rem sts. K2 tog,
patt to end.
Next row Patt to end.
Next row K2, P2 tog, patt to end.
Next row Patt to last 3 sts, K1, P2.
Complete to match first side, reversing all shaping.

Sleeves

Using No. 10 needles cast on 50[54:54:58] sts.
Work first 2 rows rib as given for back until work
measures 4in from beg, ending with a 2nd row and
dec one st in centre of last row on 34in size, inc one
st at each end of last row on 36in size and inc one
st in centre of last row on 38in size. 50[53:56:59]
sts.
Change to No. 8 needles and cont in patt as given
for back, inc one st at each end of 7th and every
foll 3rd row and working extra sts into patt, until
there are 74[77:80:83] sts. Cont without shaping
until sleeve measures 17[17½:18:18½]in from beg,
ending with a WS row.
Shape top
Cast off 2 sts at beg of every row until 10[9:8:7] sts
rem. Cast off.

Front insert and collar

Using No. 3 needles cast on 6 sts.
1st row K2, P2, K2.
2nd row P2, K2, P2.
Cont in rib, inc one st at each end of next and

every foll 4th row and working the extra sts into
rib patt, until there are 38[40:42:44] sts. Cont without shaping until work measures 6½[7:7½:8]in
from beg, ending with a WS row. Leave sts for time
being. Break off yarn.
Using No. 10 needles cast on 48[50:52:54] sts.
Leave sts for time being. Break off yarn.
Using No. 10 needles cast on 12 sts.
Next row Rib 12 sts, rib across 38[40:42:44] sts on
needle, then rib across 48[50:52:54] sts on needle.
98[102:106:110] sts.
Cont in K2, P2 rib until collar measures 4in from
cast on sts. Change to No. 8 needles and cont in
rib for a further 8in.
Cast off loosely in rib.

To make up

Press each piece lightly under a damp cloth with a
warm iron. Join shoulder seams. Set in sleeves.
Join side and sleeve seams. Join seam of collar. Sew
insert and collar to neck edge, having collar seam
to left shoulder seam and point of insert to centre
front neck.
Press seams.

49 *Back buttoning evening cardigan*

Sizes

To fit 34[36:38]in bust
Length to shoulder, 20in adjustable
Sleeve seam, 16½in adjustable
The figures in brackets [] refer to the 36 and 38in
sizes respectively

Tension

6 sts and 9 rows to 1in over main patt worked on
No.9 needles

Materials

15[16:17] balls of Twilley's Goldfingering
One pair No.9 needles
One pair No.10 needles
One pair No.11 needles
One each circular needles No.9, No.10 and No.11
14 buttons

Front

Using No.11 needles cast on 111[119:127] sts. Work
10 rows K1, P1 rib. Change to No.9 needles.
Commence main patt.
1st row K2 sts, *yfwd, K2 tog, rep from * to last st,
K1.
This row forms main patt. Cont in patt until work
measures 13in from beg, or required length to
underarm, ending with a WS row.
Shape armholes
Cast off 6[8:8] sts at beg of next 2 rows. Dec one st
at each end of next 6[8:10] RS rows.
Work 1 row.
Leave rem 87[87:91] sts on holder.

Left back

Using No.11 needles cast on 60[64:68] sts.
1st row K6 sts, *P1, K1, rep from * to end.
2nd row *P1, K1, rep from * to last 6 sts, P1, K5 sts.
Rep these 2 rows 3 times more, then 1st row once.
Next row Work in rib until 5 sts rem, turn leaving
rem 5 sts on holder for front band. 55[59:63] sts.
** Change to No.9 needles. Work in patt as given
for back until work measures same as back to
underarm, ending at armhole edge.
Shape armhole
Cast off 6[8:8] sts at beg of next row. Dec one st at
armhole edge on next 6[8:10] alt rows.
Work 1 row.
Leave rem 43[43:45] sts on holder. **

Right back

Using No.11 needles cast on 60[64:68] sts.

1st row *K1, P1, rep from * to last 6 sts, K6.
2nd row K5 sts, P1, *K1, P1, rep from * to end.
Rep these 2 rows 3 times more, then 1st row once.
Next row K5 sts and leave these sts on holder, rib
to end.
Complete as given for left back from ** to **.

Sleeves

Using No.11 needles cast on 57[61:67] sts. Work
2in K1, P1 rib. Work main patt as given for front
until work measures 3in from beg. Change to No.10
needles and cont in main patt until work measures
4in from beg. Change to No 9 needles and cont in
main patt, inc one st at each end of 9th and every
foll 8th row 8[10:10] times in all, then on every foll
12th row 4 times in all. 81[89:95] sts.
Cont in main patt without shaping until sleeve
measures 16½in from beg, or required length to
underarm.
End with a WS row.
Shape top
Cast off 6[8:8] sts at beg of next 2 rows. Dec one
st at each end of next 6[8:10] RS rows. Work 1 row.
Leave rem 57[57:59] sts on holder.

Yoke

34 and 36in sizes only
1st row Using No 9 circular needle, across 43 sts
of left back K2, (yfwd, K2 tog) 20 times then sl rem
st on to beg of 57 sts of one sleeve, yfwd, K3 tog,
(yfwd, K2 tog) 27 times, yfwd, K1, across 87 sts of
front (yfwd, K2 tog) 43 times then sl rem st on to
beg of 57 sts of 2nd sleeve, yfwd, K3 tog, (yfwd, K2
tog) 27 times, yfwd, K1, across 43 sts of right back
(yfwd, K2 tog) 21 times, K last st. 287 sts.
Work 3 rows main patt.

38in size only
1st row Using No 9 circular needle, across 45 sts
of left back K2, (yfwd, K2 tog) 21 times, yfwd, K1,
across the 59 sts of one sleeve (yfwd, K2 tog)
29 times, yfwd, K1, across 91 sts of front (yfwd, K2
tog) 45 times, yfwd, K1, across 59 sts of 2nd sleeve
(yfwd, K2 tog) 29 times, yfwd, K1, across 45 sts of
right back (yfwd, K2 tog) 22 times, K1. 303 sts.
Work 3 rows main patt, inc one st in 2nd st, one st
in centre and one st in 2nd st from end of last row.
306 sts.

All sizes
Commence yoke patt.
1st row K1, *sl 1, K1, psso, K3, (yfwd, sl 1, K1,
psso) twice, yfwd, sl 1, K1, yfwd, (K2 tog, yfwd) twice,
K3, K2 tog, rep from * to last st, K1.
2nd and every alt row P to end.
3rd, 5th and 7th rows As 1st row.
9th row K1, *sl 1, K1, psso, K2, (yfwd, K2 tog)
twice, yfwd, K3, yfwd, (sl 1, K1, psso, yfwd) twice,
K2, K2 tog, rep from * to last st, K1.
11th row K1, *sl 1, K1, psso, K1, (yfwd, K2 tog)
twice, yfwd, K5, yfwd, (sl 1, K1, psso, yfwd) twice,
K1, K2 tog, rep from * to last st, K1.
13th row K1, *sl 1, K1, psso, (yfwd, K2 tog)
twice, yfwd, K7, yfwd, (sl 1, K1, psso, yfwd) twice,
K2 tog, rep from * to last st, inc one in last st.
15th row *Sl 1, K1, psso, (yfwd, K2 tog) twice,
yfwd, K3, K2 tog, K4, yfwd, (sl 1, K1, psso, yfwd)
twice, rep from * to last 3 sts, sl 1, K1, psso, K1.
16th row P to end.
Change to No 10 circular needle.
17th row K1, *(yfwd, K2 tog) twice, yfwd, K3,
K2 tog, sl 1, K1, psso, K3, yfwd, (sl 1, K1, psso,
yfwd) twice, K1, rep from * to last st, K1.
19th, 21st and 23rd rows As 17th row.
25th row K1, *K1, (yfwd, sl 1, K1, psso) twice,
yfwd, K2, K2 tog, sl 1, K1, psso, K2, (yfwd, K2
tog) twice, yfwd, K2, rep from * to last st, K1.
27th row K1, *K2, (yfwd, sl 1, K1, psso) twice,
yfwd, K1, K2 tog, sl 1, K1, psso, K1, yfwd, (K2 tog,
yfwd) twice, K3, rep from * to last st, K1.
29th row K1, *K3, (yfwd, sl 1, K1, psso) twice,
yfwd, K2 tog, sl 1, K1, psso, yfwd, (K2 tog, yfwd)
twice, K4, rep from * to last st, K1.

31st row K1, *K4, (yfwd, sl 1, K1, psso) 3 times, yfwd, (K2 tog, yfwd) twice, K3, K2 tog, rep from * to last st, K1.

32nd row P to end.

Change to No.11 circular needle. Rep 1st to 7th patt rows once more.

1st dec row P5, *P2 tog, P2 tog, P3, P2 tog, P2 tog, P8, rep from * ending last rep P5. 227[227: 242] sts.

2nd dec row K1, sl 1, K1, psso, K4, *sl 1, K2 tog, psso, K5, sl 1, K1, psso, K5, rep from * to last 10 sts, sl 1, K2 tog, psso, K4, sl 1, K1, psso, K1. 181[181: 193] sts.

1st rib row K2, *P1, K1, rep from * to last st, K1.

2nd rib row K1, *P1, K1, rep from * to end.

Rep these 2 rows twice more.

3rd dec row K2, *sl 1, P2 tog, psso, rib 5, rep from * to last 3[3:7] sts, P1, K2[P1, K2: rib 5, K2].

Work 7 rows rib.

4th dec row K2, P1, K1, *sl 1, K2 tog, psso, rib 7, rep from * to last 3 sts, P1, K2. 111[111:119] sts.

Work 4 rows rib. Mark each end of last row with coloured thread.

Work collar

Cont in rib on these sts for a further 11in. Cast off in rib.

Button band

Using No.11 needles and with WS of work facing rejoin yarn to 5 sts left on holder of left back and cont in g st until band is long enough, when slightly stretched, to fit up centre back edge to coloured marker. Do not cast off. Mark positions for 11 buttons, first to come 4 rows below sts on needle and rem 10 at 2in intervals. Cont in g st for a further 11in to match edge of collar.

Cast off.

Sew on band.

Buttonhole band

Using No.11 needles and with RS of work facing rejoin yarn to 5 sts left on holder of right back and work as given for button band making first 11 buttonholes as markers are reached as foll:

Buttonhole row K1, cast off 2 sts, K2.

Next row K2, cast on 2 sts, K1.

When 11th buttonhole has been worked, K2 rows g st, when band should reach coloured marker. Work 1in g st.

** Work 2 buttonhole rows, then work 2in g st.** Rep from ** to ** once more. Work 2 buttonhole rows then work 1in g st. Rep from ** to ** twice more. Work 2 buttonhole rows then work 1in g st. Cast off.

Sew on band.

To make up

Do not press. Set in sleeves. Join side and sleeve seams. Fold collar in half to RS so that 3 double buttonholes match. Neaten buttonholes. Sew on buttons.

Cocktail suit

Sizes

To fit 34[36:38:40:42]in bust
36[38:40:42:44]in hips

Jacket length to shoulder, 23[23½:24:24½:25]in
Sleeve seam, 6in

Skirt length, 20[20½:21:21½:22]in

The figures in brackets [] refer to the 36, 38, 40 and 42in sizes respectively

Tension

7 sts and 9 rows to 1in over st st worked on No.10 needles

Materials

22[24:26:28:30] balls Lister Bel Air Starspun
One pair No.10 needles
One pair No.12 needles
Six buttons
Waist length of elastic
One 7in zip fastener

Jacket back

Using No.12 needles cast on 123[129:137:143:151] sts.

1st row K1, *P1, K1, rep from * to end.

2nd row P1, *K1, P1, rep from * to end.

Rep these 2 rows for 1in, ending with a 2nd row and inc one st at end of last row on 36 and 40in sizes only. 123[130:137:144:151] sts.

Change to No.10 needles. Beg with a K row cont in st st until work measures 16in from beg, ending with a P row.

Shape armholes

Cast off at beg of next and every row 6 sts twice and 2[2:3:3:4] sts 4 times. Dec one st at each end of next and foll 5[7:7:9:9] alt rows. 91[94:97:100: 103] sts. Cont without shaping until armholes measure 7[7½:8:8½:9]in from beg, ending with a P row.

Shape neck and shoulders

Next row K30[31:32:33:34] sts, turn and leave rem sts on holder.

Next row Cast off 4 sts, P to end.

Next row Cast off 6[6:7:7:7] sts, K to end.

Rep last 2 rows once more, then first of them once more. Cast off rem 6[7:6:7:8] sts.

With RS of work facing, sl first 31[32:33:34:35] sts on holder, rejoin yarn to rem sts and K to end.

Complete to match first side, reversing shaping.

Jacket left front

Using No.12 needles cast on 75[79:83:87:91] sts.

1st row *K1, P1, rep from * to last 21 sts, K10, sl 1, K10.

2nd row P21 sts, *K1, P1, rep from * to end.

Rep these 2 rows for 1in, ending with a 2nd row. Change to No.10 needles.

Next row K to last 11 sts, sl 1, K10.

Next row P to end.

Rep last 2 rows until work measures same as back to underarm, ending at armhole edge.

Shape armhole

Cast off at beg of next and foll alt rows 6 sts once and 2[2:3:3:4] sts twice, ending at armhole edge.

Shape neck

Next row K2 tog, K to last 29[30:31:32:33] sts, turn and leave rem sts on holder.

Dec one st at armhole edge on foll 5[7:7:9:9] alt rows, *at the same time* cast off at neck edge on next and foll alt rows 4 sts once, 3 sts once, 2 sts once and one st 3 times. 18[19:20:21:22] sts. Cont without shaping until armhole measures same as back to shoulder, ending at armhole edge.

Shape shoulder

Cast off at beg of next and every alt row 6[6:7:7:7] sts twice and 6[7:6:7:8] sts once. Mark positions for 6 buttons, the first to come ½in above hem and last to come in neckband ½in above sts on holder, with 4 more evenly spaced between.

Jacket right front

Using No.12 needles cast on 75[79:83:87:91] sts.

1st row K10, sl 1, K10, *P1, K1, rep from * to end.

2nd row *P1, K1, rep from * to last 21 sts, P21.

Rep these 2 rows once more.

Next row (buttonhole row) K3 sts, cast off 4 sts, K2, sl 1, K3, cast off 4 sts, patt to end.

Next row Patt to end, casting on 4 sts above those cast off in previous row.

Complete to match left front, reversing all shaping and making buttonholes as markers are reached, as before.

Sleeves

Using No.12 needles cast on 69[73:77:81:85] sts. Work 1in rib as given for back, ending with a 2nd row. Change to No.10 needles. Beg with a K row cont in st st, inc one st at each end of 5th and every foll 6th row until there are 83[87:91:95:99] sts. Cont without shaping until sleeve measures 6in from beg, ending with a P row.

Shape top

Cast off 6 sts at beg of next 2 rows. Dec one st at each end of next and foll 11[12:13:14:15] alt rows. Cast off at beg of next and every row 2 sts 10[10:12: 12:14] times, 3 sts 4 times and 4 sts twice. Cast off rem 7[9:7:9:7] sts.

Neckband

Join shoulder seams. Using No.12 needles and with RS of work facing, patt across sts of right front neck, K up 45 sts up side of front neck and 20 sts down side of back neck, K across back neck sts inc one st in centre on 36 and 40in sizes only, K up 20 sts up side of back neck and 45 sts down side of front neck, patt across sts of left front neck. 219[223:225:229: 231] sts.

Next row P21 sts, rib to last 21 sts, P21.

Next row K10, sl 1, K10, rib to last 21 sts, K10, sl 1, K10.

Rep last 2 rows for 1in making buttonholes as before on 5th and 6th rows. Cast off in patt.

To make up

Press lightly under a dry cloth with a cool iron. Set in sleeves. Join side and sleeve seams. Fold front bands in half to WS and sl st down. Work round double buttonholes. Press seams. Sew on buttons.

Skirt back

Using No.12 needles cast on 91[97:105:111:119] sts and beg at waist. Work 1in rib as given for jacket back, ending with a 2nd row and inc one st at end of last row on 36 and 40in sizes only. 91[98: 105:112:119] sts. Change to No.10 needles. Beg with a K row work 4 rows st st.

Shape darts

Next row K14 sts, pick up loop between sts and K tbl – called inc 1 –, K19[21:23:25:27] sts, inc 1, K25[28:31:34:37] sts, inc 1, K19[21:23:25:27] sts, inc 1, K14 sts.

Beg with a P row work 9 rows st st.

Next row K14 sts, inc 1, K20[22:24:26:28] sts, inc 1, K27[30:33:36:39] sts, inc 1, K20[22:24:26:28] sts, inc 1, K14 sts.

Beg with a P row work 9 rows st st.

Cont inc in this way on next and every foll 10th row until there are 143[150:157:164:171] sts. Cont without shaping until work measures 20[20½: 21:21½:22]in from beg, ending with a P row and inc one st at end of last row on 36 and 40in sizes only.

Next row (picot edge) K1, *yfwd, K2 tog, rep from * to end

Change to No.12 needles. Beg with a P row work 1½in st st. Cast off.

Skirt front

Work as given for back.

To make up

Press as given for jacket. Join side seams leaving 7in open at top of left seam for zip. Turn hem to WS at picot row and sl st down. Sew in zip. Sew elastic inside waist ribbing with casing st. Press seams.

Aran cardigan for father and son

Sizes
Boy's cardigan to fit 26 [28:30]in chest
Length to shoulder, 14 [15:16]in
Sleeve seam, 9½ [10½:11½]in
Man's cardigan to fit 38 [40:42]in chest
Length to shoulder, 25 [26:27]in
Sleeve seam, 18 [18½:19]in
The figures in brackets [] refer to the 28 and 30in boys' sizes and 40 and 42in mens' sizes respectively

Tension
6 sts and 8 rows to 1in over st st worked on No.9 needles

Materials
Wendy Double Knitting Nylonised
Boy's cardigan 12 [14:16] balls
Man's cardigan 24 [26:28] balls
One pair No.9 needles
One pair No.11 needles
One cable needle
6 buttons for boy's cardigan
7 buttons for man's cardigan

Note
Abbreviations are given in patt rows of boy's cardigan

Boy's cardigan back
Using No.11 needles cast on 81 [87:93] sts.
1st row K1, *P1, K1, rep from * to end.
2nd row P1, *K1, P1, rep from * to end.
Rep these 2 rows for 1¼in, ending with a 2nd row and inc one st in centre of last row. 82 [88:94] sts. Change to No.9 needles. Commence patt.
1st row P9 [11:13] sts, (insert needle behind first st and K 2nd st then K first st and sl both sts off tog – called Tw2L –) twice, K1, P7, K3, P1, K1, P11 [12:13], K4, P11 [12:13], K3, P1, K3, P7, K1, (insert needle in front of first st and K 2nd st then K first st and sl both sts off tog – called Tw2R –) twice, P9 [11:13] sts.
2nd row K9 [11:13] sts, P5, K7, P3, K1, P3, K11 [12:13], sl next 2 sts on to cable needle and hold at front of work to WS, P2 then P2 from cable needle – called C4P –, K11 [12:13], P3, K1, P3, K7, P5, K9 [11:13] sts.
3rd row P9 [11:13] sts, K1, (Tw2L) twice, P7, sl 1, K2, P1, K2, sl 1, P10 [11:12], sl next st on to cable needle and hold at back of work, K2 then P1 from cable needle – called Cr3R –, sl next 2 sts on to cable needle and hold at front of work, P1 then K2 from cable needle – called Cr3L –, P10 [11:12], sl 1, K2, P1, K2, sl 1, P7, (Tw2R) twice, K1, P9 [11:13] sts.
4th row K9 [11:13] sts, P5, K7, sl 1, P2, K1, P2, sl 1, K10 [11:12], P2, K2, P2, K10 [11:12], sl 1, P2, K1, P2, sl 1, K7, P5, K9 [11:13] sts.
5th row P9 [11:13] sts, K1, (Tw2L) twice, K1, sl next st on to cable needle and hold at front of work, K2 then K1 from cable needle – called C3F –, P1, sl next 2 sts on to cable needle and hold at back of work, K1 then K2 sts from cable needle – called C3B –, P9 [10:11], Cr3R, P2, Cr3L, P9 [10:11], C3F, P1, C3B, P7, K1, (Tw2R) twice, K1, P9 [11:13] sts.
6th row K9 [11:13] sts, P5, K7, P3, K1, P3, K9 [10:11], P2, K4, P2, K9 [10:11], P3, K1, P3, K7, P5, K9 [11:13] sts.
7th row P9 [11:13] sts, K1, (Tw2L) twice, P7, sl 1, K2, P1, K2, sl 1, P8 [9:10], Cr3R, P4, Cr3L, P8 [9:10], sl 1, K2, P1, K2, sl 1, P7, (Tw2R) twice, K1, P9 [11:13] sts.
8th row K9 [11:13] sts, P5, K7, sl 1, P2, K1, P2, sl 1, K8 [9:10], P2, K6, P2, K8 [9:10], sl 1, P2, K1, P2, sl 1, K7, P5, K9 [11:13] sts.
9th row P9 [11:13] sts, (Tw2L) twice, K1, P7,

C3F, P1, C3B, P7 [8:9], Cr3R, P6, Cr3L, P7 [8:9], C3F, P1, C3B, P7, K1, (Tw2R) twice, P9 [11:13] sts.
10th row K9 [11:13] sts, P5, K7, P3, K1, P3, K7[8:9], P2, K8, P2, K7 [8:9], P3, K1, P3, K7, P5, K9 [11:13] sts.
11th row Patt 28 [30:32] sts as given for 3rd row, P6 [7:8], Cr3R, P8, Cr3L, P6 [7:8], patt to end as given for 3rd row.
12th row Patt 28 [30:32] sts as given for 4th row, K6 [7:8], P2, K10, P2, K6 [7:8], patt to end as given for 4th row.
13th row Patt 28 [30:32] sts as given for 5th row, P6 [7:8], Cr3L, P8, Cr3R, P6 [7:8], patt to end as given for 5th row.
14th row As 10th.
15th row Patt 28 [30:32] sts as given for 3rd row, P7 [8:9], Cr3L, P6, Cr3R, P7 [8:9], patt to end as given for 3rd row.
16th row As 8th.
17th row Patt 28 [30:32] sts as given for 5th row, P8 [9:10], Cr3L, P4, Cr3R, P8 [9:10], patt to end as given for 5th row.
18th row As 6th.
19th row Patt 28 [30:32] sts as given for 3rd row, P9 [10:11], Cr3L, P2, Cr3R, P9 [10:11], patt to end as given for 3rd row.
20th row As 4th.
21st row Patt 28 [30:32] sts as given for 5th row, P10 [11:12], Cr3L, Cr3R, P10 [11:12], patt to end as given for 5th row.
22nd row As 2nd.
Rows 3-22 form patt. Cont in patt until work measures 8½ [9:9½]in from beg, ending with a WS row.
Shape armholes
Keeping patt correct, cast off 2 [3:4] sts at beg of next 2 rows and 2 sts at beg of next 6 rows. 66 [70:74] sts. Cont without shaping until armholes measure 3½ [4:4½]in from beg, ending with a WS row.
Shape shoulders
Cast off at beg of next and every row 7 sts 4 times and 7 [8:9] sts twice. Leave rem 24 [26:28] sts on holder.

Right front
Using No.11 needles cast on 55 [57:61] sts. Work 1¼in rib as given for back, ending with a 2nd row and inc one st at beg of last row on 28in size only. 55 [58:61] sts.
Next row Rib 8 sts and leave these sts on holder for front band, change to No.9 needles, P8 [9:10] sts, K4, P9, K3, P1, K3, P5, (Tw2R) twice, K1, P9 [11:13] sts. 47 [50:53] sts.
2nd row K9 [11:13] sts, P5, K5, P3, K1, P3, K9, C4P, K8 [9:10] sts.
3rd row P7 [8:9] sts, Cr3R, Cr3L, P8, sl 1, K2, P1, K2, sl 1, P5, K1, (Tw2R) twice, P9 [11:13] sts.
4th row K9 [11:13] sts, P5, K5, sl 1, P2, K1, P2, sl 1, K8, P2, K2, P2, K7 [8:9] sts.
5th row P6 [7:8] sts, Cr3R, P2, Cr3L, P7, C3F, P1, C3B, P5, (Tw2R) twice, K1, P9 [11:13] sts.
Cont in patt as now set until work measures same as back to underarm, ending with a RS row.
Shape armhole
Cast off at beg of next and every alt row 2 [3:4] sts once and 2 sts 3 times. 39 [41:43] sts. Cont without shaping until armhole measure 2 [2½:3] in from beg, ending with a RS row.
Shape neck
Next row Patt 33 [34:35] sts, turn and leave rem 6 [7:8] sts on holder.
Cast off at beg of next and every alt row 4 sts once, 3 sts once and 2 sts once. Dec one st at neck edge on foll 3 alt rows, ending with a RS row.
Shape shoulder
Cast off at beg of next and every alt row 7 sts twice and 7 [8:9] sts once.

Left front
Using No.11 needles cast on 55 [57:61] sts. Work ¾in rib as given for back, ending with a WS row.
Next row (buttonhole row) Rib to last 6 sts, cast off 3 sts, rib to end.
Next row Rib to end, casting on 3 sts above those cast off in previous row.
Cont in rib until work measures 1¼in from beg, ending with a WS row and inc one st at end of last row on 28in size only. 55 [58:61] sts. Change to No.9 needles.
Next row P9 [11:13] sts, K1, (Tw2L) twice, P5, K3, P1, K3, P9, K4, P8 [9:10] sts, turn and leave rem 8 sts on holder for front band. 47 [50:53] sts.
Next row K8 [9:10] sts, C4P, K9, P3, K1, P3, K5, P5, K9 [11:13] sts.
Complete to match right front, reversing all shaping.

Sleeves
Using No.11 needles cast on 41 [45:49] sts. Work 1¼in rib as given for back, ending with a 2nd row and inc one st in centre of last row. 42 [46:50] sts. Change to No.9 needles.
1st row P1 [2:3] sts, K3, P1, K3, P11 [12:13], K4, P11 [12:13], K3, P1, K3, P1 [2:3] sts.
2nd row K1 [2:3] sts, P3, K1, P3, K11 [12:13], C4P, K11 [12:13], P3, K1, P3, K1 [2:3] sts.
3rd row P1 [2:3] sts, sl 1, K2, P1, K2, sl 1, P10 [11:12], Cr3R, Cr3L, P10 [11:12], sl 1, K2, P1, K2, sl 1, P1 [2:3] sts.
Cont in patt as now set, inc one st at each end of every 6th row until there are 62 [68:74] sts. Cont without shaping until sleeve measures 9½ [10½:11½]in from beg, ending with a WS row.
Shape top
Cast off at beg of next and every row 2 sts 2 [4:6] times and one st 4 [6:8] times. 54 sts. (Cast off at beg of next and every row 2 sts twice and one st twice) 3 times. 36 sts. Cast off 2 sts at beg of next 10 rows. 16 sts. Cont on these sts for length of shoulder, ending with a WS row. Leave sts on holder.

Right front band
Using No.11 needles and with WS of work facing, rejoin yarn to sts of right front, inc in first st, rib to end. Cont in rib until band fits up front edge, when slightly stretched, ending with a WS row. Leave sts on holder. Mark positions for 6 buttons on right front, first to come in welt and last to come on neckband, with 4 more evenly spaced between.

Left front band
Work as given for right front band, making buttonholes as before as markers are reached.

Neckband
Sew saddle tops of sleeves to front and back shoulders. Using No.11 needles and with RS of work facing, rib across 8 sts of right front band, K next st tog with first st of front neck, K rem 5 [6:7] sts of front neck, K up 13 sts up side of neck, K across sts of right sleeve, back neck and left sleeve K2 tog at each seam and at centre back, K up 13 sts down other side of neck, K5 [6:7] front neck sts, K next st tog with first st of left front band, rib to end. 107 [111:115] sts. Work 9 rows rib, making buttonhole as before on 4th and 5th rows. Cast off in rib.

To make up
Press each piece under a damp cloth with a warm iron. Set in sleeves. Join side and sleeve seams. Sew on front bands. Press seams. Sew on buttons.

Man's cardigan back
Using No.11 needles cast on 117 [123:129] sts. Work 1½in rib as given for back of boy's cardigan,

ending with a 2nd row. Change to No.9 needles.
1st row P14 [16:18] sts, (Tw2L) twice, K1, P7, K3, P1, K3, P12, K4, P19 [21:23], K4, P12, K3, P1, K3, P7, K1, (Tw2R) twice, P14 [16:18] sts.
2nd row K14 [16:18] sts, P5, K7, P3, K1, P3, K12, C4P, K19 [21:23], C4P, K12, P3, K1, P3, K7, P5, K14 [16:18] sts.
3rd row P14 [16:18] sts, K1, (Tw2L) twice, P7, sl 1, K2, P1, K2, sl 1, P11, Cr3R, Cr3L, P17 [19:21], Cr3R, Cr3L, P11, sl 1, K2, P1, K2, sl 1, P7, (Tw2R) twice, K1, P14 [16:18] sts.
4th row K14 [16:18] sts, P5, K7, sl 1, P2, K1, P2, sl 1, K11, P2, K2, P2, K17 [19:21], P2, K2, P2, K11, sl 1, P2, K1, P2, sl 1, K7, P5, K14 [16:18] sts.
5th row P14 [16:18] sts, (Tw2L) twice, K1, P7, C3F, P1, C3B, P10, Cr3R, P2, Cr3L, P15 [17:19], Cr3R, P2, Cr3L, P10, C3F, P1, C3B, P7, K1, (Tw2R) twice, P14 [16:18] sts.
6th row K14 [16:18] sts, P5, K7, P3, K1, P3, K10, P2, K4, P2, K15 [17:19], P2, K4, P2, K10, P3, K1, P3, K7, P5, K14 [16:18] sts.
7th row Patt 33 [35:37] sts as given for 3rd row, P9, Cr3R, P4, Cr3L, P13 [15:17], Cr3R, P4, Cr3L, P9, patt to end as given for 3rd row.
8th row Patt 33 [35:37] sts as given for 4th row, K9, P2, K6, P2, K13 [15:17], P2, K6, P2, K9, patt to end as given for 4th row.
9th row Patt 33 [35:37] sts as given for 5th row P8, Cr3R, P6, Cr3L, P11 [13:15], Cr3R, P6, Cr3L, P8, patt to end as given for 5th row.
10th row Patt 33 [35:37] sts as given for 6th row, K8, P2, K8, P2, K11 [13:15], P2, K8, P2, K8, patt to end as given for 6th row.
11th row Patt 33 [35:37] sts as given for 3rd row, P7, Cr3R, P8, Cr3L, P9 [11:13], Cr3R, P8, Cr3L, P7, patt to end as given for 3rd row.
12th row Patt 33 [35:37] sts as given for 4th row, K7, P2, K10, P2, K9 [11:13], P2, K10, P2, K7, patt to end as given for 4th row.
13th row Patt 33 [35:37] sts as given for 5th row, P7, Cr3L, P8, Cr3R, P9 [11:13], Cr3L, P8, Cr3R, P7, patt to end as given for 5th row.
14th row As 10th.
15th row Patt 33 [35:37] sts as given for 3rd row, P8, Cr3L, P6, Cr3R, P11 [13:15], Cr3L, P6, Cr3R, P8, patt to end as given for 3rd row.
16th row As 8th.
17th row Patt 33 [35:37] sts as given for 5th row, P9, Cr3L, P4, Cr3R, P13 [15:17], Cr3L, P4, Cr3R, P9, patt to end as given for 5th row.
18th row As 6th.
19th row Patt 33 [35:37] sts as given for 3rd row, P10, Cr3L, P2, Cr3R, P15 [17:19], Cr3L, P2, Cr3R, P10, patt to end as given for 3rd row.
20th row As 4th.
21st row Patt 33 [35:37] sts as given for 5th row, P11, Cr3L, Cr3R, P17 [19:12], Cr3L, Cr3R, P11, patt to end as given for 5th row.
22nd row As 2nd.
Rows 3-22 form patt. Cont in patt until work measures 15½ [16:16½]in from beg, ending with a WS row.
Shape armholes
Cast off 3 sts at beg of next 2 rows.
****Next row** K2 sts, sl 1, K1, psso, patt to last 4 sts, K2 tog, K2 sts.
Next row P3 sts, patt to last 3 sts, P3. **
Rep last 2 rows until 39 [41:43] sts rem, ending with a WS row. Leave sts on holder.

Right front
Using No.11 needles cast on 69 [73:75] sts. Work 1½in rib as given for back, ending with a 2nd row and inc one st at beg of last row on 38 and 42in sizes only. 70 [73:76] sts.
Next row Rib 12 sts and leave these sts on holder for front band, change to No.9 needles, P9 [10:11] sts, K4, P12, K3, P1, K3, P7, K1, (Tw2R) twice, P14 [16:18] sts. 58 [61:64] sts.
Next row K14 [16:18] sts, P5, K7, P3, K1, P3, K12, C4P, K9 [10:11] sts.
Next row P8 [9:10] sts, Cr3R, Cr3L, P11, sl 1, K2, P1, K2, sl 1, P7, (Tw2R) twice, K1, P14 [16:18] sts.
Next row K14 [16:18] sts, P5, K7, sl 1, P2, K1, P2, sl 1, K11, P2, K2, P2, K8 [9:10] sts.
Next row P7 [8:9] sts, Cr3R, P2, Cr3L, P10, C3F, P1, C3B, P7, K1, (Tw2R) twice, P14 [16:18] sts.
Cont in patt as now set until work measures same as back to underarm, ending with a RS row.
Shape armhole
Cast off 3 sts at beg of next row.
Next row Patt to last 4 sts, K2 tog, K2 sts.
Next row P3 sts, patt to end.
Rep last 2 rows until 31 [32:33] sts rem, ending with a RS row.
Shape neck
Next row Patt 23 sts, turn and leave rem 8 [9:10] sts on holder.
Cont dec at armhole edge on next and every alt row, *at the same time* cast off at neck edge 3 sts once, 2 sts twice and one st 4 times, ending with a WS row. 5 sts.
Next row K1, K2 tog, K2 sts.
Next row P4 sts.
Next row K2 tog, K2 sts.
Cast off.

Left front
Using No.11 needles cast on 69 [73:75] sts. Work ¾in rib as given for back, ending with a 2nd row.
Next row (buttonhole row) Rib to last 8 sts, cast off 3 sts, rib to end.
Next row Rib to end, casting on 3 sts above those cast off in previous row.
Cont in rib until work measures 1½in from beg, ending with a 2nd row and inc one st at end of last row on 38 and 42in sizes only. 70 [73:76] sts. Change to No.9 needles.
Next row P14 [16:18] sts, (Tw2L) twice, K1, P7, K3, P1, K3, P12, K4, P9 [10:11] sts, turn and leave rem 12 sts on holder for front band. 58 [61:64] sts.
Next row K9 [10:11] sts, C4P, K12, P3, K1, P3, K7, P5, K14 [16:18] sts.
Complete to match right front, reversing all shaping.

Sleeves
Using No.11 needles cast on 55 [59:63] sts. Work 2¼in rib as given for back, ending with a 2nd row and inc one st in centre of last row. 56 [60:64] sts. Change to No.9 needles.
1st row (Tw2L) 0 [1:2] times, P7, K3, P1, K3, P12, K4, P12, K3, P1, K3, P7, (Tw2R) 0 [1:2] times.
2nd row P0 [2:4] sts, K7, P3, K1, P3, K12, C4P, K12, P3, K1, P3, K7, P0 [2:4] sts.
Cont in patt as now set, inc one st at each end of every 8th row, working first 5 [3:1] of inc sts into patt panel of 5 sts then rem sts into reversed st st, until there are 86 [90:94] sts. Cont without shaping until sleeve measures 18 [18½:19]in from beg, ending with a WS row.
Shape top
Cast off 3 sts at beg of next 2 rows. 80 [84:88] sts. Rep from ** to ** as given for back until 8 sts rem, ending with a WS row. Leave sts on holder.

Right front band
Using No.11 needles and with WS of work facing, rejoin yarn to 12 sts on holder, inc in first st, rib to end.
Cont in rib until band fits up front edge to neck when slightly stretched, ending with a WS row. Leave sts on holder.
Mark positions for 7 buttons on right front, first to come in welt and last to be in neck band, with 5 more evenly spaced between.

Left front band
Work as given for right front band making buttonholes as before as markers are reached.

Neckband
Join raglan seams. Using No.11 needles and with RS of work facing, rib across 12 sts of right front band, K next st tog with first st of front neck, K rem 7 [8:9] sts of front neck, K up 18 sts up side of neck, K across sts of right sleeve, back neck and left sleeve K2 tog at each seam, K up 18 sts down other side of neck, K7 [8:9] front neck sts, K next st tog with first st of front band, rib to end. 129 [133:137] sts. Work 2in rib, making buttonhole as before after 1in. Cast off in rib.

To make up
Press each piece under a damp cloth with a warm iron. Join side and sleeve seams. Sew on front bands. Press seams. Sew on buttons.

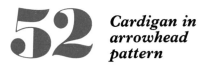

52 *Cardigan in arrowhead pattern*

Sizes
To fit 36 [38:40:42]in chest
Length to shoulder, 25 [26:27:28]in
Sleeve seam, 17½ [18:18½:19]in
The figures in brackets [] refer to the 38, 40 and 42in sizes respectively
Tension
6 sts and 8 rows to 1in over patt worked on No.9 needles
Materials
24 [26:28:30] balls Jaeger Spiral-spun in main shade, A
1 ball of contrast colour, B
2 balls of contrast colour, C
One pair No.9 needles
One pair No.11 needles
One 22 [22:24:24]in open ended zip fastener

Back
Using No.11 needles and A, cast on 121 [127:133:139] sts.
1st row K1, *P1, K1, rep from * to end.
2nd row P1, *K1, P1, rep from * to end.
Rep these 2 rows once more, then 1st row once. Join in C. P 1 row, then rib 3 rows. Join in A. P 1 row, then rib 1 row. Join in B. P 1 row, then rib 3 rows. Break off B. With A, P 1 row, then rib 1 row. With C, P 1 row, then rib 3 rows. Break off C. With A, P 1 row, then rib 3 rows.
** Change to No.9 needles. P 1 row. Commence patt.
1st row K1 [0:3:2] sts, *P1, K3, rep from * to last 4 [3:2:1] sts, P1, K3 [2:1:0].
2nd row P3 [2:1:0] sts, K1, *P3, K1, rep from * to last 1 [0:3:2] sts, P1 [0:3:2].
3rd row K2 [K5:K2, P1, K5:K1, P1, K3, P1, K5] sts, *P1, K3, P1, K5, rep from * to last 9 [2:5:8] sts, P1, K3, P1, K4 [P1, K1:P1, K3, P1:P1, K3, P1, K3].
Cont in patt working from chart, beg and ending rows as set, until work measures 16½ [17:17½:18]in from beg, ending with a WS row.
Shape armholes
Keeping patt correct, cast off at beg of next and every row 5 sts twice, 3 sts twice and 2 sts 2 [2:4:4] times. 101 [107:109:115] sts. Dec one st at each end of next and foll 3 [5:5:7] alt rows 93 [95:97:99] sts. Cont without shaping until armholes measure 8½ [9:9½:10]in from beg, ending with a WS row.
Shape shoulders
Cast off at beg of next and every row 6 sts 8 times and 6 [7:7:8] sts twice. Cast off rem

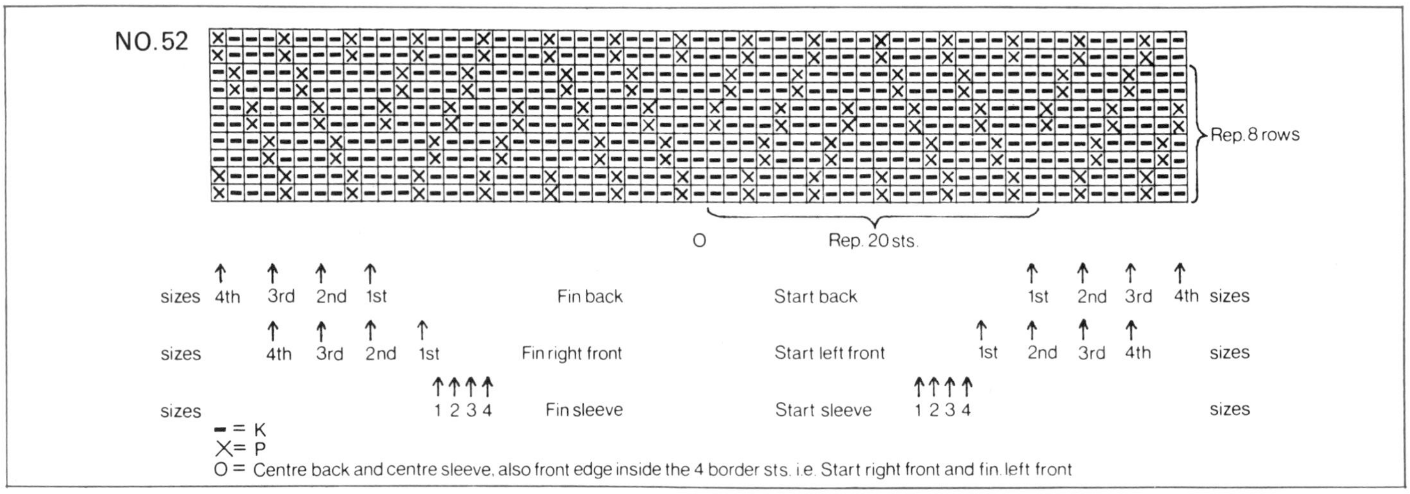
NO.52
Rep. 8 rows
O
Rep. 20 sts.
sizes 4th 3rd 2nd 1st
Fin back
Start back
1st 2nd 3rd 4th sizes
sizes 4th 3rd 2nd 1st
Fin right front
Start left front
1st 2nd 3rd 4th sizes
sizes 1 2 3 4
Fin sleeve
Start sleeve
1 2 3 4 sizes
▬ = K
X = P
O = Centre back and centre sleeve, also front edge inside the 4 border sts. i.e. Start right front and fin. left front

33 [33:35:35] sts.

Right front
Using No.11 needles and A, cast on 61 [65:67: 71] sts.
1st row K3 sts, *P1, K1, rep from * to end.
2nd row *P1, K1, rep from * to last 3 sts, P1, K2.
Keeping 2 sts at front edge in g st, work as given for back to **. Change to No.9 needles.
Next row Inc 1 [0:1:0] st, P to last 4 sts, K1, P1, K2. 62 [65:68:71] sts.
Commence patt.
1st row K3 sts, P1, K1, *P1, K3, rep from * to last 1 [0:3:2] sts, P1 [0:P1, K2:P1, K1].
Keeping 4 sts at front edge as now set, cont in patt working from chart until front measures same as back to underarm, ending at armhole edge.
Shape armhole
Keeping patt correct, cast off at beg of next and every alt row 5 sts once, 3 sts once and 2 sts 1 [1:2:2] times. Dec one st at armhole edge on next and foll 3 [5:5:7] alt rows. 48 [49:50:51] sts. Cont without shaping until armhole measures 6 [6½:7:7½]in from beg, ending at centre front edge.
Shape neck
Cast off at beg of next and every alt row 6 [6:7: 7] sts once, 3 sts once and 2 sts twice. Dec one st at neck edge on foll 5 alt rows. 30 [31:31:32] sts. Cont without shaping until armhole measures same as back to shoulder, ending at armhole edge.
Shape shoulder
Cast off at beg of next and every alt row 6 sts 4 times and 6 [7:7:8] sts once.

Left front
Using No.11 needles and A, cast on 61 [65:67: 71] sts.
1st row *K1, P1, rep from * to last 3 sts, K3.
2nd row K2, P1, *K1, P1, rep from * to end.
Keeping 2 sts at front edge in g st work as given for back to **, inc one st at end of last row on 36 and 40in sizes only. 62 [65:68:71] sts. Change to No.9 needles.
Next row K2, P1, K1, P to end.
Complete to match right front, reversing all shaping and noting that 1st patt row is as foll:
1st row K2 [1:0:3] sts, *P1, K3, rep from * to end.

Sleeves
Using No.11 needles and A, cast on 67 [69:71: 73] sts. Work as given for back to **. Change to No.9 needles. P 1 row. Commence patt.
1st row K2 [3:0:1] sts, *P1, K3, rep from * to last 1 [2-3-4] sts, P1, K0 [1:2:3].
This row sets patt. Cont in patt working from chart and inc one st at each end of 3rd and every foll 8th row until there are 93 [95:99:101] sts, working extra sts into patt. Cont without shaping until sleeve measures 17½ [18:18½:19]in from beg, ending with a WS row.
Shape top
Cast off 5 sts at beg of next 2 rows. Dec one st at each end of next and foll 12 [13:13:14] alt rows. 57 [57:61:61] sts. Cast off at beg of next and every row 2 sts 12 [12:14:14] times and 3 sts 4 times. Cast off rem 21 sts.

Collar
Using No.11 needles and A, cast on 117 [121: 125:129] sts. Work 1in K1, P1 rib as given for back, ending with a 2nd row.
Next row Rib to last 9 sts, turn, sl 1, rib to last 9 sts, turn.
Next row Sl 1, rib to last 13 sts, turn, sl 1, rib to last 13 sts, turn.
Cont in this way working 4 sts less on every row until 33 sts rem unworked at each end.
Next row (RS) Rib to end.
Work 4 more row rib. Join in B. K 1 row, then rib 3 rows. With A, K 1 row, then rib 1 row. Join in C. K 1 row, then rib 3 rows. Break off C. With A, K 1 row, then rib 1 row. With B, K 1 row, then rib 3 rows. Break off B. With A, K 1 row, then rib 5 rows. Cast off in rib.

To make up
Press each piece under a damp cloth with a warm iron. Join shoulder, side and sleeve seams. Set in sleeves. Sew on collar. Sew in zip. Press seams.

See chart above.

53 *Family jerseys in cables and moss stitch*

Sizes
To fit 24 [26:28:30:32:34:36:38:40:42:44]in bust/chest
Length to shoulder, 16 [18:20:22:24:24½:25: 25½:27:27½:28]in
Sleeve seam, 12 [13½:15:16:17:17½:17½:18:18: 18½:18½]in
The figures in brackets [] refer to the 26, 28, 30, 32, 34, 36, 38, 40, 42 and 44in sizes respectively
Tension
5 sts and 7 rows to 1in over st st worked on No. 7 needles
Materials
10 [12:14:16:18:19:20:22:24:25:26] balls Lister Lavenda Double Six
One pair No.7 needles
One pair No.9 needles
Set of 4 No.9 needles pointed at both ends
One cable needle
Note
Abbreviations are given in patt rows of Jersey A

Jersey A back
Using No.9 needles cast on 73 [79:85:91:97:103: 109:115:121:127:133] sts.
1st row K1, *P1, K1, rep from * to end.
2nd row P1, *K1, P1, rep from * to end.
Rep these 2 rows for 1½ [1½:1½:1½:2:2:2:2:2½: 2½:2½]in, ending with a 2nd row and inc one st in centre of last row. 74 [80:86:92:98:104:110:116: 122:128:134] sts. Change to No.7 needles.
Commence patt.
1st row K24 [27:30:33:36:39:42:45:48:51:54] sts, P2, K3, P2, K12, P2, K3, P2, K to end.
2nd and every alt row P24 [27:30:33:36:39: 42:45:48:51:54] sts, K2, P3, K2, P12, K2, P3, K2, P to end.
3rd row as 1st.
5th row K24 [27:30:33:36:39:42:45:48:51:54] sts, P2, sl next st on to cable needle and hold at front of work, K2 sts then K1 from cable needle – called C3F –, P2, sl next 3 sts on to cable needle and hold at back of work, K3 then K3 from cable needle, sl next 3 sts on to cable needle and hold at front of work, K3 then K3 from cable needle – called C12 –, P2, sl next 2 sts on to cable needle and hold at back of work, K1 then K2 from cable needle – called C3B –, P2, K to end.
7th row As 1st.
9th row As 1st.
11th row K24 [27:30:33:36:39:42:45:48:51: 54] sts, P2, C3F, P2, K12, P2, C3B, P2, K to end.
12th row As 2nd.
These 12 rows form patt. Cont in patt until work measures 10½ [12:13½:15:16½:16½:16½:16½:17½: 17½:17½]in from beg, ending with a WS row.
Shape armholes
Cast off at beg of next and every row 4 [4:4:4:5: 5:5:5:6:6:6] sts twice, 3 sts twice and 2 sts 2 [2:2:4:4:4:6:6:6:8:8] times. Dec one st at each end of next and foll 1 [2:3:2:2:3:2:3:3:2:3] alt rows. 52 [56:60:64:68:72:76:80:84:88:92] sts. Cont without shaping until armholes measure 4½ [5: 5½:6:6¼:6¾:7¼:7¾:8:8½:9]in from beg, ending with a WS row.
Shape shoulders
Cast off at beg of next and every row 5 [5:6:6:7: 7:6:6:7:7:7] sts 4 [4:4:4:4:4:6:6:6:6:6] times and 4 [6:5:7:6:8:5:7:5:7:8] sts twice. Leave rem 24 [24:26:26:28:28:30:30:32:32:34] sts on holder.

Jersey A front
Work as given for back until armholes measure 4 [4:4:4:6:6:6:6:8:8:8] rows less than back, ending with a WS row.
Shape neck
Next Row Patt 16 [18:19:21:23:25:26:28:30:

32:33] sts, turn and leave rem sts on holder.
Work 3 [3:3:3:5:5:5:5:7:7:7] rows on these sts,
dec one st at neck edge on first and every alt row.

Shape shoulder
Cast off at beg of next and every alt row 5 [5:6:6:
7:7:6:6:7:7:7] sts 2 [2:2:2:2:2:3:3:3:3:3] times
and 4 [6:5:7:6:8:5:7:5:7:8] sts once.
With RS of work facing, miss first 20 [20:22:22:
22:22:24:24:24:24:26] sts for centre
neck, rejoin yarn to rem sts, K2 tog, patt to
end. Complete to match first side, reversing
shaping.

Jersey A sleeves
Using No.9 needles cast on 39 [41:43:45:47:49:
51:53:55:57:59] sts. Work 1½ [1½:1½:1½:2:2:2:
2½:2½:2½]in rib as given for back, ending with a
2nd row and inc one st in centre of last row.
40 [42:44:46:48:50:52:54:56:58:60] sts. Change
to No.7 needles.
1st row K14 [15:16:17:18:19:20:21:22:23:24]
sts, P2, K3, P2, K3, P2, K to end.
2nd and every alt row P14 [15:16:17:18:19:
20:21:22:23:24] sts, K2, P3, K2, P3, K2, P to
end.
3rd row As 1st.
5th row K14 [15:16:17:18:19:20:21:22:23:24]
sts, P2, C3B, P2, C3F, P2, K to end.
6th row As 2nd.
These 6 rows form patt. Cont in patt, inc one st
at each end of 6th [6th:8th:8th:8th:8th:8th:
8th:8th:8th:8th] row until there are 60 [62:64:
66:70:72:74:76:80:82:84] sts. Cont without
shaping until sleeve measures 12 [13½:15:16:17:
17½:17½:18:18:18½:18½]in from beg, ending
with a WS row.

Shape top
Cast off 4 [4:4:4:5:5:5:6:6:6] sts at beg of next
2 rows. Dec one st at each end of next and every
alt row until 28 [28:32:32:34:34:38:38:40:40:
40] sts rem, ending with a WS row.
Cast off 2 sts at beg of next 6 [6:8:8:8:8:10:10:
10:10:10] rows. Cont on rem 16 [16:16:16:16:
18:18:18:20:20:20] sts for length of shoulder,
ending with a WS row. Leave sts on holder.

Jersey A neckband
Sew saddle tops of sleeves to front and back
shoulders. Using set of 4 No.9 needles and with
RS of work facing, K across all sts on holders,
K2 tog at each back seam and K up 3 [3:3:3:4:4:
4:4:5:5:5] sts at each side of front neck. 80
[80:84:84:92:92:96:96:104:104:108] sts. Work
in rounds of K1, P1 rib for 5 [5:5:6:6:6:7:7:8:
8]in. Cast off loosely in rib.

To make up
Press each piece under a damp cloth with a
warm iron. Join side, sleeve and underarm
seams. Press seams.

Jersey B back
Using No.9 needles cast on 74 [80:86:92:98:
104:110:116:122:128:134] sts. Beg with a K row
work 6 [6:6:6:8:8:8:8:10:10:10] rows st st.
Next row P all sts to form hemline.
Change to No.7 needles. P 1 row. Commence patt.
1st row K2 [5:8:8:11:14:14:17:20:20:23] sts,
*P2, K3, P2, K12, P2, K3, P2, *, K18 [18:18:
24:24:24:30:30:30:36:36] sts, rep from * to *,
K to end.
2nd and every alt row P2 [5:8:8:11:14:14:17:
20:20:23] sts, *K2, P3, K2, P12, K2, P3, K2,
*, P18 [18:18:24:24:24:30:30:30:36:36] sts, rep
from * to *, P to end.
3rd row As 1st.
5th row K2 [5:8:8:11:14:14:17:20:20:23] sts,
*P2, C3F, P2, C12, P2, C3B, P2, *, K18 [18:18:
24:24:24:30:30:30:36:36] sts, rep from * to *,
K to end.
Keeping 2 panels of 26 sts in patt as on Jersey

A, complete as given for jersey A.

Jersey B front
Keeping patt correct as given for jersey B back,
work as given for jersey A front.

Jersey B sleeves
Using No.9 needles cast on 39 [41:43:45:47:49:
51:53:55:57:59] sts. Work 1½ [1½: 1½: 1½: 2: 2:
2:2:2½:2½:2½]in rib as given for jersey A,
ending with a 2nd row and inc one st in centre
of last row. 40 [42:44:46:48:50:52:54:56:58:60]
sts. Change to No.7 needles.
1st row K12 [13:14:15:16:17:18:19:20:21:22]
sts, P2, K12, P2, K to end.
2nd and every alt row P12 [13:14:15:16:17:
18:19:20:21:22] sts, K2, P12, K2, P to end.
3rd row As 1st.
5th row K12 [13:14:15:16:17:18:19:20:21:22]
sts, P2, C12, P2, K to end.
Cont in patt as now set, working C12 on every
12th row and complete as given for jersey A
sleeves.

Jersey B neckband
Work as given for jersey A neckband.

To make up
Press and make up as given for jersey A. Fold
hemline in half to WS and sl st down.

Jersey C back
Using No.9 needles cast on 73 [79:85:91:97:
102:109:115:121:127:133] sts. Work 1½ [1½:1½:
1½:2:2:2:2½:2½:2½]in rib as given for jersey A
back, ending with a 2nd row and inc one st in
centre of last row. 74 [80:86:92:98:104:110:116:
122:128:134] sts. Change to No.7 needles.
1st row K0 [1:0:0:1:0:0:1:0:0:1] st, (P1, K1)
2 [3:5:5:5:7:7:8:9:9:10] times, *P2, K2 [2:2:2:
3:3:3:3:4:4:4], P2, K12, P2, K2 [2:2:2:3:3:3:3:
4:4:4], P2, *, (sl next 2 sts on to cable needle
and hold at back of work, K1 then P2 from cable
needle – called C3B –, sl next st on to cable
needle and hold at front of work, P2 then K1
from cable needle – called C3F –) 3 [3:3:4:4:
5:5:5:6:6] times, rep from * to *, (K1, P1) 2
[3:5:5:5:7:7:8:9:9:10] times, K0 [1:0:0:1:0:0:
1:0:0:1] st.
2nd row P0 [1:0:0:1:0:0:1:0:0:1] st, (K1, P1)
2 [3:5:5:5:7:7:8:9:9:10] times, *K2, P2 [2:2:2:
3:3:3:3:4:4:4], K2, P12, K2, P2 [2:2:2:3:3:3:3:3:
4:4:4], K2, *, (P1, K4, P1) 3 [3:3:4:4:5:5:5:
6:6] times, rep from * to *, (K1, P1) 2 [3:5:5:5:
7:7:8:9:9:10] times, P0 [1:0:0:1:0:0:1:0:0:1].
3rd row P0 [1:0:0:1:0:0:1:0:0:1] st, (K1, P1)
2 [3:5:5:5:7:7:8:9:9:10] times, *P2, K2 [2:2:2:
3:3:3:3:4:4:4], P2, K12, P2, K2 [2:2:2:3:3:3:3:3:
4:4:4], P2, *, (P1, K4, P1) 3 [3:3:4:4:5:5:5:
6:6] times, rep from * to *, (K1, P1) 2 [3:5:5:5:
7:7:8:9:9:10] times, P0 [1:0:0:1:0:0:1:0:0:1].
4th row K0 [1:0:0:1:0:0:1:0:0:1] st, (P1, K1)
2 [3:5:5:5:7:7:8:9:9:10] times, *K2, P2 [2:2:2:
3:3:3:3:4:4:4], K2, P12, K2, P2 [2:2:2:3:3:3:3:3:
4:4:4], K2, *, (K1, P4, K1) 3 [3:3:4:4:5:5:5:5:
6:6] times, rep from * to *, (K1, P1) 2 [3:5:5:5:
7:7:8:9:9:10] times, K0 [1:0:0:1:0:0:1:0:0:1].
5th row Patt 4 [7:10:10:10:11:14:14:17:18:18:21]
sts as given for 1st row, *P2, K2 [2:2:2:2:3:3:3:
3:4:4], P2, C12, P2, K2 [2:2:3:3:3:3:3:4:4:4],
P2, *, (K1, P1) 3 [3:3:4:4:5:5:5:6:6] times,
rep from * to *, patt to end as given for 1st row.
6th row As 2nd.
7th row Patt 28 [31:34:34:37:40:40:43:46:46:
49] sts as given for 3rd row, (C3F, C3B) 3 [3:3:
4:4:4:5:5:5:6:6] times, patt to end as given for
3rd row.
8th row Patt 28 [31:34:34:37:40:40:43:46:46:
49] sts as given for 4th row, (K2, P2, K2) 3 [3:3:
4:4:4:5:5:5:6:6] times, patt to end as given for
4th row.
9th row Patt 28 [31:34:34:37:40:40:43:46:46:

49] sts as given for 1st row, (P2, K2, P2) 3 [3:
3:4:4:4:5:5:5:6:6] times, patt to end as given
for 1st row.
10th row Patt 28 [31:34:34:37:40:40:43:46:46:
49] sts as given for 2nd row, (K2, P2, K2) 3 [3:
3:4:4:4:5:5:5:6:6] times, patt to end as given
for 2nd row.
11th row Patt 28 [31:34:34:37:40:40:43:46:46:
49] sts as given for 3rd row, (P2, K2, P2) 3[3:3:
4:4:4:5:5:5:6:6] times, patt to end as given for
3rd row.
12th row As 8th.
These 12 rows form patt. Keeping patt correct
throughout, complete as given for Jersey A
back.

Jersey C front
Keeping patt correct as given for jersey C
back, work as given for jersey A front.

Jersey C sleeves
Using No.9 needles cast on and work in rib as
given for jersey A sleeves. Change to No.7
needles.
1st row K0 [1:0:1:0:1:0:0:1:0] st, (P1, K1)
4 [4:5:5:6:6:7:7:7:8] times, P2, K2 [2:2:2:3:
3:3:3:4:4], P2, K12, P2, K2 [2:2:2:3:3:3:3:3
4:4:4], P2, (K1, P1) 4 [4:5:5:5:6:6:7:7:7:8]
times. K0 [1:0:1:1:0:1:0:0:1:0].
2nd row P0 [1:0:1:0:1:0:0:1:0] st, (K1, P1)
4 [4:5:5:6:6:7:7:7:8] times, K2, P2 [2:2:2:3:
3:3:3:4:4:4], K2, P12, K2, P2 [2:2:2:3:3:3:3:
4:4:4], K2, (P1, K1) 4 [4:5:5:5:6:6:7:7:7:8]
times, P0 [1:0:1:1:0:1:0:0:1:0].
3rd row P0 [1:0:1:0:1:0:0:1:0] st, (K1, P1)
4 [4:5:5:6:6:7:7:7:8] times, patt 24 [24:24:
24:26:26:26:26:28:28:28] sts as given for 1st row,
(P1, K1) 4 [4:5:5:5:6:6:7:7:7:8] times, P0
[1:0:1:1:0:1:0:0:1:0].
4th row K0 [1:0:1:0:1:0:0:1:0] st, (P1, K1)
4 [4:5:5:6:6:7:7:7:8] times, patt 24 [24:
24:24:26:26:26:26:28:28:28] sts as given for 2nd
row, (K1, P1) 4 [4:5:5:5:6:6:7:7:7:8] times,
K0 [1:0:1:1:0:1:0:0:1:0].
Cont in patt as now set, working C12 on next
and every 12th row. Complete as given for
jersey A sleeves.

Jersey C neckband
Work as given for jersey A neckband.

To make up
As given for jersey A.

54 *Chunky Aran cardigan*

Sizes
To fit 34 [36:38:40:42:44]in chest
Length to top of shoulder, 24½ [25:25½:26:26½:
27]in
Sleeve seam, 18½ [18½:19½:19½:20½:20½]in
The figures in brackets [] refer to the 36, 38, 40,
42 and 44in sizes respectively

Tension
9 sts and 12 rows to 2in over st st worked on
No.7 needles

Materials
16 [17:18:18:20:21] balls Mahony's Blarney
Bainin
One pair No.7 needles
One pair No.10 needles
Cable needle. 5 buttons

Back
Using No.10 needles cast on 84 [88:92:98:102:
106] sts. Work 11 rows K1, P1 rib.
Next row (inc row) Rib 3 [5:7:11:13:15] sts,
*inc in next st, rib 1, rep from * to last 5 [7:9:

11:13:15] sts, inc in next st, rib to end. 123 [127:131:137:141:145] sts.
Change to No.7 needles. Commence patt.
1st row P1 [3:5:2:4:6] sts, * make a sl loop in a short length of contrasting yarn and place on needle and on the foll rows sl this marker from one needle to another until patt is established – called sl marker –, K9, (P1 [1:1:2:2:2], K2, P4, K2) 4 times, P1 [1:1:2:2:2], K9, sl marker, *, P1 [1:1:2:2:2], K9, P1 [1:1:2:2:2], rep from * to * once more, P1 [3:5:2:4:6] sts.
2nd row K1 [3:5:2:4:6] sts, *P9, (K1 [1:1:2:2: 2], P2, K4, P2) 4 times, K1 [1:1:2:2:2], P9, *, K1 [1:1:2:2:2], P9, K1 [1:1:2:2:2], rep from * to * once more, K1 [3:5:2:4:6] sts.
3rd row P1 [3:5:2:4:6] sts, *sl next 2 sts on to cable needle and hold at back of work, K2 sts then K2 sts from cable needle – called C4B –, K1, sl next 2 sts on to cable needle and hold at front of work, K2 sts then K2 sts from cable needle – called C4F –, (P1 [1:1:2:2:2], sl next 2 sts on to cable needle and hold at front of work, P2 sts then K2 sts from cable needle – called T4F –, sl next 2 sts on to cable needle and hold at back of work, K2 sts then P2 sts from cable needle – called T4B –,) 4 times, P1 [1:1:2:2:2], C4B, K1, C4F, *, P1 [1:1:2:2:2], C4B, K1, C4F, P1 [1:1:2:2:2], rep from * to * once more, P1 [3:5:2:4:6] sts.
4th row K1 [3:5:2:4:6] sts, *P9, K3 [3:3:4:4:4], (P4, K5 [5:5:6:6:6]) 3 times, P4, K3 [3:3:4:4:4], P9, *, K1 [1:1:2:2:2], P9, K1 [1:1:2:2:2], rep from * to * once more, K1 [3:5:2:4:6] sts.
5th row P1 [3:5:2:4:6] sts, *K9, P3 [3:3:4:4:4], (K4, P5 [5:5:6:6:6]) 3 times, K4, P3 [3:3:4:4:4], K9, *, P1 [1:1:2:2:2], K9, P1 [1:1:2:2:2], rep from * to * once more, P1 [3:5:2:4:6] sts.
6th row As 4th.
7th row P1 [3:5:2:4:6] sts, *C4B, K1, C4F, (P1 [1:1:2:2:2], T4B, T4F) 4 times, P1 [1:1:2:2: 2], C4B, K1, C4F, *, P1 [1:1:2:2:2], C4B, K1, C4F, P1 [1:1:2:2:2], rep from * to * once more, P1 [3:5:2:4:6] sts.
8th row As 2nd.
These 8 rows form patt. Cont in patt until work measures 15in from beg, ending with a WS row.
Shape raglan
** Cast off 3 [2:1:3:2:1] sts at beg of next 2 rows.
3rd row K2 sts, sl 1, K1, psso, patt to last 4 sts, K2 tog, K2 sts.
4th row P3 sts, patt to last 3 sts, P3 sts. **
Rep last 2 rows until 101 [103:105:107:109:111] sts rem, ending with a WS row.
*** **Next row** K2 sts, sl 1, K2 tog, psso, patt to last 5 sts, K3 tog, K2 sts.
Next row P3 sts, patt to last 3 sts, P3 sts.
Next row K2 sts, sl 1, K1, psso, patt to last 4 sts, K2 tog, K2 sts.
Next row P3 sts, patt to last 3 sts, P3 sts. ***
Rep last 4 rows until 35 [37:39:41:43:45] sts rem, ending with a RS row.
Next row P3 [4:5:3:4:5] sts, *P2 tog, P1, rep from * to last 5 [6:7:5:6:7] sts, P2 tog, P to end.
Cast off rem 25 [27:29:29:31:33] sts.

Left front
Using No.7 needles cast on 25 [25:25:29:29:29] sts for pocket lining. Beg with a K row work 19 [19:27:27:27:27] rows st st.
Next row P1, *inc in next st, P1, rep from * to last 2 [2:2:4:4:4] sts, inc in next st, P to end. 37 [37:37:42:42:42] sts.
Next row P3 [3:3:4:4:4] sts, (K4, P5 [5:5:6:6: 6]) 3 times, K4, P3 [3:3:4:4:4] sts.
Next row K3 [3:3:4:4:4] sts, (P4, K5 [5:5:6:6: 6]) 3 times, P4, K3 [3:3:4:4:4] sts.
Next row (P1 [1:1:2:2:2] sts, T4B, T4F) 4 times, P1 [1:1:2:2:2] sts.
Next row (K1 [1:1:2:2:2] sts, P2, K4, P2) 4 times, K1 [1:1:2:2:2] sts.
Next row (P1 [1:1:2:2:2] sts, K2, P4, K2) 4

times, P1 [1:1:2:2:2] sts.
Leave sts on holder.
Using No.10 needles cast on 42 [44:46:48:50:52] sts. Work 11 rows K1, P1 rib. ****
Next row (inc row) Rib 3 [5:7:11:13:15] sts, *inc in next st, rib 1, rep from * to last 9 [9:9: 7:7:7] sts, inc in next st, rib to end. 58 [60:62: 64:66:68] sts.
Change to No.7 needles. Commence patt.
1st row P1 [3:5:2:4:6] sts, sl marker, work from * to * as given for 1st row of back, sl marker, P2.
This row sets patt. Cont in patt as given for back until 16 [16:24:24:24:24] rows have been worked, ending with an 8th patt row.
Place pocket
1st row Patt 11 [13:15:13:15:17] sts, (K2 tog, P1, P2 tog, P1, K2 tog, P1 [1:1:2:2:2]) 4 times, patt to end. 46 [48:50:52:54:56] sts.
2nd row Patt 11 sts, beg with K1 work 25 [25:25:30:30:30] sts in K1, P1 rib, patt to end.
3rd row Patt 10 [12:14:11:13:15] sts, work across next 25 [25:25:30:30:30] sts in rib as set, patt to end.
Rep 2nd and 3rd rows twice more, then 2nd row once.
Next row Patt 10 [12:14:11:13:15] sts, cast off next 25 [25:25:30:30:30] sts, patt to end.
Next row Patt 11 sts, work in patt across 37 [37:37:42:42:42] sts of pocket lining, patt to end. 58 [60:62:64:66:68] sts.
Cont in patt until work measures same as back to underarm, ending with a WS row.
Shape raglan
Next row Cast off 3 [2:1:3:2:1] sts, patt to end.
Next row Patt to last 3 sts, P3.
Shape front
Next row K2 sts, sl 1, K1, psso, patt to last 2 sts, K2 tog.
Keeping 3 sts at raglan edge in st st cont to dec one st at raglan edge on every alt row, *at the same time* dec one st at neck edge on every 4th row until 43 sts rem, ending with a WS row.
Next row K2 sts, sl 1, K2 tog, psso, patt to last 2 sts, K2 tog.
Next row Patt to last 3 sts, P3.
Next row K2 sts, sl 1, K1, psso, patt to end.
Next row Patt to last 3 sts, P3.
Rep last 4 rows until 8 sts rem. Keeping neck edge straight, cont to dec at raglan edge until 5 sts rem, ending with a WS row.
Next row K2 sts, K2 tog, P1.
Next row Patt to last 3 sts, P3.
Next row K3 tog, P1.
Next row P2 sts.
Next row K2 tog. Fasten off.

Right front
Work as given for left front to ****.
Next row (inc row) Rib 9 [9:9:7:7:7] sts, *inc in next st, rib 1, rep from * to last 3 [5:7:11:13: 15] sts, inc in next st, rib to end. 58 [60:62:64: 66:68] sts.
Change to No.7 needles. Commence patt.
1st row P2 sts, sl marker, work from * to * as given for 1st row of back, sl marker, P1 [3:5:2: 4:6] sts.
Cont in patt as given for back until 16 [16:24: 24:24:24] rows have been worked, ending with an 8th patt row.
Place pocket
1st row Patt 12 [12:12:13:13:13] sts, (K2 tog, P1, P2 tog, P1, K2 tog, P1 [1:1:2:2:2]) 4 times, patt to end. 46 [48:50:52:54:56] sts.
2nd row Patt 10 [12:14:11:13:15] sts, beg with a K st work 25 [25:25:30:30:30] sts in K1, P1 rib, patt to end.
3rd row Patt 11 sts, work across next 25 [25:25: 30:30:30] sts in rib as set, patt to end.
Rep 2nd and 3rd rows twice more, then 2nd row once.
Next row Patt 11 sts, cast off next 25 [25:25: 30:30:30] sts, patt to end.

Next row Patt 10 [12:14:11:13:15] sts, work in patt across 37 [37:37:42:42:42] pocket lining sts, patt to end. 58 [60:62:64:66:68] sts.
Complete to match left front, reversing all shapings and shaping front as foll:
Next row K2 tog, patt to last 4 sts, K2 tog, K2 sts.

Sleeves
Using No.10 needles cast on 40 [42:44:48:50:52] sts. Work 11 rows K1, P1 rib.
Next row (inc row) Rib 3 [5:5:7:7:9] sts, *inc in next st, rib 1, rep from * to last 5 [5:7:7:9:9] sts, inc in next st, rib to end. 57 [59:61:66:68:70] sts.
Change to No.7 needles. Commence patt.
1st row P1 [2:3:3:4:5] sts, sl marker, work from * to * as given for 1st row of back, sl marker, P1 [2:3:3:4:5] sts.
This row sets patt. Cont in patt as given for back, inc one st at each end of 3rd and every foll 6th [6th:6th:8th:8th:8th] row until there are 83 [85:87:90:92:94] sts, working extra sts into reversed st st. Cont without shaping until sleeve measures 18½ [18½:19½:19½:20½:20½]in from beg, ending with a WS row.
Shape raglan
Work as given for back from ** to **, then rep last 2 rows until 41 [41:41:22:22:22] sts rem, ending with a WS row. Work as given for back from *** to ***. Rep last 4 rows until 9 [9:9:10: 10:10] sts rem, ending with a WS row.
Cast off.
Front band
Using No.10 needles cast on 10 sts. Work in K1, P1 rib until band, when slightly stretched, fits up right front, round neck and down left front to beg of front shaping. Mark positions for 5 buttons on right front, first to come ½in above cast on edge and last to come ½in below front shaping with 3 more evenly spaced between. Cont in rib, making buttonholes as markers are reached, as foll:
Next row (buttonhole row) Rib 4 sts, cast off 2 sts, rib to end.
Next row Rib to end, casting on 2 sts above those cast off in previous row.
Cont in rib until band fits down left front to lower edge. Cast off in rib.

To make up
Press each piece lightly on WS under a damp cloth with a warm iron. Join raglan seams. Join side and sleeve seams. Sew front band in place. Sew pocket linings down. Press seams. Sew on buttons.

 *Check cardigan with shawl collar*

Sizes
To fit 38 [40:42:44:46]in chest
Length to shoulder, 24 [24¼:24½:24¾:25]in, adjustable
Sleeve seam, 17½ [18:18½:18½:19]in, adjustable
The figures in brackets [] refer to the 40, 42, 44 and 46in sizes respectively
Tension
5¼ sts and 7 rows to 1in over patt worked on No.8 needles
Materials
14 [15:16:17:18] balls Lee Target Motoravia Double Knitting in main shade, A
9 [9:10:11:11] balls of contrast colour, B
One pair No.8 needles
One pair No.9 needles
7 buttons

Note

Always weave colour not in use across back of work

Back

Using No.9 needles and A, cast on 101 [107:113: 119:125] sts.

1st row K1, *P1, K1, rep from * to end.
2nd row P1, *K1, P1, rep from * to end.
Rep these 2 rows until work measures 2in from beg, ending with a 2nd row. Change to No.8 needles. Commence patt.
1st row Join in B, K0 [K3B: K2B, 1A, 3B: K2A, 3B, 1A, 3B: K0], *K5A, 3B, 1A, 3B, rep from * to last 5 [8:11:14:5] sts, K5A, K0 [K3B: K3B, 1A, 2B: K3B, 1A, 3B, 2A: K0].
2nd row P0 [P3B: P2B, 1A, 3B: P2A, 3B, 1A, 3B: P0], *P5A, 3B, 1A, 3B, rep from * to last 5 [8:11:14:5] sts, P5A, P0 [P3B: P3B, 1A, 2B: P3B, 1A, 3B, 2A: P0].
Rep 1st and 2nd rows twice more.
7th row K0 [K3A: K2A, 1B, 3A: K2B, 3A, 1B, 3A: K0], *K5B, 3A, 1B, 3A, rep from * to last 5 [8:11:14:5] sts, K5B, K0 [K3A: K3A, 1B, 2A: K3A, 1B, 3A, 2B: K0].
8th row P0 [P3A: P2A, 1B, 3A: P2B, 3A, 1B, 3A: P0], *P5B, 3A, 1B, 3A, rep from * to last 5 [8:11:14:5] sts, P5B, P0 [P3A: P3A, 1B, 2A: P3A, 1B, 3A, 2B: P0].
Rep 7th and 8th rows once more.
11th row As 1st.
12th row As 2nd.
13th row As 7th.
14th row As 8th.
15th row As 7th.
16th row As 8th.
These 16 rows form patt and are rep throughout. Cont in patt until work measures 16in from beg, or required length to underarm ending with a WS row.

Shape armholes

Keeping patt correct, cast off 6 [6:7:8:8] sts at beg of next 2 rows. Dec one st at each end of next and foll 6 [7:7:7:8] alt rows. 75 [79:83:87: 91] sts. Cont without shaping until armholes measure 8 [8¼:8½:8¾:9]in from beg, ending with a WS row.

Shape shoulders

Cast off at beg of next and every row 6 sts 6 times and 6 [7:8:9:10] sts twice. Cast off rem 27 [29:31:33:35] sts.

Left front

Using No.9 needles and A, cast on 26 sts for pocket lining. Beg with a K row work 32 rows st st, dec one st at each end of last row. Leave sts on holder.
Using No.9 needles and A, cast on 51 [57:57:63: 63] sts. Work 2in K1, P1 rib as given for back.
Change to No.8 needles. Commence patt. **
1st row Join in B, K0 [K1A, 3B, 5A: K1B, 5A: K3A: K0], *K3B, 1A, 3B, 5A, rep from * to last 3 [0:3:0:3] sts, K3B [K0:K3B:K0:K3B].
2nd row P3B [P0: P3B: P0: P3B], *P5A, 3B, 1A, 3B, rep from * to last 0 [9:6:3:0] sts, P0 [P5A, 3B, 1A: P5A, 1B: P3A: P0].
These 2 rows set patt. Cont in patt until 24 rows have been worked.

Place pocket

Next row Patt 12 sts, sl next 24 sts on to holder, with RS of work facing cont in patt across pocket lining sts, patt to end.
Cont in patt until work measures same as back to underarm, ending at armhole edge.

Shape armhole and front edge

Next row Cast off 6 [6:7:8:8] sts, patt to last 2 sts, dec one st.
Dec one st at armhole edge on foll 7 [8:8:8:9] alt rows, *at the same time* cont to dec one st at front edge on every foll 3rd row, until 24 [25:26:27:28] sts rem.
Cont without shaping until armhole measures same as back to shoulder, ending at armhole edge.

Shape shoulder

Cast off at beg of next and every alt row 6 sts 3 times and 6 [7:8:9:10] sts once.

Right front

Work as given for left front to **.
1st row Join in B, K3B [K0: K3B: K0: K3B], *K5A, 3B, 1A, 3B, rep from * to last 0 [9:6:3:0] sts, K0 [K5A, 3B, 1A: K5A, 1B: K3A: K0].
2nd row P0 [P1A, 3B, 5A: P1B, 5A: P3A: P0], *P3B, 1A, 3B, 5A, rep from * to last 3 [0:3:0:3] sts, P3B [P0: P3B: P0: P3B].
Cont as given for left front until 24 rows have been worked.

Place pocket

Next row Patt 15 [21:21:27:27] sts, sl next 24 sts on to holder, with RS of pocket lining sts facing, cont in patt across sts on holder, patt to end.
Complete to match left front, reversing all shapings.

Sleeves

Using No.9 needles and A, cast on 53 [53:59:59: 59] sts.
Work 2½in K1, P1 rib as given for back.
Change to No.8 needles. Commence patt.
1st row Join in B, K5A [K5A: K3B, 5A: K3B, 5A: K3B, 5A], *K3B, 1A, 3B, 5A, rep from * to last 0 [0:3:3:3] sts, K0 [K0: K3B: K3B: K3B].
2nd row P0 [P0: P3B: P3B: P3B], *P5A, 3B, 1A, 3B, rep from * to last 5 [5:8:8:8] sts, P5A [P5A: P5A, 3B: P5A, 3B: P5A, 3B].
These 2 rows set patt. Cont in patt, inc one st at each end of 3rd and every foll 6th row until there are 77 [79:81:83:85] sts, and working extra sts into patt when possible. Cont without shaping until sleeve measures 17½ [18:18½:18½: 19]in from beg, or required length to underarm, ending with a WS row.

Shape top

Cast off 6 [6:7:8:8] sts at beg of next 2 rows. Dec one st at each end of next and every alt row until 35 sts rem. Cast off at beg of next and every row 2 sts 6 times and 3 sts 4 times. Cast off rem 11 sts.

Right shawl collar and button band

Join shoulder seams. Using No.9 needles and A, cast on 11 sts. Work in K1, P1 rib as given for back until band measures 19in from beg, or required length of front edge to beg of front shaping, ending with a 2nd row.

Shape collar

Next row (RS) Rib to last st, inc one st.
Next row Rib to end.
Rep last 2 rows until there are 40 sts. Cont without shaping until collar fits up front neck to shoulder, ending at outer edge.

Shape curve

** **Next row** Rib 30 sts, turn.
Next row Sl 1, rib to end.
Next row Rib 20 sts, turn.
Next row Sl 1, rib to end.
Next row Rib 10 sts, turn.
Next row Sl 1, rib to end. **
Cont in rib across all sts for a further 1¼in, ending at outer edge. Rep from ** to ** once more. Cont in rib across all sts until collar fits to centre back neck, ending at inner edge. Cast off 10 sts at beg of next and foll 3 alt rows. Mark positions for 7 buttons on right front band, first to come ½in above cast on edge and last to come ¾in below collar shaping, with 5 more evenly spaced between.

Left shawl collar and buttonhole band

Work as given for right half, reversing shaping and making buttonholes as markers are reached, as foll:
Next row (RS) Rib 4 sts, cast off 3 sts, rib to end.
Next row Rib to end, casting on 3 sts above those cast off in previous row.

To make up

Press each piece under a damp cloth with a warm iron. Join side and sleeve seams. Set in sleeves. Join right and left shawl collar at centre back. Sew on bands and collar to front edges, having collar seam at centre neck.
Pocket tops Using No.9 needles, A, and with RS of work facing, rejoin yarn to 24 sts on holder, and work in K1, P1 rib to end. Work 5 more rows rib. Cast off loosely in rib.
Sew down pocket linings and pocket tops. Press all seams. Sew on buttons.

 56 *Crisp textured sleeveless cardigan for man or woman*

Sizes

To fit 32 [34:36:38:40:42:44]in bust/chest
Length to shoulder, 22 [22½:23:23½:24:24½: 25]in
The figures in brackets [] refer to the 34, 36, 38, 40,42 and 44in sizes respectively

Tension

7 sts and 12 rows to 1in over patt worked on No.8 needles

Materials

14 [16:17:19:20:21:22] balls Emu Scotch Double Knitting, Double Crepe or Bri-Nylon Double Knitting
One pair No.8 needles
One pair No.10 needles
6 buttons

Back

Using No.10 needles cast on 94 [100:104:110: 116:122:126] sts. Work 2in K1, P1 rib, ending with a RS row.
Next row Rib 11 [11:10:10:13:13:12] sts, *inc in next st, rib 2 sts, rep from * to last 11 [11:10: 10:13:13:12] sts, inc in next st, rib to end. 119 [127:133:141:147:155:161] sts.
Change to No.8 needles. Commence patt.
1st row (RS) K to end.
2nd row K to end.
3rd row K1, *sl 1 p-wise, K1, rep from * to end.
4th row K1, *yfwd, sl 1 p-wise, ybk, K1, rep from * to end.
These 4 rows form patt. Cont in patt until work measures 13½ [13½:14:14:14½:14½:15]in from beg, ending with a WS row.

Shape armholes

Keeping patt correct, cast off 4 [4:5:5:5:6:6] sts at beg of next 2 rows. Dec one st at each end of next and every alt row until 91 [95:101:107: 111:115:119] sts rem. Cont without shaping until armholes measure 8 [8½:8½:9:9:9½:9½]in from beg, ending with a WS row.

Shape shoulders

Cast off at beg of next and every row 7 [7:8:8:7: 9:10] sts 6 [2:6:2:2:4:4] times and 8 [8:9:9:10: 10:10] sts 2 [6:2:6:4:4:4] times. Cast off rem 33 [33:35:37:37:39:39] sts.

Left front

Using No.10 needles cast on 46 [50:52:56:58:60: 62] sts. Work 2in K1, P1 rib, ending with a RS row.
Next row Rib 5 [7:5:7:8:6:4] sts, *inc in next st, rib 2 sts, rep from * to last 5 [7:5:7:8:6:4] sts, inc in next st, rib to end. 59 [63:67:71:73: 77:81] sts.
Change to No.8 needles. Work in patt as given for back until front measures same as back to underarm, ending with a WS row.

Shape armhole and neck edge

Next row Cast off 4 [4:5:5:5:6:6] sts, patt to last 2 sts, work 2 tog.

Keeping patt correct, dec one st at armhole edge on every alt row, *at the same time* dec one st at neck edge on every foll 6th [6th:5th:5th:6th:6th:5th] row until 41 [42:46:49:50:52:53] sts rem. Keeping armhole edge straight, cont to dec at neck edge only as before until 29 [31:33:35:37:38:40] sts rem. Cont without shaping until armhole measures same as back to shoulder, ending at armhole edge.

Shape shoulder

Cast off at beg of next and every alt row 7 [7:8:8:7:9:10] sts 3 [1:3:1:1:2:2] times and 8 [8:9:9:10:10:10] sts 1 [3:1:3:3:2:2] times.

Right front

Work as given for left front, reversing all shapings.

Front band

Using No.10 needles cast on 11 sts.

1st row K1, *P1, K1, rep from * to end.

2nd row P1, *K1, P1, rep from * to end.

Rep these 2 rows for ½in.

Next row (buttonhole row) Rib 4 sts, cast off 3 sts, rib to end.

Next row Rib to end, casting on 3 sts above those cast off in previous row.

Cont in rib, making 5 more buttonholes in this way at intervals of 2¼ [2¼:2½:2½:2½:2½:2½]in measured from base of previous buttonhole.

Cont until band is long enough, when slightly stretched, to fit up left front, across back neck and down right front. Cast off in rib.

Armbands

Join shoulder seams. Using No.10 needles and with RS of work facing, K up 100 [104:104:108:108:112:112] sts evenly around armhole edge.

Next row P to end.

Beg with a K row work 4 rows st st.

Next row P all sts to mark foldline.

Beg with a P row work 7 rows st st. Cast off loosely.

To make up

Press each piece under a damp cloth with a warm iron for wool, or under a dry cloth with a cool iron for Bri-Nylon, omitting ribbing. Join side seams. Fold armband in half to WS and sl st down. Sew on front band, placing buttonholes on right front for her and left front for him. Sew on buttons.

57 *Cardigans for mother and daughter*

Sizes

To fit 24 [27:30:33:36]in chest/bust

Length to shoulder, 14 [16:18:20:22]in

Sleeve seam, 11 [13:15:17:17½]in

The figures in brackets [] refer to the 27, 30, 33 and 36in sizes respectively

Tension

7½ sts to 1in and 32 rows to 3in over patt worked on No.10 needles

Materials

8[10:12:14:16] balls Patons Purple Heather 4 ply

One pair No.10 needles

One pair No.12 needles

4[4:5:6:6] buttons

Back

Using No.12 needles cast on 93[105:117:129:141] sts.

1st row K1, *P1, K1, rep from * to end.

2nd row P1, *K1, P1, rep from * to end.

Rep these 2 rows 3 times more, then first of them again. Change to No.10 needles.

Commence patt.

1st row (WS) K3 sts, *P3, K3, rep from * to end.

2nd row P3 sts, *K3, P3, rep from * to end.

3rd row As 1st.

4th row K 3rd st in front of first 2 sts, then K first and 2nd sts and sl all 3 sts off needle tog – called Cr3 –, *K3, Cr3, rep from * to end.

5th row As 2nd.

6th row As 1st.

7th row As 2nd.

8th row K3 sts, *Cr3, K3, rep from * to end.

These 8 rows form patt. Cont in patt until work measures 9 [10½:12:13:14]in from beg, ending with a WS row.

Shape armholes

Cast off at beg of next and every row 4[5:5:6:6] sts twice and 2 sts 2[2:4:4:6] times. 81[91:99:109:117] sts. Dec one st at each end of next and foll 2[3:3:4:4] alt rows. 75[83:91:99:107] sts.

Cont without shaping until armholes measure 5[5½:6:7:8]in from beg, ending with a WS row.

Shape shoulders

Cast off at beg of next and every row 6[6:5:6:6] sts 6[6:8:8:8] times and 5[7:7:5:7] sts twice.

Leave rem 29[33:37:41:45] sts on holder.

Left front

Using No.12 needles cast on 61[67:73:85:91] sts.

1st row *K1, P1, rep from * to last 19[19:19:25:25] sts, K9[9:9:12:12] sts, sl 1, K to end.

2nd row P19[19:19:25:25] sts, *K1, P1, rep from * to end.

Rep these 2 rows 3 times more, then first of them again. Change to No.10 needles.

Commence patt.

1st row (WS) P19[19:19:25:25] sts, *P3, K3, rep from * to end.

2nd row *K3, P3, rep from * to last 19[19:19:25:25] sts, K9[9:9:12:12] sts, sl 1, K to end.

3rd row As 1st.

4th row *Cr3, K3, rep from * to last 19[19:19:25:25] sts, K9[9:9:12:12] sts, sl 1, K to end.

5th row P19[19:19:25:25] sts, *K3, P3, rep from * to end.

6th row *K3, P3, rep from * to last 19[19:19:25:25] sts, K9[9:9:12:12] sts, sl 1, K to end.

7th row As 5th.

8th row *K3, Cr3, rep from * to last 19[19:19:25:25] sts, K9[9:9:12:12] sts, sl 1, K to end.

These 8 rows form patt. Cont in patt until work measures same as back to underarm, ending at armhole edge with a WS row.

Shape armhole

Cast off at beg of next and every alt row 4[5:5:6:6] sts once and 2 sts 1[1:2:2:3] times. 55[60:64:75:79] sts. Dec one st at armhole edge of next 3[4:4:5:5] alt rows. 52[56:60:70:74] sts.

Cont without shaping until armhole measures 3½[4:4½:5:6]in from beg, ending at front edge.

Shape neck

Cast off at beg of next and foll alt rows 19[19:19:25:25] sts once, 4[4:5:5:6] sts once, 2[3:3:3:4] sts once and 2 sts 1[1:1:2:2] times. Dec one st at neck edge on foll 2[3:4:4:4] alt rows. Cont without shaping until armhole measures same as back to shoulder, ending at armhole edge.

Shape shoulder

Cast off at beg of next and every alt row 6[6:5:6:6] sts 3[3:4:4:4] times and 5[7:7:5:7] sts once.

Right front

Mark positions for buttons on left front edge, first on last row of welt and last ½in below neck edge, with rem equally spaced between.

Using No.12 needles cast on 61[67:73:85:91] sts.

1st row K9[9:9:12:12] sts, sl 1, K9[9:9:12:12] sts, *P1, K1, rep from * to end.

2nd row *P1, K1, rep from * to last 19[19:19:25:25] sts, P to end.

Rep these 2 rows 3 times more.

Next row (buttonhole row) K3[3:3:5:5] sts, cast off 3 sts, K3[3:3:4:4] sts, sl 1, K3[3:3:4:4] sts, cast off 3 sts, K3[3:3:5:5] sts, *P1, K1, rep from * to end.

Change to No.10 needles.

Next row *K3, P3, rep from * to last 19[19:19:25:25] sts, P to end casting on 3 sts above those cast off in previous row.

Complete to match left front, reversing all shapings and making buttonholes as before as markers are reached.

Sleeves

Using No.12 needles cast on 45[45:51:51:57] sts. Work 9 rows rib as given for back. Change to No.10 needles. Cont in patt as given for back, inc one st at each end of every 8th row until there are 61[61:67:67:73] sts, then at each end of every foll 6th row until there are 71[77:83:89:95] sts, working extra sts into patt when possible. Cont without shaping until sleeve measures 11[13:15:17:17½]in from beg, ending with a WS row.

Shape top

Cast off 4[5:5:6:6] sts at beg of next 2 rows. Dec one st at each end of next and every alt row until 45[47:51:53:57] sts rem, ending with a WS row. Cast off at beg of next and every row 2 sts 8[8:10:10:12] times, 3 sts 4 times and 4 sts twice. Cast off rem 9[11:11:13:13] sts.

Neckband

Join shoulder seams. Using No.12 needles and with RS of work facing, rejoin yarn at beg of patt at right front neck edge, K up 25[27:29:31:33] sts up right front neck, K across back neck sts, K up 25[27:29:31:33] sts down left front neck to beg of patt. Beg with a P row work 5[5:5:9:9] rows st st.

Next row (picot row) K1, *yfwd, K2 tog, rep from * to end.

Beg with a P row work 6[6:6:10:10] rows st st. Cast off.

To make up

Press each piece under a damp cloth with a warm iron. Set in sleeves. Join side and sleeve seams. Fold front bands in half to WS at sl st line and sl st down. Fold neckband in half to WS at picot row and sl st down. Neaten double buttonholes. Press all seams. Sew on buttons.

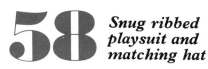

58 *Snug ribbed playsuit and matching hat*

Sizes

To fit 22 [24]in chest

Length to shoulder, 26½ [30½]in

Sleeve seam, 8 [9½]in

The figures in brackets [] refer to the 24in size only

Tension

6 sts and 8 rows to 1in over st st worked on No.9 needles.

Materials

15[17] balls Sirdar Double Crepe

One pair No.9 needles

One pair No.11 needles

12 [14]in zip fastener

Body stocking

Using No.11 needles cast on 62[66] sts.

1st row K2, *P2, K2, rep from * to end.

2nd row P2, *K2, P2, rep from * to end.

These 2 rows form patt. Cont in patt until work measures 1½in from beg. Change to No.9 needles. Cont in patt, inc one st at each end of

every 8th row until there are 82[90] sts. Cont without shaping until work measures 12 [15]in from beg, ending with a WS row.

Shape crutch
Cast off at beg of next and every row 4 sts twice and 2 sts 2[4] times. Dec one st at each end of next row. 68[72] sts. Rib 1 row, ending with a WS row. Leave sts on holder.
Work a 2nd piece in same way.

Join body
Next row K3 sts, rib 65[69] sts, with RS of first piece facing, rib 65[69] sts, K3 sts. 136[144] sts.
Next row K3 sts, rib to last 3 sts, K3 sts.
Keeping 3 sts at each end in g st throughout, cont in rib until work measures 17 [20½]in from beg, ending with a WS row.

Shape seat
Next row K3 sts, rib 104[108] sts, turn.
Next row Rib 78 sts, turn.
Next row Rib 72 sts, turn.
Next row Rib 66 sts, turn.
Cont in this way, working 6 sts less on every row until there are 30 sts in centre. Cont in rib across all sts until work measures 22 [25½]in from beg, ending with a WS row.

Divide for armholes
Next row Rib 31[33] sts, cast off 6 sts, rib to last 37[39] sts, cast off 6 sts, rib to end.
Complete left front first. Rib 1 row. Dec one st at beg of next and foll 2[3] alt rows. 28[29] sts.
Cont without shaping until armhole measures 3½ [4]in from beg, ending with a WS row.

Shape shoulder
Next row Cast off 14 sts, turn and leave rem 14[15] sts on holder for neck. Break off yarn. With WS of work facing, rejoin yarn to centre 62[66] sts for back. Rib 1 row. Dec one st at each end of next and foll 2[3] alt rows. 56[58] sts. Cont without shaping until armholes measure 3½ [4]in from beg, ending with a WS row.

Shape shoulder
Next row Cast off 14 sts, rib to last 14 sts, cast off to end.
Leave rem 28[30] sts on holder. With WS of work facing, rejoin yarn to rem sts and work right front to match left front, reversing shaping.

Sleeves
Using No.11 needles cast on 46[50] sts. Beg first row with P2, work 2in K2, P2 rib. Change to No.9 needles. Cont in rib, inc one st at each end of next and every foll 4th[6th] row until there are 66[70] sts. Cont without shaping until sleeve measures 8 [9½]in from beg, ending with a WS row.

Shape top
Cast off at beg of next and every row 3 sts twice and 2 sts twice. Dec one st at each end of every alt row until 20[22] sts rem. Cont without shaping on these 20[22] sts for length of shoulder, ending with a WS row. Leave sts on holder.

Neckband
Join saddle tops of sleeves to front and back shoulders. Using No.11 needles and with RS of work facing, rib across all sts on holders. 96[104] sts. Keeping 3 sts at each end in g st, cont in rib for 3in. Cast off loosely in rib.

To make up
Do not press. Set in sleeves. Join sleeve seams. Fold neckband in half to WS and sl st down. Join front seam leaving 12 [14]in open for zip. Sew in zip. Join leg seams. Press seams very lightly under a damp cloth with a warm iron.

Hat
Using No.11 needles cast on 102 sts. Work 3in K2 P2 rib. Change to No.9 needles. Cont in

rib until work measures 7½in from beg, ending with a WS row.

Shape top
Next row Rib 8 sts, *sl 1, K2 tog, psso, K3 tog, rib 20 sts, (P3 tog) twice, *, rib 20 sts, rep from * to * once, rib 10 sts. 86 sts.
Work 5 rows rib without shaping.
Next row Rib 6 sts, *(P3 tog) twice, rib 16 sts, sl 1, K2 tog, psso, K3 tog, *, rib 16 sts, rep from * to *, rib 8 sts. 70 sts.
Work 5 rows rib without shaping.
Next row Rib 4 sts, *sl 1, K2 tog, psso, K3 tog, rib 12 sts, (P3 tog) twice, *, rib 12 sts, rep from * to *, rib 6 sts. 54 sts.
Work 3 rows rib without shaping.
Next row K2, *(P3 tog) twice, rib 8 sts, sl 1, K2 tog, psso, K3 tog, *, rib 8 sts, rep from * to *, P2, K2. 38 sts.
Work 3 rows rib without shaping.
Next row *Sl 1, K2 tog, psso, K3 tog, rib 4 sts, (P3 tog) twice, *, rib 4 sts, rep from * to *, K2. 22 sts.
Rib 1 row. Break off yarn, thread through rem sts, draw up and fasten off.

To make up
Do not press. Join seam. Make a pompon and sew to top. Press seam very lightly under a damp cloth with a warm iron.

 ### Girl's suit, beret and socks in lobster claw stitch

Sizes
To fit 28 [31:34]in chest
Jacket length to shoulder, 16½ [18:19½]in
Sleeve seam, 14 [15:16]in
Skirt length, 18 [19:20]in
The figures in brackets [] refer to the 31 and 34in sizes respectively

Tension
5½ sts and 7½ rows to 1in over st st worked on No.8 needles

Materials
16[17:19] balls Patons Limelight Courtelle Double Crepe
One pair No.8 needles; One pair No.10 needles
One cable needle
Five buttons
Waist length of elastic

Jacket back
Using No.10 needles cast on 77[81:85] sts.
1st row K1, *P1, K1, rep from * to end.
2nd row P1, *K1, P1, rep from * to end.
Rep these 2 rows for 1in, ending with a 2nd row. Change to No.8 needles. Beg with a K row cont in st st until work measures 10½ [11½: 12½]in from beg, ending with a P row.

Shape armholes
Cast off 5[4:3] sts at beg of next 2 rows. Dec one st at each end of next and every alt row until 61[65:69] sts rem. Cont without shaping until armholes measure 6 [6½:7]in from beg, ending with a P row.

Shape shoulders
Cast off at beg of next and every row 6 sts 4 times and 6[7:8] sts twice. Leave rem 25[27:29] sts on holder.

Jacket left front
Using No.10 needles cast on 51[59:67] sts. Work 1in rib as given for back, ending with a 2nd row. Change to No.8 needles. Commence patt.
1st row (RS) P2, *K6, P2, rep from * to last 9 sts, turn and leave 9 sts on holder. 42[50:58] sts.
2nd row K2, *P2, P2 winding yarn twice round needle on each st, P2, K2, rep from * to end.

3rd row P2, *sl next 2 sts on cable needle and hold at back of work, K next st dropping extra loop, K2 from cable needle, sl next st on cable needle and hold at front of work dropping extra loop, K2 sts, K1 from cable needle – called C6 –, P2, rep from * to end.
4th row K2, *P6, K2, rep from * to end.
These 4 rows form patt. Cont in patt until work measures same as back to underarm, ending with a WS row.

Shape armhole
Cast off 5[6:8] sts at beg of next row. Work 1 row. Dec one st at beg of next and every alt row until 34[40:45] sts rem. Cont without shaping until armhole measures 4 [4½:5]in from beg, ending at armhole edge.

Shape neck
Next row Patt 28[32:35] sts, turn and leave rem 6[8:10] sts on holder.
Cast off 3 sts at beg of next row and 2 sts at beg of foll 2 alt rows. Dec one st at neck edge on foll 3 alt rows, then cont without shaping until armhole measures same as back to shoulder, ending at armhole edge.

Shape shoulder
Cast off at beg of next and every alt row 6[7:8] sts twice and 6[8:9] sts once.

Jacket right front
Work as given for left front, reversing all shaping.

Sleeves
Using No.10 needles cast on 41[45:49] sts. Work 2in rib as given for back, ending with a 2nd row and inc one st in centre of last row. 42[46: 50] sts. Change to No.8 needles. Commence patt.
1st row K4[6:8] sts, P2, *K6, P2, rep from * 3 times more, K4[6:8] sts.
2nd row P4[6:8] sts, K2, *P2, P2 winding yarn twice round needle on each st, P2, K2, rep from * 3 times more, P4[6:8] sts.
3rd row K4[6:8] sts, P2, *C6, P2, rep from * 3 times more, K4[6:8] sts.
4th row P4[6:8] sts, K2, *P6, K2, rep from * 3 times more, P4[6:8] sts.
These 4 rows set patt. Cont in patt, inc one st at each end of next and every foll 8th row, working extra sts in st st, until there are 62[66: 70] sts. Cont without shaping until sleeve measures 14 [15:16]in from beg, ending with a WS row.

Shape top
Cast off 5 sts at beg of next 2 rows. Dec one st at each end of next and every alt row until 40[42:44] sts rem. Cast off at beg of next and every row 2 sts 8[8:10] times and 3 sts 4 times. Cast off rem 12[14:12] sts.

Left front band
Sl 9 sts on holder on to No.10 needle, with RS of work facing inc in loop before first st, rib to end. Cont in rib until band fits along front edge to neck edge, when slightly stretched, ending with a WS row. Leave sts on holder. Tack band in place and mark positions for 5 buttons, first in first row above welt and last on last RS row, with 3 more equally spaced between.

Right front band
Sl 9 sts on holder on to No. 10 needle, with WS of work facing inc in loop before first st, rib to end.
Next row Rib 3 sts, cast off 3 sts, rib to end.
Next row Rib 4 sts, cast on 3 sts, rib to end.
Complete to match left front band, making buttonholes as markers are reached as before.

Neckband
Join shoulder seams. Using No.10 needles and with RS of work facing, rib across sts of right

front band and right front neck working last st of band tog with first st of front neck, K up 18 sts up side of neck, K across back neck sts, K up 18 sts down other side of neck, work across left front neck and left front band sts, working 2 tog as before. 91[97:103] sts. Cont in rib for 1in. Cast off in rib.

To make up
Do not press. Set in sleeves. Join side and sleeve seams. Sew on front bands. Sew on buttons.

Skirt back
Using No.10 needles cast on 89[97:105] sts. Work ½in rib as given for jacket back, inc one st in centre of last row. 90[98:106] sts. Change to No. 8 needles. Cont in patt as given for jacket left front until work measures 17 [18: 19]in from beg, or 1in less than required length, ending with a WS row and dec one st in centre of last row. Change to No.10 needles. Work 2in rib as given at beg. Cast off in rib.

Skirt front
Using No.10 needles cast on 97[105:113] sts. Work as given for skirt back.

To make up
Do not press. Join side seams. Fold ribbing at top in half to WS and sl st down. Thread elastic through waist.

Socks
Using No.10 needles cast on 55[59:63] sts. Work 1in rib as given for jacket back, ending with a 2nd row and inc one st in centre of last row. 56[60:64] sts.
Change to No.8 needles.
Next row K11[13:15] sts, P2, *K6, P2, rep from * 3 times more, K11[13:15] sts.
This row sets patt. Cont in patt until work measures 4 [4½:5]in from beg, ending with a WS row.
Shape leg
Next row K1, K2 tog, patt to last 3 sts, sl 1, K1, psso, K1.
Cont dec in this way on every foll 6th row until 44[46:48] sts rem. Cont without shaping until work measures 12 [13:14]in from beg, ending with a WS row.
Divide for heel
Next row K10 sts, turn, sl next 24[26:28] sts on holder and leave for instep.
Next row P10 sts, then P across the 10 sts at other end of row.
Cont on these sts in st st for 2 [2¼:2½]in, ending with a P row.
Turn heel
Next row K12 sts, K2 tog, turn.
Next row P5 sts, P2 tog, turn.
Next row K6 sts, K2 tog, turn.
Cont to work one more st on every row until all sts are worked in, ending with a P row. 12 sts. Break off yarn.
With RS of work facing, rejoin yarn to beg of heel, K up 10[11:12] sts down side of heel, K12 heel sts, then K up 10[11:12] sts up other side of heel. 32[34:36] sts.
Next row P to end.
Next row K1, K2 tog, K to last 3 sts, sl 1, K1, psso, K1.
Rep last 2 rows 5 times more. Cont without shaping until work measures 5 [5½:6]in from where sts were picked up at heel, ending with a P row.
Shape toe
Next row K1, K2 tog, K to last 3 sts, sl 1, K1, psso, K1.
Next row P to end.
Rep last 2 rows 4[5:6] times more. Leave sts on holder to graft.
Work instep
Sl instep sts on to No.8 needle, with RS of work

facing rejoin yarn, K3[4:5] sts, patt 18 sts, K3[4:5] sts. Cont in patt as now set until instep measures same as under part of foot to toe, ending with a RS row.
Next row P3[4:5] sts, (K2 tog, P6) twice, K2 tog, P3[4:5] sts.
Shape toe
Work as given for under part of foot and P2 tog in centre of last row. Graft sts.

To make up
Do not press. Join back seam. Join side seams of foot.

Beret
Using No.10 needles cast on 101 sts. Work 1in rib as given for jacket back, ending with a 2nd row.
Change to No.8 needles.
Next row K into front and back of every st. 202 sts.
Next row K2, *P6, K2, rep from * to end. Cont in patt as given for Jacket front for 28 rows.
Next row P2 tog, *patt 6 sts, P2 tog, rep from * to end. 176 sts.
Work 7 more rows patt working P1 instead of P2 throughout.
Next row P1, *patt 5 sts, sl 1, K1, psso, rep from * to last 7 sts, patt 6 sts, P1. 152 sts.
Work 7 more rows patt without any P sts between. Change to No.10 needles.
Next row K2 tog, *P1, K1, rep from * to end. 151 sts.
Next row P1, *K1, P1, rep from * to end.
Next row Rib 14 sts, (sl 1, K2 tog, psso, rib 27 sts) 4 times, sl 1, K2 tog, psso, rib 14 sts. 141 sts.
Next row Rib to end.
Next row Rib 12 sts, (sl 1, K1, psso, K1, K2 tog, rib 23 sts) 4 times, sl 1, K1, psso, K1, K2 tog, rib 12 sts. 131 sts.
Next row Rib 12 sts, (P3, rib 23 sts) 4 times, P3, rib 12 sts.
Next row Rib 12 sts, (sl 1, K2 tog, psso, rib 23 sts) 4 times, sl 1, K2 tog, psso, rib 12 sts. 121 sts.
Next row Rib to end.
Cont to dec in this way on every alt row until 71 sts rem, ending with a RS row.
Next row Rib 6 sts, (P3 tog, rib 11 sts) 4 times, P3 tog, rib 6 sts.
Next row Rib 4 sts, (sl 1, K1, psso, K1, K2 tog, rib 7 sts) 4 times, sl 1, K1, psso, K1, K2 tog, rib 4 sts.
Next row Rib 4 sts, (P3 tog, rib 7 sts) 4 times, P3 tog, rib 4 sts. 41 sts.
Cont dec in this way on every row until 21 sts rem.
Next row K1, *K2 tog, rep from * to end. Break off yarn, thread through rem sts and fasten off.

To make up
Do not press. Join seam.

60 Summer dress with cabled bodice

Sizes
To fit 22 [24:26:28]in chest
Length to shoulder, 13½ [14½:16½:19½]in
Sleeve seam, 1½ [1½:2:2]in
The figures in brackets [] refer to the 24, 26 and 28in sizes respectively
Tension
6 sts and 8 rows to 1in over st st worked on No. 9 needles

Materials
8[9:11:12] balls Patons Four Seasons Courtelle
One pair No.9 needles
One pair No.11 needles
One cable needle
Set of 4 No.11 needles pointed at both ends

Back
Using No.11 needles cast on 100[106:120:130] sts. Beg with a K row work 1in st st, ending with a K row.
Next row K all sts tbl to form hemline.
Change to No.9 needles. Beg with a K row cont in st st until work measures 1½ [1½:2:2]in from hemline, ending with a P row.
Shape skirt
Next row K19[20:23:25] sts, K2 tog, K19[20: 23:25] sts, sl 1, K1, psso, K16[18:20:22] sts, K2 tog, K19[20:23:25] sts, sl 1, K1, psso, K19 [20:23:25] sts.
Beg with a P row work 3[3:5:5] rows st st.
Next row K19[20:23:25] sts, K2 tog, K17[18: 21:23] sts, sl 1, K1, psso, K16[18:20:22] sts, K2 tog, K17[18:21:23] sts, sl 1, K1, psso, K19 [20:23:25] sts.
Beg with a P row work 3[3:5:5] rows st st.
Cont dec in this way on next and every foll 4th [4th:6th:6th] row until 68[74:80:86] sts rem. Cont without shaping until work measures 5½ [6½:8:9½]in from hemline, ending with a P row. Commence bodice patt.
1st row P2, *K4, P2, rep from * to end.

2nd row K2, *P4, K2, rep from * to end. Rep these 2 rows once more.
5th row P2, *sl next 2 sts on cable needle and hold at front of work, K2 sts, then K2 from cable needle — called C4F —, P2, rep from * to end.
6th row As 2nd.
7th row As 1st.
8th row As 2nd.
These 8 rows form patt. Cont in patt until work measures 9 [9½:11:13½]in from hemline, ending with a WS row.
Shape armholes
Cast off 4 sts at beg of next 2 rows.
Next row K3 sts, K2 tog, patt to last 5 sts, sl 1, K1, psso, K3.
Next row P4 sts, patt to last 4 sts, P4.
Next row K4 sts, patt to last 4 sts, K4.
Next row P4 sts, patt to last 4 sts, P4.
Cont to dec in this way at each end of next and every foll 4th row until 46[50:56:60] sts rem. Work 1[1:3:3] rows after last dec row.
Shape shoulders
Cast off at beg of next and every row 6[7:7:8] sts twice and 7[7:8:8] sts twice. Leave rem 20 [22:26:28] sts on holder.

Front
Work as given for back until 48[52:58:62] sts rem, then work 1 row after last dec row, ending with a WS row.
Shape neck
Next row Patt 16[17:18:19] sts, turn and leave rem sts on holder.
Next row Dec one st, patt to end.
Next row K3 sts, K2 tog, patt to end.
Next row Dec one st, patt to end.
Work 0[0:2:2] more rows without shaping.
Shape shoulder
Cast off at beg of next and foll alt row 6[7:7:8] sts once and 7[7:8:8] sts once.
With RS of work facing, sl first 16[18:22:24] sts on holder and leave for centre neck, rejoin yarn to rem sts and patt to end. Complete to match first side, reversing all shapings.

Sleeves
Using No.11 needles cast on 46[50:50:54] sts.
1st row K2, *P2, K2, rep from * to end.

2nd row P2, *K2, P2, rep from * to end.
Rep these 2 rows 1[1:2:2] times more. Change to No.9 needles. Beg with a K row cont in st st, inc one st at each end of first row, then cont without shaping until sleeve measures 1½ [1½:2: 2]in from beg, ending with a P row. 48[52:52: 56] sts.
Shape top
Cast off 4 sts at beg of next 2 rows. Dec one st at each end of next and every foll 4th row as given for back until 38[42:38:42] sts rem. Work 3 rows without shaping after last dec row. Cont to dec in this way at each end of next and every alt row until 16[16:18:18] sts rem. Cont on these sts without shaping for length of shoulder, ending with a P row. Leave sts on holder.

Neckband
Sew saddle top of sleeves to back and front shoulders. Using set of 4 No.11 needles and with RS of work facing, K across all sts on holders dec one st at each back seam and K up 3[3:5:5] sts up each side of front neck. 72[76:92:96] sts. Work in rounds of K2, P2 rib for 1¼ [1¼:2:2]in. Cast off loosely in rib.

To make up
Press each piece under a dry cloth with a cool iron. Set in sleeves. Join side and sleeve seams. Fold neckband in half to WS and sl st down. Turn hem to WS at lower edge and sl st down. Press seams.

61 Wrapover judo dressing gown for boy or girl

Sizes
To fit 24 [26:28]in chest
Length to shoulder, 20 [23:26]in
Sleeve seam, 9½ [11:12½]in
The figures in brackets [] refer to the 26 and 28in sizes respectively
Tension
7½ sts and 10 rows to 1in over patt worked on No.11 needles
Materials
11[12:14] balls Robin Vogue 4 ply in main shade, A
2 balls of contrast colour, B
One pair No.11 needles
One pair No.13 needles

Back
Using No.13 needles and A, cast on 120[127: 134] sts. Beg with a K row work ¾in st st, ending with a K row.
Next row K all sts tbl to form hemline. Change to No.11 needles. Commence patt.
1st row K to end.
2nd row K1, *P6, K1, rep from * to end.
These 2 rows form patt and are rep throughout. Cont in patt until work measures 1½ [2:2½]in from hemline, ending with a WS row. Dec one st at each end of every foll 10th[12th: 14th] row until 98[105:112] sts rem. Cont without shaping until work measures 14½ [17: 19½]in from hemline, ending with a WS row.
Shape armholes
Cast off at beg of next and every row 5 sts twice and 2 sts 6 times. Dec one st at each end of next and foll 2[3:4] alt rows. 70[75:80] sts. Cont without shaping until armholes measure 5½ [6:6½]in from beg, ending with a WS row.
Shape shoulders
Cast off at beg of next and every row 4[5:5] sts 4 times and 5[5:6] sts 4 times. Break off A and join in B. Change to No.13 needles. K 1 row dec one st in centre of row on 24 and 28in

sizes only. 33[35:35] sts.
**Next row P1, *K1, P1, rep from * to end.
Next row K1, *P1, K1, rep from * to end.
Next row P1, *K1, P1, rep from * to end.
Next row (picot hem) K1, *yfwd, K2 tog, rep from * to end.
Next row P1, *K1, P1, rep from * to end.
Next row K1, *P1, K1, rep from * to end.
Cast off loosely in rib. ******

Left front
Using No.13 needles and A, cast on 78[85:92] sts. Beg with a K row work ¾in st st, ending with a K row.
Next row K all sts tbl to form hemline. Change to No.11 needles. Cont in patt as given for back until work measures 1½ [2:2½]in from hemline, ending with a WS row. Dec one st at beg of next and every foll 10th[12th:14th] row until 67[74:81] sts rem. Cont without shaping until work measures 20[24:28] rows less than back to underarm, ending with a WS row.
Shape front edge
Dec one st at end of next and every alt row until 57[62:67] sts rem, ending with a WS row.
Shape armhole
Cont dec at front edge on every alt row as before, *at the same time* cast off 5 sts at beg of next row, then 2 sts at beg of foll 3 alt rows, then dec one st at beg of foll 3[4:5] alt rows. Cont to dec at front edge only on every alt row until 18[20:22] sts rem. Cont without shaping until armhole measures same as back to shoulder, ending with a WS row.
Shape shoulder
Cast off at beg of next and every alt row 4[5:5] sts twice and 5[5:6] sts twice.

Right front
Work as given for left front, reversing all shaping.

Sleeves
Using No.11 needles and A, cast on 59[61:63] sts.
1st row K to end.
2nd row P1[2:3] sts, K1, *P6, K1, rep from * to last 1[2:3] sts, P1[2:3].
These 2 rows set patt. Cont in patt, inc one st at each end of 13th and every foll 12th row until there are 71[75:79] sts. Cont without shaping until sleeve measures 9½ [11:12½]in from beg, or required length to underarm, ending with a WS row.
Shape top
Cast off 5 sts at beg of next 2 rows. Dec one st at each end of next and foll 13[14:15] alt rows. 33[35:37] sts. Cast off at beg of next and every row 2 sts 6 times and 3 sts 4 times. Cast off rem 9[11:13] sts.
Sleeve edging
Using No.13 needles, B and with RS of work facing, K up 53[55:57] sts round lower edge of sleeve. Work as given for back neck from ** to **.

Front borders
Using No.13 needles, B and with RS of work facing, K up 151[163:175] sts up right front edge beg at hemline. Work as given for back neck from ** to **. Work left front border in same way, beg at shoulder.

To make up
Press each piece under a damp cloth with a warm iron. Join shoulder seams. Set in sleeves. Join side and sleeve seams. Turn hem to WS at lower edge and sl st down. Turn front borders, back neck border and sleeve edges to WS at picot row and sl st down.
Press seams. Using B, make a thick cord sash to tie round waist.

62 Plaid blanket on jumbo pins

Size
Before doubling approximately 72in by 142in
Tension
4 sts and 5 rows to 4in
Materials
Pingouin Double Knitting (25 grm balls)
69 balls main shade A, grey
66 balls first contrast B, black
18 balls 2nd contrast C, gold
18 balls 3rd contrast D, flame
One pair Aero Jumbo needles
One No.7·00 (ISR) Aero crochet hook
Note. 6 strands are used together throughout. Take both ends of each of 3 balls to obtain 6 threads.

Blanket
1st strip
Using 6 strands of B cast on 18 sts.
1st row *K1, P1, rep from * to end.
Work 6 rows st st beg with a K row.
Continue in st st working in stripes thus:
*2 rows A, 1 row B, 2 rows C, 1 row B, 2 rows A, 7 rows B, 7 rows A, 2 rows D, 1 row A, 2 rows C, 1 row A, 2 rows D, 7 rows A, 7 rows B, rep from *3 times then work 2 rows A, 1 row B, 2 rows C, 1 row B, 2 rows A and 6 rows B.
Last row Using B, *K1, P1, rep from * to end. Cast off. Work 3 more strips in the same way.

To make up
Finish off all ends securely.
Sew strips together lengthwise.
Using No.7·00 (ISR) hook and 6 strands of C work a chain the same length as the strip seam. Finish off ends. Work 2 more chains the same length. Pin chains in place along seam and from wrong side sew securely in place.
Using 6 strands of D crochet 10 chains the length of the strip.
Sew one chain on either side of gold chains. Sew rem 4 chains in place, one in the centre of each strip.
Fold blanket in half and slip stitch cast on and off edges together.
Fringe
For each tassel use 6 strands of yarn 8 in long. Place one tassel on each st or each row round sides matching colours.

63 Spherical lampshade

Size
To fit a round lampshade 22in diameter
Tension
4 sts and 7 rows to 1in measured over st st
Materials
Cordonnet du Pingouin
16 50gm balls
One No.9 16 in Aero Twinpin
One No.9 30in Aero Twinpin
Note. Yarn is used double throughout.

Lampshade (top section)
Using No.9 16in Twinpin cast on 70 sts.
K 1 row.

Place marker thread before first st and join work into a circle.
K 6 rounds.
K one more round dec 20 sts evenly.   50 sts.
1st patt round * P2, K1tbl, P2, yrn 7 times, rep from * to end of round.   10 bells.
2nd patt round * P2, K1tbl, P2, K into back of each of 7 loops to form 7 sts, rep from * to end.
3rd patt round * P2, K1tbl, P2, K5, K2 tog, rep from * to end.
4th patt round * P2, K1 tbl, P2, K4, K2 tog. rep from * to end.
5th patt round * P2, K1 tbl, P2, K3, K2 tog, rep from * to end.
6th patt round * P2, K1 tbl, P2, K2, K2 tog, rep from * to end.
7th patt round * P2, K1 tbl, P2 K1, K2 tog, rep from * to end.
8th patt round * P2, K1 tbl, P2, K2 tog, rep from * to end.
9th patt round * P1, P up 1, K1 tbl, P up 1, P1, yrn 7 times, rep from * to end. 20 bells.
Rep from 2nd – 8th patt rounds once.
Change to No.9 30in Twinpin.
17th patt round As 9th patt round.   40 bells.
Rep 2nd – 8th patt rounds once.
25th patt round * P2, K1 tbl, P2, K1 tbl, P1, P2 tog, yrn 7 times, P2, K1 tbl, rep from * to end.   20 bells.
Work 2nd – 8th patt rows once noting that there are now 11 sts between bells.
33rd patt round As 9th patt round.   40 bells.
Rep 2nd – 8th patt rounds once.
41st patt round As 25th patt round.   20 bells.
Rep 2nd – 8th patt rounds once.
49th patt round As 9th patt round.   40 bells.
Rep 2nd – 8th patt rounds once.
57th patt round As 25th patt round.   20 bells.
Rep 2nd – 8th patt rounds once.
65th patt round As 9th patt round.   80 bells.
Rep 2nd – 8th patt rounds once.
73rd patt round * P2, K1 tbl, P2, K1 tbl, P1, P2 tog, yrn 7 times, P2, K1 tbl, P2, yrn 7 times, P2 tog, P1, K1 tbl, P2, yrn 7 times, P2 tog, K1 tbl, rep from * to end.   60 bells.
Rep 2nd – 8th rounds once.
81st patt round As 9th patt round.   80 bells.
Rep 2nd – 8th patt rounds once.
Thread sts on to a length of yarn longer than the circumference of the lampshade or cast off if preferred.
Work the bottom section in the same way.

To make up
Fit the two sections on to the lampshade and graft or seam invisibly together.

64

Bunny nightdress case

Size
10in high and 15in long without tail
Tension
2 sts to 1in
Materials
Twilley's 747 yarn
3 hanks
One pair Twilley's ½in Whizzpins
One 10in zip
Scraps of black and white felt for eyes

Body
Using ½in Whizzpins cast on 8 sts.
1st row K.

2nd row Inc once in each of first 2 sts, K to end of row.
3rd row Inc in first st, K to end of row.
4th row K.
Rep 2nd – 4th rows twice more, then 2nd row once. K 12 rows.
23rd row K2 tog, K to end of row.
24th row K.
Rep 23rd and 24th rows twice more.
K 3 rows.
32nd row K to last st, inc.
33rd row Inc, K to end.
K 2 rows.
Rep 23rd and 24th rows twice then 23rd row once.
41st row K2 tog, K to last 2 sts, K2 tog.
42nd row K.
Rep 41st and 42nd rows 3 times more.
Cast off.
Work a second piece in the same way.

Ear
Using ½in Whizzpins cast on 3 sts.
K 2 rows.
3rd row K to last st, inc.
K 2 rows.
6th row As 3rd row.
K 2 rows.
9th row As 3rd row.
K 8 rows.
18th row K2 tog, K to last 2 sts, K2 tog.
K 2 rows.
21st row As 18th row.
K one row.
Cast off.
Make 2nd ear in the same way.

To make up
Press all pieces on the wrong side under a damp cloth using a warm iron.
Place the two body pieces together and seam ½in from front edge leaving 1in open at back of head for ears and 10in open at bottom edge for zip. Place ears from the right side into their spaces and secure.
Make a pompon from rem yarn for tail and sew on. Cut 2 white felt ovals 2in long and 1½in wide for eyes. Cut 2 black felt circles 1½in diameter. Sew black circle to white oval and sew in place. Cut white felt oval 2½in long and 2in wide for nose and sew in place.
Cut 2 white felt teeth 1½in deep and also some strips for whiskers. Sew in place.

65

Hot water bottle cover

Size
11½in by 10in
Tension
8 sts to 1in
Materials
Twilley's Cortina
2oz purple
2oz mulberry
2oz lavender
One pair No. 7 needles
One No.4·00 (ISR) Aero crochet hook
2 buttons
Note. Use yarn double throughout.

Back
Using No. 7 needles and 2 strands of purple cast on 65 sts.
1st row (WS) P.

2nd row (K1, yfwd, K4, sl1, K2tog, psso, K4, yfwd, K1) 5 times.
Rep last 2 rows twice more.
Break off yarn
leaving ends to darn in.
Join in 2 strands of mulberry. Rep first and 2nd rows 3 times.
Break off yarn as before.
Join in 2 strands of lavender. Rep first and 2nd rows 3 times. Break off yarn as before.
These 18 rows form the patt and are rep throughout. Continue in patt until work measures 11½in ending with the last row of a colour stripe.
Cast off purlwise.

Front
Work as given for back.

To make up
Press pieces lightly under a damp cloth with a warm iron.
Using No.4·00 (ISR) hook and 2 strands of purple work 1 row of dc round each edge of front and back.
With RS of front facing join front and back by working 1 row dc through both thicknesses from front edge down side and to within 1½in of centre on lower edge. Break off yarn. Leave a 3in gap for base of bottle and rejoin yarn finishing lower edge and other side, then complete by working 1 row dc across top of front only making 2 button loops of 3ch each 1in in from either side. Fasten off.
Finish off ends and re-press.
Sew buttons to correspond with button loops.

66

Dog's jacket

Size
To fit 13½ [17¼:21¼]in chest
Length from neck to tail 11¾ [14½:17¼]in
Tension
6 sts to 1in slightly stretched
Materials
Wendy Double Knitting Wool
4[4:6] balls
One pair No.8 needles

Back
Using No.8 needles cast on 24 sts.
1st row (WS row) K1, *P2, K2, rep from * to last 3 sts, P2, K1.
2nd row (RS row) K3, * P2, K2, rep from * to last st, K1.
Rep 1st and 2nd rows twice more.
Next row K1, P2, inc by lifting thread before next st, rib to last 3 sts, inc by lifting thread before next st, P2, K1.
Next row K3, rib to last 3 sts, K3.
Rep last 2 rows until there are 56[72:88] sts, keeping 3 edge sts as set and working inc sts into central ribs as they are made.
Work without shaping until 8¾[10¼:11¾]in from cast on edge ending with a WS row.
Next row K2, S11, work 1, psso, rib to last 4 sts, K2 tog, K2.
Next row K1, P2, rib to last 3 sts, P2, K1.
Rep last 2 rows until 32[40:48] sts rem.
Work until 11¾[14½:17¼]in. Slip sts on to a holder.

Front
Using No.8 needles cast on 20[24:28] sts.

1st row (WS) K3, * P2, K2, rep from * to last st, K1.
2nd row (RS) K1, * P2, K2, rep from * to last 3 sts, P2, K1.
Rep 1st and 2nd rows until work measures 7¼[8¾:10¼]in from cast on edge, ending with a WS row.

Collar

1st row With RS facing rib to last 2 sts, P2 tog, continue across sts for front from holder, K2 tog, rib to end. 50[62:74]sts.
Work in rib until collar measures 3¼[3½:4]in.
Cast off in rib.

To make up

Sew collar seam. Continue seam below collar joining front and back for 1¼[1½:2¼]in.
Leave 3¼[3½:4]in unjoined for leg opening.
Seam remainder. Join other side of front and back in the same way.

Initialled face flannel

Size
12in square
Tension
7 sts to 1in
Materials
Twilley's Stalite
1 2oz ball in main shade, A
1 2oz ball in contrast shade, B
One pair of No.10 needles

Face flannel

Using No.10 needles and B cast on 83 sts.
1st row K1, *P1, K1, rep from * to end.
2nd row P1, * K1, P1, rep from * to end.
Continue in rib for 2 rows more, dec 1 st at each end of both rows.
79 sts.
K 1 row. Break off B leaving an end to darn in.
Join in A and P 1 row.
1st patt row P1, *K1, P1, rep from * to end.
2nd patt row K1, *P1, K1, rep from * to end.
3rd patt row As 2nd.
4th patt row As first.
These 4 rows form the patt.
Continue in patt until work measures 11½in from cast on edge, ending with a 2nd patt row.
K 1 row.
Break off A as before.
Join in B. * P 1 row.
Next row K1, * P1, K1, rep from * to end.
Work 3 rows more in rib inc 1 st at each end of next 2 rows only.
Cast off in rib. *

Side borders

Using B and with right side facing K up 77 sts along side of centre section. Work from * to * as for last border.
Rep along rem side.

To make up

Finish off ends and sew corner border mitres together.
Using one strand of B embroider the outline of initials in one corner. Using 2 strands of B fill in the space between outlines.
Press lightly under a damp cloth on the wrong side using a warm iron.

Ribbed square bedspread

Size
About 30in by 40in or as required
Tension
9 sts and 8 rows to 1in over patt worked on No.8 needles, unstretched
Materials
Lister Lavenda Double Knitting
14 oz balls red, A
7 oz balls pale pink, B; 7 oz balls deep pink, C
One pair No.8 Aero needles
Square
Using No.8 needles and A cast on 44 sts.
1st row K1, * K4, P2, rep from * to last st, K1.
2nd row K1, * K2, P4, rep from * to last st, K1.
Repeat first row until work measures 5in.
Cast off.
Work 23 squares more using A.
Work 12 squares more using B.
Work 12 squares more using C.
To make up
Join squares together as shown in the diagram, alternating the direction of the rib.

See below for chart for assembling the ribbed squares.

Pompon trimmed blanket

Size
About 50in by 80in
Tension
One square of 23 sts and 39 rows measures 5in
Materials
Patons Double Knitting Wool
3 50grm balls in each of 9 colours
One pair No.7 Aero needles
Square
Using No. 7 needles cast on 23 sts.
Work in garter st (every row knit) for 39 rows.
Cast off.
To make up
Sew squares together on the wrong side.
Make pompons from leftover wool and sew on corners of squares as shown in the illustration.

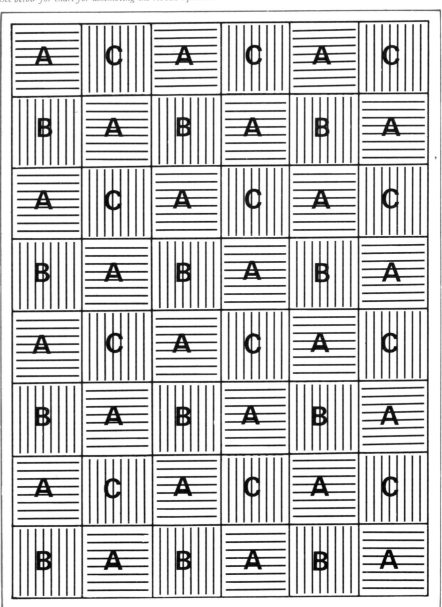

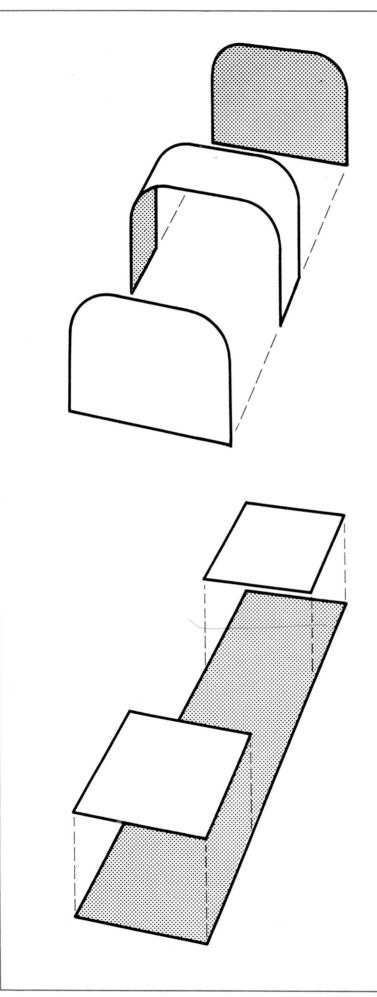

70,71

Toaster cover and oven mitts

Size
Toaster cover: to fit a Morphy Richards toaster
Oven mitts: 30in long
Tension
6½ sts and 8 rows to 2in measured over st st
Materials
Twilley's Knitcot
For Toaster cover
3 2oz balls scarlet, A
1 2oz ball white, B
1 2oz ball gentian blue, C
For Oven mitts
3 2oz balls scarlet, A
1 2oz ball white, B
1 2oz ball gentian blue, C
2 pieces of wadding 6½in square
For both
One pair No.4 Aero needles
One No.6·00 (ISR) Aero crochet hook
Note. Knitcot is used double throughout.

Toaster cover
Side pieces
Using No.4 needles and 2 strands of A cast on 33 sts.
K 4 rows.
** **5th row** K.
6th row P.
Continue in st st working patt thus:
1st patt row K1B, * 3A, 1B, rep from * to end.
2nd patt row P1C, * 1B, 1A, 1B, 1C, rep from * to end.
3rd patt row K1A, * 1C, 1B, 1C, 1A, rep from * to end.
4th patt row P2A, * 1C, 3A, rep from * to last 3 sts, 1C, 2A.
Using A K 1 row, P 1 row, K 1 row. **
8th patt row P7A, * 1B, 8A, rep from * once more, 1B, 7A.
9th patt row K6A, * 1B, 1C, 1B, 6A, rep from * once more, 1B, 1C, 1B, 6A.
10th patt row P5A, * 1B, 3C, 1B, 4A, rep from * twice more, 1A.
11th patt row K4A, * 1B, 5C, 1B, 2A, rep from * twice more, 2A.
Rep 10th, 9th and 8th rows once.
Using A K 1 row, P 1 row, K 1 row.
Rep 4th, 3rd, 2nd and first rows once.
Using A and dec one st at each end of every row P 1 row, K 1 row, P 1 row, K 1 row.
Cast off rem sts loosely.
Work another piece in the same way.
Centre piece
Using 2 strands of A cast on 18 sts. Work in garter st for 22in when slightly stretched.
Cast off.

To make up
Press pieces lightly.
Using No.6 (ISR) hook and 2 strands of B work 1 row dc round centre piece and side and top edges on side pieces.
Pin centre piece between side pieces and work 1 row dc using 2 strands of B through previous row. Work 1 row more dc.

Oven mitts
Main part
Using No.4 needles and 2 strands of A cast on 21 sts. K 4 rows.
Work as side pieces of toaster cover from ** to **

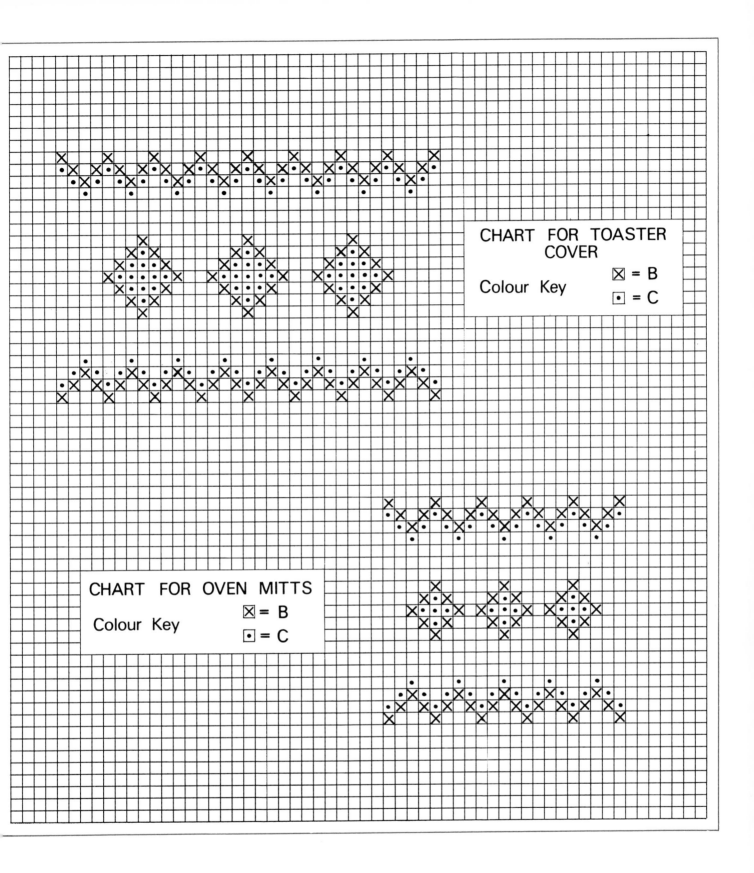

CHART FOR TOASTER
COVER

Colour Key   ⊠ = B
               · = C

CHART FOR OVEN MITTS

Colour Key   ⊠ = B
               · = C

*** **8th patt row** P4A, * 1B, 5A, rep from *
once more, 1B, 4A.
9th patt row K3A, * 1B, 1C, 1B, 3A, rep
from * once more, 1B, 1A.
10th patt row P2A, * 1B, 3C, 1B, 1A, rep
from * twice more, 1A.
Rep 9th and 8th rows once.
Using A K 1 row, P 1 row, K 1 row.
Rep 4th, 3rd, 2nd and first rows once.
Continue using A only. ***

P 1 row, K 1 row, P 1 row.
Work in garter st for 25in when slightly
stretched ending with a WS row.
Rep from ** to ** as for sides of toaster cover
then from *** to *** as for other end.
P 1 row, K 5 rows.
Cast off knitwise.
Lining pieces
Using 2 strands of A cast on 19 sts.
Work 6in using st st. Cast off.

To make up

Press lightly. Sew linings to WS of each end of
garter st strips enclosing wadding, so that they
are covered by patterned section when folded
back. Fold patterned sections into place. Using
2 strands of B work 1 row dc round all edges
working through both thicknesses at ends.
Work 1 more round of dc.
Finish off.

72, 73

Patchwork tea and coffee cosy

Size
To fit a teapot 6½in high
To fit a slender coffee pot 8in high
Tension
5 sts and 7 rows to 1in
Materials
Twilley's Cortina
1oz red
1oz mango
1oz old gold
1oz honeysuckle
One pair of No. 7 needles
One No 4·00 (ISR) Aero crochet hook
Note. Yarn is used double throughout.
When changing colours across rows twist colours together to prevent holes. When changing colours from previous row work st above to correspond with sts on previous row, ie K the Pst and P the Kst.

Tea cosy
Using No. 7 needles and 2 strands of honeysuckle cast on 44 sts.
Work from chart reading right side rows from right to left and wrong side rows from left to right. Cast off.
Work 2nd side in same way.

Edging
Using No.4·00 (ISR) hook and 2 strands of honeysuckle work 1 row dc round outer edges of each piece. Then work in dc through both edges to join side and top leaving 3in spaces at each side to correspond with spout and handle and working topknot in centre of top edge thus, 1dc into centre dc (12ch, slip st to last dc) 3 times, then complete in dc.

To make up
Press cosy on wrong side under a damp cloth using a warm iron.

Coffee cosy
Work as given for tea cosy casting on 28 sts instead of 44 sts. Work from coffee cosy chart.

Read the charts from right to left on right side rows, and from left to right for wrong side rows.

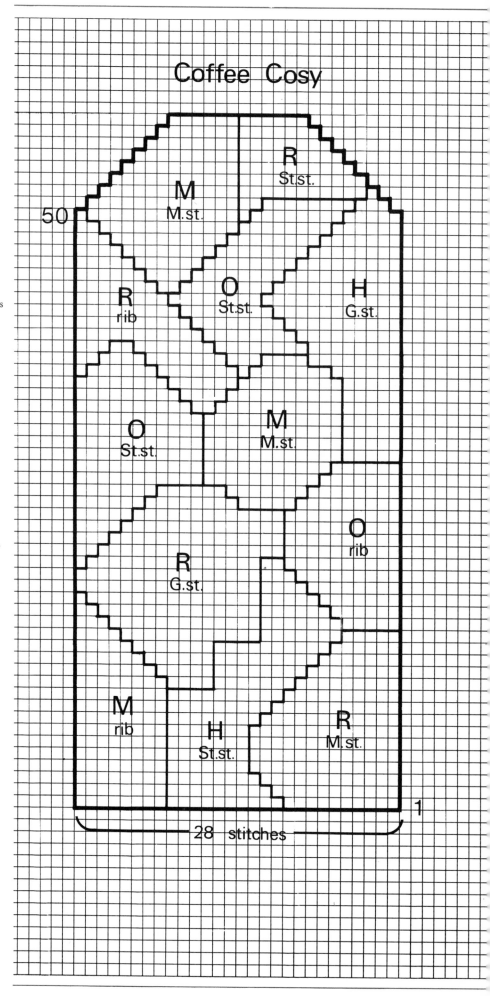

Coffee Cosy

Tea Cosy

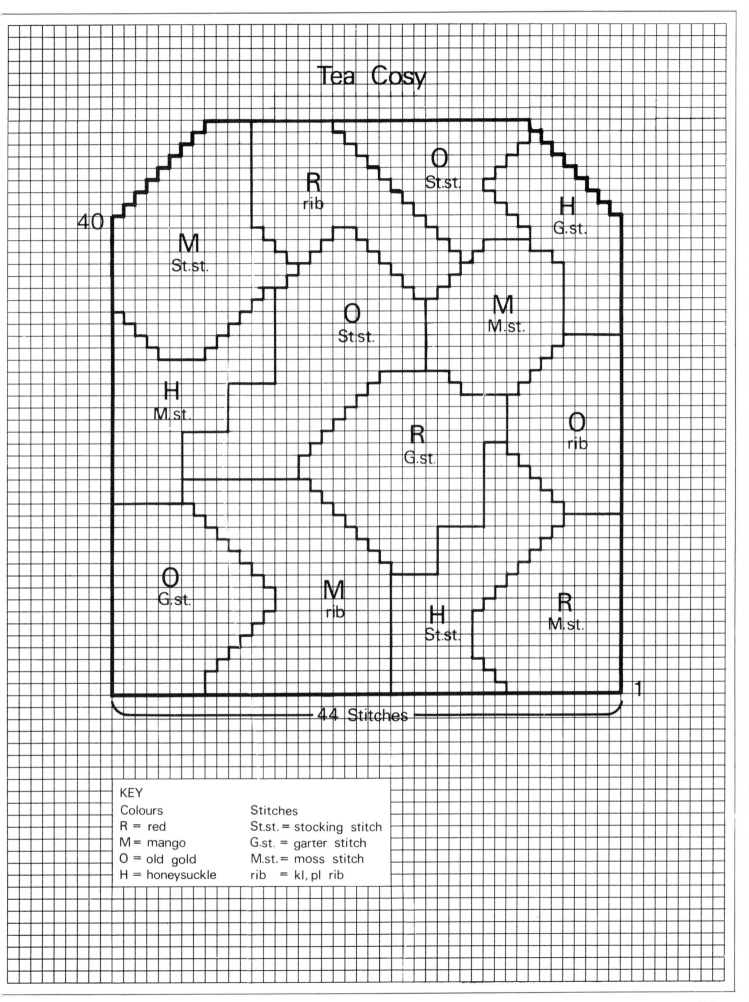

40

O
St.st.

R
rib

H
G.st.

M
St.st.

O
St.st.

M
M.st.

H
M.st.

R
G.st.

O
rib

O
G.st.

M
rib

H
St.st.

R
M.st.

1

44 Stitches

KEY

Colours
R = red
M = mango
O = old gold
H = honeysuckle

Stitches
St.st. = stocking stitch
G.st. = garter stitch
M.st. = moss stitch
rib = k1, p1 rib

74,75

*Two
floor cushions
or footstools*

Size
18in square by 3½in deep
Tension
5½ sts to 1in
Materials
Pingouin Double Knitting
Green cushion
6 25 grm balls green, A
1 25 grm ball pink, B
1 25 grm ball blue, C
1 25 grm ball lemon, D
Blue cushion
6 25 grm balls blue, A
1 25 grm ball pink, B
1 25 grm ball green, C
1 25 grm ball lemon, D
For both
One pair No.9 Aero needles
One cushion pad

Green cushion
Using No.9 needles and B cast on 8 sts.
1st row K.
2nd and every alt row K each st in the colour in which it was worked on the previous row, keeping all threads on WS when working in more than one colour.
3rd row K twice into each st. 16 sts.
5th row Keeping threads behind work on WS, *K2B, K up 1A, K2B, rep from * 3 times more.
7th row * (K1, K up 1, K1) B, (K up 1, K1, K up 1) A, (K1, K up 1, K1) B, rep from * 3 times more.
9th row * K3B, (K1, K up 1, K1, K up 1, K1) A, K3B, rep from * 3 times more.
11th row *K2B, 7A, 2B, rep from * 3 times more
13th row * K1B, (K2, K up 1, K5, K up 1, K2) A, K1B, rep from * 3 times more.
15th row Using C, K.
17th row Using C, K, inc 12 sts evenly across row. 64 sts.
19th row * K3A, (K1, K up 1, K1,) C, K3A, rep from * 7 times more.
21st row * K2A, 5C, 2A, rep from * 7 times more.
23rd row * K2A, (K3, K up 1, K2) C, K2A, rep from * 7 times more.
25th row * K3A, K4C, (K3, K up 1) A, rep from * 7 times more.
27th row * (K1, K up 1, K3) A, K2C, K5A, rep from * 7 times more.
29th row Using C, K.
31st row * (K6, K up 1) C, rep from * 15 times more.
33rd row * K3D, 9A, 2D, rep from * 7 times more.
35th row * K4D, (K4, K up 1, K3) A, K3D, rep from * 7 times more.
37th row * K5D, 6A, (K3, K up 1, K1) D, rep from * 7 times more.
39th row * K5D, (K3, K up 1, K3) A, K5D, rep from * 7 times more.
41st row * K4D, (K5, K up 1, K4) A, K4D, rep from * 7 times more.
43rd row * K3D, (K6, K up 1, K6) A, K3D, rep from * 7 times more.
45th row Using C, K.
47th row Using C, K, inc 24 sts evenly across

49th row * K2A, (K1, K up 1) C, 5A, 2C, 3A, 2C, 5A, (K1, K up 1), C, 1A, rep from * 7 times more.
51st row * K 3 times into next st B, 1A, 2C, 5A, 2C, 1A, K 4 times into next st D, 1A, 2C, 5A, 2C, 1A, rep from * 7 times more.
53rd row * (K3tog tbl, K1, K up 1) A, 2C, 5A, 2C, (K up 1, K1, K4 tog tbl, K1, K up 1) A, 2C, 5A, 2C, (K up 1, K1) A, rep from * 7 times more.
55th row * K1A, K3 times into next st B, 2A, 2C, 3A, 2C, 1A, K 4 times into next st D, 3A, K 4 times into next st D, 1A, 2C, 3A, 2C, 2A, K 3 times into next st B, rep from * 7 times more.
57th row * (K1, K3tog tbl, K2) A, 2C, 3A, 2C, (K1, K4tog tbl, K3, K4tog tbl, K1) A, 2C, 3A, 2C, (K2, K3tog tbl), A, rep from * 7 times more.
59th row * K 3 times into next st B, 2A, 2C, (K2, K up 1, K1) A, 2C, 1A, K 4 times into next st D, 2A, K 4 times into next st D, 1A, 2C, (K1, K up 1, K2) A, 2C, 2A, rep from * 7 times more
61st row * (K3tog tbl, K1) A, 2C, 6A, 2C, (K4 tog tbl, K2, K4 tog tbl) A, 2C, 6A, 2C, 1A, rep from * 7 times more.
63rd row * K3C, (K4, K up 1, K4) A, 2C, 2A, K 4 times into next st D, 2A, 2C, (K4, K up 1, K4) A, 2C, rep from * 7 times more.
65th row * K13A, 2C, (K1, K4tog tbl, K1) A, 2C, 12A, rep from * 7 times more.
67th row * K14A, 2C, 1A, 2C, 27A, 2C, 1A, 2C, (K13, K up 1) A, turn.
Work on these sts only to complete first quarter.
69th row (K2, K up 1, K13) A, 3C, 29A, 3C, (K13, K up 1, K2) A.
71st row (K2, K up 1, K15) A, 1C, 31A, 1C, (K15, K up 1, K2) A.
73rd row Using A, K2, K up 1, K to last 2 sts, K up 1, K2.
75th row (K2, K up 1, K9) A, K 4 times into next st D, (15A, K 4 times into next st D) 3 times, (K9, K up 1, K2) A.
77th row Using A, K2, K up 1, K to last st working clusters K4tog tbl as before, K up 1, K2.
79th row K2, K up 1, K to last 2 sts, K up 1, K2.
81st, 83rd and 85th rows As 79th row.
87th row (K2, K up 1) A, * 3C, 3A, rep from * 12 times more, 3C, (K up 1, K2) A.
89th row Using C, as 79th row.
91st row (K2, K up 1, K2) C, * 3A, 3C, rep from * 12 times more, 3A, (K2, K up 1, K2) C.
93rd – 99th rows Using A, as 79th row.
** K 32 rows without shaping for side, cast off or leave sts for grafting.
Rejoin yarn to next group of sts and work from 67th row in the same way. Work other 2 sections to match. Do not cast off last section but work 198 rows on rem sts for under section. **

Blue cushion
Using No.9 needles and B cast on 8 sts.
1st row K.
2nd and every alt row K each st in the colour in which it was worked on the previous row, keeping all threads on WS when using 1 or more colours.
3rd row K twice into every st. 16 sts.
5th row * K1B, K up 1 A, K1B, rep from * 7 times more.
7th row * K1B, (K up 1, K1) A, 1B, rep from * 7 times more.
9th row * K1B, (K up 1, K2) A, 1B, rep from * 7 times more.
11th row * K1B, (K up 1, K3) A, 1B, rep from * 7 times more.
13th row * K1B, (K up 1, K4) A, 1B, rep from * 7 times more.

15th row * K1B, (K up 1, K5) A, 1B, rep from * 7 times more.
17 – 21st rows Using C, K.
23rd – 36th rows Using A, K, inc 16 sts evenly on 23rd, 27th and 31st rows. 112 sts.
37th row * K5A, 4C, 5A, rep from * 7 times more.
39th row * (K2, K up 1, K1) A, 8C, (K1, K up 1, K2) A, rep from * 7 times more.
41st row * K2A, 5C, (K1, K up 1, K1, K up 1) A, 5C, 2A, rep from * 7 times more.
43rd row * K5C, 3A, (K1, K up 1, K1, K up 1) D, 3A, 5C, rep from * 7 times more.
45th row * 3C, 4A, 6D, 4A, 3C, rep from * 7 times more.
47th row * (K1, K up 1) C, 6A, 6D, 6A, (K up 1, K1) C, rep from * 7 times more.
49th row * (K1, K up 1, K7) A, 6D, 16A, 6D, (K7, K up 1, K1) A, turn and complete this section on these sts only.
51st row (K1, K up 1, K9) A, 4D, 18A, 4D, (K9, K up 1, K1) A.
53rd row (K2, K up 1, K10) A, 2D, 20A, 2D, (K10, K up 1, K2) A.
55th – 59th rows Using A, K2, K up 1 K to last 2 sts, K up 1, K2.
61st row (K2, K up 1) A, (5C, 7A) twice, (K2, K up 1, K2) C, (7A, 5C) twice, (K up 1, K2) A.
63rd row (K2, K up 1) A, 8C, (3A, 9C) 3 times, 3A, 8C, (K up 1, K2) A.
65th row (K2, K up 1) A, 4C, K 3 times into next st B, (11C, K 3 times into next st B) 4 times, 4C, (K up 1, K2) A.
67th row (K2, K up 1) A, 2C, (1A, 2C, 3B, 2C, 1A, 5C) 5 times, 2C, (K up 1, K2) A.
69th row (K2, K up 1) A, 1C, 2A, 2C, (K 3 times into next st B, K3 tog tbl C, K3 times into next st B, 2C, 2A, 1C, 2A, 2C) 5 times, (K up 1, K2) A.
71st row (K2, K up 1, K1) C, 3A, (2C, 3B, 1C, 3B, 2C, 5A) 5 times, 3A, (K1, K up 1, K2) C.
73rd row (K2, K up 1, K6) A, (1C, K3 tog tbl C, K 3 times into next st B, K3 tog tbl C, 1C, 7A) 5 times, (K6, K up 1, K2) A.
75th row (K2, K up 1, K7) A, (2C, 3B, 2C, 7A) 5 times, (K up 1, K2) A.
77th row K1A, K 3 times into next st B, 9A, *(K1, K3 tog tbl, K1) C, 2A, (K 3 times into next st B, 1A) 3 times, 1A, rep from * 3 times more, (K1, K3 tog tbl, K1) C, 9A, K 3 times into next st B, 1A.
79th row (K1, K up 1) A, 3B, 9A, * 3C, 2A, (3B, 1A) 3 times, 1A, rep from * 3 times more, 3C, 9A, 3B, (K up 1, K1) A.
81st row K 3 times into next st B, (K1, K3tog tbl, K10) A, *1C, 3A, (K3 tog tbl, K1) A3 times, 2A, rep from * 3 times, 1C, (K10, K3 tog tbl, K2) A.
83rd row K3B, (K1, K up 1, K71, K up 1, K2) A.
85th row Using A, K3 tog tbl, K1, K up 1, K73, K up 1, K2.
87th, 89th and 91st rows Using A, K2, K up 1, K to last 2 sts, K up 1, K2.
93rd row (K2, K up 1) A, (3B, 3A) 13 times, 3B, (K up 1, K2) A.
95th row (K2, K up 1) A, (2B, 1A) 27 times, 2B, (K up 1, K2) A.
97th row (K2, K up 1, K2) B, (3A, 3B) 13 times, 3A, (K2, K up 1, K2) B.
99th, 101st, 103rd and 105th rows Using A, as **87th row.**
Complete from ** to ** as given for green cushion, working other sections from 49th row.

To make up
DO NOT PRESS. Seam top sections together. Seam or graft under side to edges, leaving last edge open. Slip cushion pad in place. Sew or graft remaining edge.

120

Crash course in knitting

Everything a beginner needs to know and a comprehensive reference for the expert

Methods

There are two types of knitting—'flat' and 'in the round'. Flat knitting is worked backwards and forwards using two needles. Round knitting is useful for items such as socks, gloves and certain types of sweaters and is worked with a set of four needles, pointed at both ends.

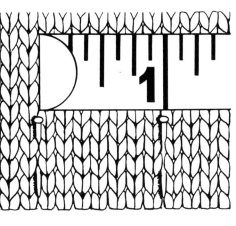

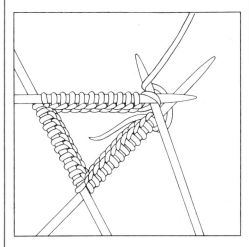

Alternatively, there are long flexible needles known as circular needles and these are used on larger items in the round to make them seamless. Circular needles can also be used for flat knitting working backwards and forwards in rows.

Needles

Needles are manufactured in varying sizes to combine with the different thicknesses of yarns to create different tensions. The range is wide, from very fine needles to those measuring one inch in diameter.

Tension

This refers to the number of stitches and rows to the inch. Unless the same tension is obtained as did the designer of the original garment, then obviously it will not fit. It is always advisable before embarking on a project to work a tension sample of a minimum of four inches square. If there are too many stitches to the inch, change to a larger size of needle until the correct number is obtained.

Conversely, if too few stitches are being made, adjust to a smaller needle until the correct tension is acquired. Even half a stitch too many or too few, although seemingly little, amounts to nine stitches too many or too few on the back of a thirty-four inch sweater. This would mean the completed garment would be two inches too large or too small.

Substituting yarns

Each design has been worked out for the knitting yarn which is stated, but if you wish to substitute another, do so only if you are absolutely sure that the same tension can be obtained. Not even two different double knitting wools will knit up exactly the same and the yardage on the different makes of the yarns will mean that you will need a different quantity.

Casting on

There are several methods of casting on, each with its own appropriate use. The following are the most often used.

Thumb method. This is worked using only one needle. It is an excellent way to begin most garments since it gives an elastic, hard-wearing edge. Make a slip loop in the yarn about three feet from the end. This length varies with the number of stitches required but one yard will cast on about one hundred stitches. Alternatively, take a guide from the width of the piece of knitting multiplied by three.

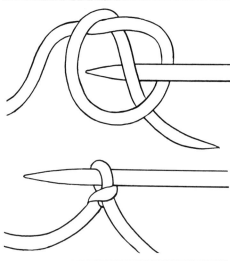

Slip the loop onto the needle, which should be held in the right hand.

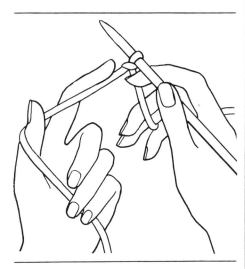

Working with the short length of yarn in the left hand, pass this round the left thumb.

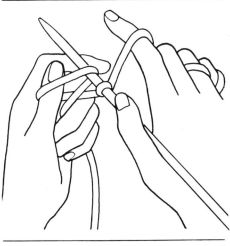

continued overleaf

Crash course in knitting

continued from previous page

Insert the point of the needle under the loop on the thumb and hook forward the long end of the yarn from the ball.

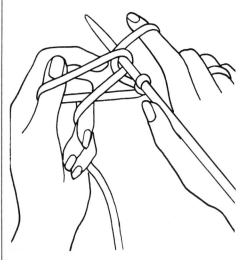

Wind the yarn under and over the needle and draw through the loop, leaving stitch on the needle.

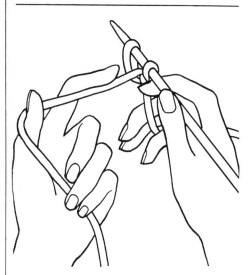

Tighten stitch on needle, noting that yarn is round the thumb ready for the next stitch.

Repeat actions 3 to 5 for the required number of stitches.

Two needle method. This method, sometimes known as the English cable version, is necessary when extra stitches are required during the knitting itself, for instance for a buttonhole or pocket although it can also be used at the beginning of a garment.

Make a slip loop in the yarn three inches from the end. It is not necessary to estimate the yarn required as the stitches are worked from the ball yarn. Slip the loop onto the left-hand knitting needle.

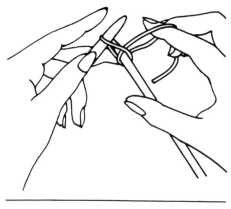

Insert right-hand needle into the loop holding yarn in the right hand and wind the yarn under and over the needle.

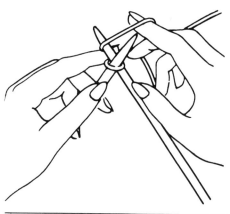

Draw the new loop through the first loop on left-hand needle thus forming a second loop. Pass newly made loop onto the left-hand needle.

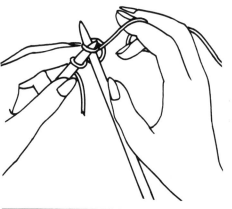

Place point of right-hand needle between two loops on the left-hand needle and wind yarn under and over the right-hand needle point and draw this new loop through between the two stitches on the left-hand needle. Slip this loop onto the left-hand needle.

Repeat action 3 between the last two stitches on the left-hand needle until the required number of stitches have been cast on.

Invisible method. This gives the flat hemmed effect of a machine knit garment. It is a flexible, strong finish which can hold ribbon or elastic and is very useful for designs which need casings.

Using a contrast yarn which is later removed, and the Thumb method, cast on half the number of stitches required, plus one. Now using the correct yarn, begin the ribbing.

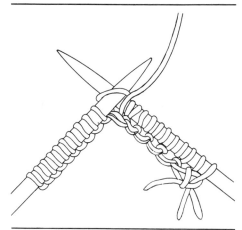

1st row K1, *yfwd, K1, rep from * to end.
2nd row K1, *yfwd, sl 1, ybk, K1, rep from * to end.
3rd row Sl 1, *ybk, K1, yfwd, sl 1, rep from * to end.

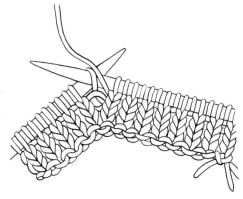

Repeat second and third rows once more.
6th row K1, *P1, K1, rep from * to end.
7th row P1, *K1, P1, rep from * to end.

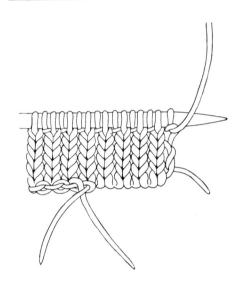

Continue in rib for the required depth. Unpick contrast yarn. The ribs should appear to run right round the edge.

Knit stitch
Take the needle with the cast on stitches in the left hand, the other needle in the right hand. Insert the right-hand needle point through the first stitch on the left-hand needle from front to back.

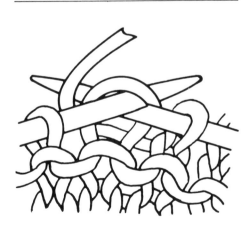

Keeping the yarn behind the needles, pass the yarn round the point of the right-hand needle so that it forms a loop.

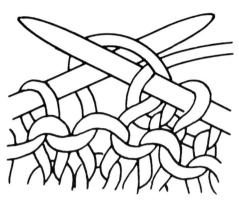

Draw this loop through the stitch on the left-hand needle, so forming a new loop on the right-hand needle.

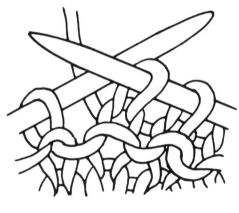

Allow the stitch on the left-hand needle to slip off.
Repeat this action until a loop has been drawn through each stitch on the left-hand needle and placed on the right-hand needle.
This completes one row. To work the next row, change the needle holding the stitches to the left hand and the free needle to the right hand. Repeat the same process as for the first row.

Purl stitch
Take the needle with the cast on stitches in the left hand, the other needle in the right hand. Insert the right-hand needle point through the first stitch on the left-hand needle from back to front.

Keeping the yarn at the front of the needles, pass the yarn round the point of the right-hand needle to form a loop.

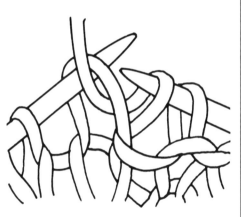

Draw this loop through the stitch on the left-hand needle, thus forming a new loop on the right-hand needle.

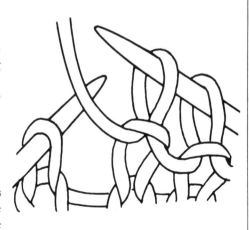

continued overleaf

Crash course in knitting

continued from previous page

Allow the stitch on the left-hand needle to slip off.

Repeat this action with each stitch along the row until all the stitches on the left-hand needle have been passed over to the right-hand needle. This completes one row. To work the next row, change the needle holding the stitches to the left hand and the free needle to the right hand. Repeat the process as for the first row.

Lifting dropped stitches

On stocking stitch, insert a crochet hook into the dropped stitch with the knit side of the work facing. Lift the first thread above the stitch onto the hook tip and hold it in the hook curve as you slowly draw the hook back until the first stitch slips off the tip, leaving the lifted thread as the new stitch. Repeat this until all the threads have been lifted then return the stitch to the needle.

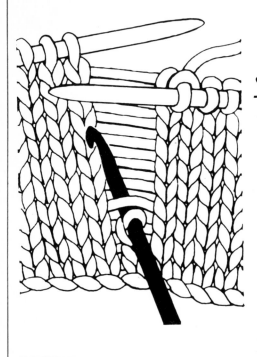

If the purl side is the right side, lift the stitch on the wrong or knit side.

Casting off

To cast off on a knit row, knit into each of the first two stitches. Then, *with the left-hand needle point, lift the first stitch over the second stitch, leaving only one stitch on the right-hand needle.

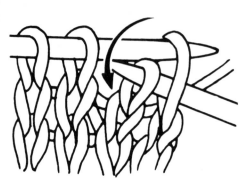

Knit the next stitch, repeat from * until one stitch remains. Cut the yarn and draw it through the last stitch, pulling tight.

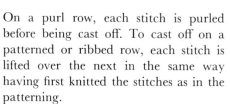

On a purl row, each stitch is purled before being cast off. To cast off on a patterned or ribbed row, each stitch is lifted over the next in the same way having first knitted the stitches as in the patterning.

Garter stitch

This consists of working every row in knit stitches. Because the wrong side of a knit row forms purl stitches, this gives a ridge of purl stitches on every second row on both sides of the work.

Stocking stitch

By working a knit row alternately with a purl row, the ridges of the purl stitches form on the same side of the work and the right side gives a smooth fabric.

Ribbing

To form a ribbed pattern both knit and purl stitches are combined on the same row. This can be done by simple alternating of one knit, one purl stitch, or two knit, two purl stitches, although it can be worked in more unusual combinations repeated systematically. On the next row, the knit stitches become purl stitches and the purl stitches knit stitches.

The slipped stitch

The slipped stitch is so called because it is transferred from the left-hand needle to the right-hand needle without being worked. The yarn is carried either behind or in front of the stitch. It is used in several different ways—decreasing, making a fold for a pleat or facing, to form lacy patterns and to form a texture on the surface of the knitting.

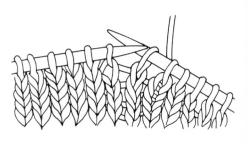

Slip stitch knitwise on a knit row.
Hold the yarn behind the work as if to knit the stitch. Insert the right-hand needle point into the stitch from front to back, as in the knit stitch, and slip it onto the right-hand needle.

Slip stitch purlwise on a knit row.
Hold the yarn behind the work as if to knit the stitch. Insert the right-hand needle point into the stitch from back to front, as in a purl stitch, and slip it onto the right-hand needle.

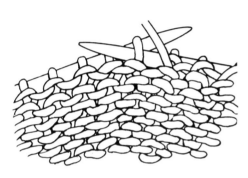

Slip stitch purlwise on a purl row.
Hold the yarn at the front of the work as if to purl the stitch. Insert the right-hand needle point from back to front as if to form a purl stitch, and slip it onto the right-hand needle.

It is important to remember that when decreasing by slipping a stitch on a knit row, the stitch must be slipped knitwise, otherwise it will become crossed. On a purl row, the stitch must be slipped purlwise. However, if the slipped stitch does not form a decrease, it must be slipped purlwise on a knit row to prevent it being crossed when purled on the following row.

Increasing

The shape of the work is determined by increasing or decreasing. The simplest way is to knit twice into the same stitch. Knit or purl the stitch in the usual way but do not slip the stitch off the needle.

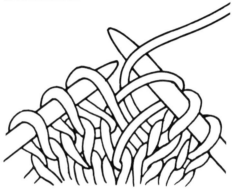

Instead, place the point of the right-hand needle into the back of the stitch and knit or purl into the stitch again. Slip both these stitches onto the right-hand needle, thus making two stitches out of one.

To increase invisibly. Insert the right-hand needle into the front of the stitch below that on the left-hand needle and knit a new stitch. If the increase is on purl work then purl the new stitch. The next stitch on the row being worked is then knitted or purled.

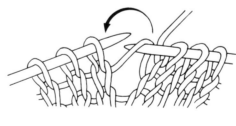

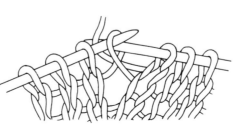

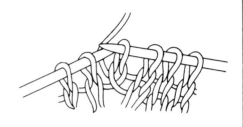

To increase between stitches on knit work. Using the right-hand needle, pick up the yarn which lies between the stitch just worked and the next one, and place it on the left-hand needle. Knit into the back of this loop. This twists and tightens the loops so that no hole is formed. Slip the loop off the left-hand needle.

To increase between stitches on purl work. Pick the loop up and purl into it from the back.

Multiple increase at the beginning of a row. Cast on the number of stitches required by the two needle method and work across the entire row in the usual manner.

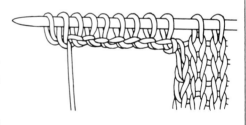

Multiple increase at the end of a row. Reverse the work and cast on.

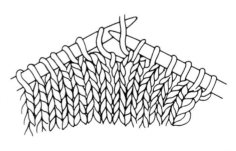

continued overleaf

Crash course in knitting

continued from previous page

Increasing between two knit stitches.
Bring the yarn forward as if to purl then taking it back over the right-hand needle ready to knit the next stitch.

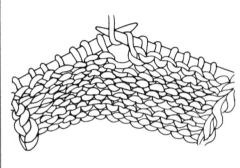

Increasing between two purl stitches.
A similar method can be used to the one previously given by taking the yarn over and round the needle before purling the next stitch.

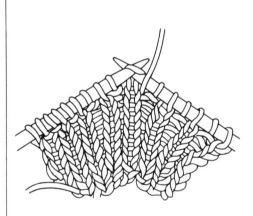

To make a stitch between a purl and a knit stitch. This is particularly useful on ribbed work. The yarn is already in position to the front and the next stitch is knitted in the usual way, the yarn taken over the needle.

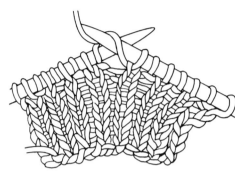

To make a stitch between a knit and a purl stitch. Bring the yarn forward and once round the needle before purling the next stitch.

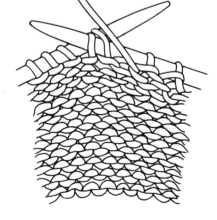

Decreasing
The simplest method of decreasing is to knit or purl two stitches together. This is sometimes worked into the back of the stitches.

Another method of decreasing is to slip one stitch, knit the next one and then slip the slipped stitch off the needle over the knitted one.

Multiple decreases. These are worked by casting off, maintaining the continuity of the pattern by knitting knit stitches and purling purl stitches before slipping one over the other.

Working with several colours

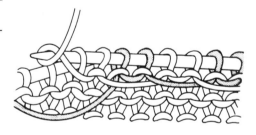

Stranding. The colour which is not in use is taken across the back of the work while the colour in use is being worked. It is important not to pull the yarn too tight or the work will pucker and there should be sufficient elasticity when the garment is worn. However, there should not be so much slackness that loops form.

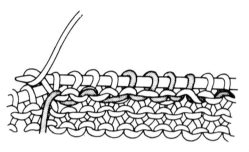

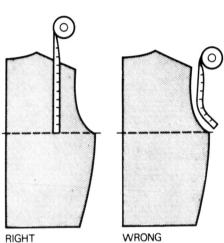

RIGHT   WRONG

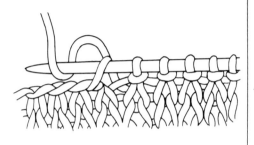

Weaving. This method takes more care but it is worth it for the professional finish it gives, especially if a colour is out of use across a fairly large number of stitches. The principle is to weave the colour not in use under the colour being used. This is done by taking the colour in use under the out-of-work strand before working the next stitch.

Marker threads

Sometimes it is necessary to mark a particular point in the work as a visual guide later. A short length of contrasting yarn is threaded through the stitch and tied in place so that it does not accidentally come out. Once it has served its purpose, simply pull it out.

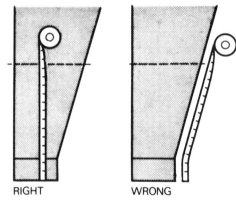

RIGHT   WRONG

Measuring

Always lay knitting on a flat surface for accuracy. Always use a rigid rule and not a tape measure. Never measure round curves but measure the depth of, for example, an armhole on a straight line. In the same way a sleeve should be measured up the centre of the work and not along the shaped edge.

Picking up the stitches

As a general rule, when picking up stitches along a side edge, one stitch should be picked up for every two rows. However, whether the stitches are being picked up along the ends of the rows or along a cast off edge, it will save time and aggravation to divide by marking with pins the length into eight. Spacing the number of stitches evenly can then be adjusted early on to avoid having to pull them all out at the end and begin again. Insert the needle into the fabric edge, wrap the yarn round the needle and draw the loop through. This can be done with a crochet hook and then transferred to the knitting needle.

Making up

The finishing of a garment is just as important as the working of it. First check whether the yarn can be pressed or not. Many man-made fibres stretch to an incredible degree and lose their texture when pressed.

Darn in all ends of yarn securely. Place each piece of knitting, right side down, on an ironing pad and pin evenly round the edges. Always use rustless pins and never stretch the knitting. Check the measurements against those given in the instructions once the pieces are pinned out and adjust if necessary.

Wring out a clean white cotton cloth or a piece of old sheeting in warm water and place over the top of the work, but not over any ribbing. This has an elasticity which would be lost with pressing. With a warm iron press evenly but not heavily on the surface by pressing the iron down and lifting it up without moving along the surface.

continued overleaf

Crash course in knitting

continued from previous page

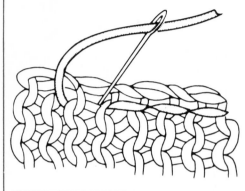

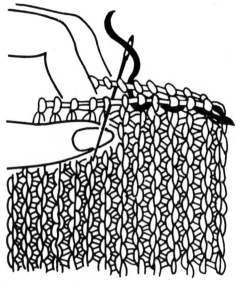

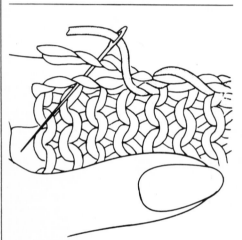

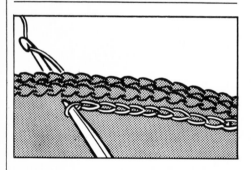

alt	alternate
beg	beginning
cm	centimetre
dec	decrease
grm(s)	gramme(s)
g st	garter stitch
in	inch(es)
inc	increase
K	knit
KB	knit into back of stitch
M1K	make one knitwise
M1P	make one purlwise
No.	number
P	purl
patt	pattern
PB	purl into back of stitch
psso	pass slip stitch over
rem	remaining
rep	repeat
RS	right side
sl 1	slip one knitwise
sl 1P	slip one purlwise
st(s)	stitch(es)
st st	stocking stitch
tbl	through back of loop(s)
tog	together
WS	wrong side
ybk	yarn backward
yfwd	yarn forward
yon	yarn over needle
yrn	yarn round needle

Sew seams with a blunt ended needle using either a back stitch seam or overcasting stitches. Alternatively, work a crocheted slip stitch along the seam line. For a flat seam, such as on ribbing, pass the threaded needle through the edge stitch on the right-hand side directly across to the edge stitch on the left-hand side and pull the yarn through. Turn the needle and work through the next stitch on the left-hand side directly across to the edge stitch on the right-hand side, again pulling the yarn through. Continue in this way.

An asterisk (*) shown in a pattern row denotes that the stitches shown after this sign must be repeated from that point. Square brackets [] denote instructions for larger sizes in the pattern. Round brackets denote that this section of the pattern is to be worked for all sizes.

Knitting Pattern

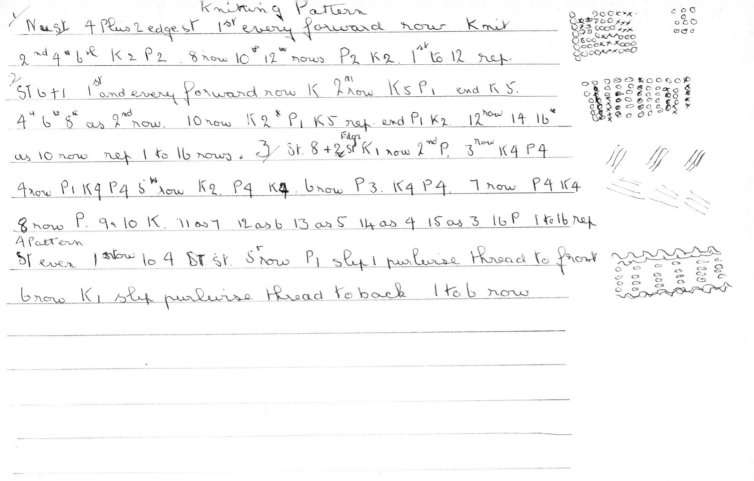

1/ N cast 4 Plus 2 edge st 1st every forward row Knit 2nd 4th 6th K2 P2. 8 row 10th 12th rows P2 K2. 1st to 12 rep.

2/ St 6+1 1st and every forward row K 2nd row K5 P1 end K5. 4th 6th 8th as 2nd row. 10 row K2 P1 K5 rep end P1 K2. 12th row 14 16th as 10 row rep 1 to 16 rows. 3/ St. 8+2 st K1 row 2nd P, 3rd row K4 P4 Fdge 4 row P1 K4 P4 5th row K2 P4 K4. 6 row P3. K4 P4. 7 row P4 K4 8 row P. 9 & 10 K. 11 as 7 12 as 6 13 as 5 14 as 4 15 as 3 16 P 1 to 16 rep

4 Pattern St even 1st row to 4 St. St. 5 row P1 slip 1 purlwise thread to front 6 row K1 slip purlwise thread to back 1 to 6 row